Moira Martingale is a journalist and author. For many years she was a columnist and feature writer for national and regional newspapers and magazines in the United Kingdom, including the *Birmingham Post*, the *Liverpool Echo*, *The Sunday Times* and *The Sun*. In the 1980s, she wrote substantially in newspapers about the formerly taboo subject of child sexual abuse, especially within families. Prior to this, no newspapers had been courageous enough to expose this hidden issue; afterwards many campaigners continued to publicise the topic within national UK media and, later, internationally. Martingale's previous books were published in the UK and worldwide by various publishers. She has B.Ed. and M.Sc. degrees in English Literature and Psychology and a doctorate in Gothic Literature. Studying abnormal psychology gave her a particular interest in the darker aspects of the human psyche – child abuse remains a *bête noire* – and she has just completed a novel which explores multiple personality disorder. She lives in Worcestershire, England and Carcassonne, France.

Cannibal Killers

Monsters with a Taste for Murder

MOIRA MARTINGALE

First published in Great Britain in 1993
by Robert Hale Ltd

This edition first published in Great Britain in 2022
by Ad Lib Publishers Ltd
15 Church Road
London SW13 9HE
www.adlibpublishers.com
Text © 2022 Moira Martingale

Paperback ISBN 978-1-802470-33-8
eBook ISBN 978-1-802471-06-9

A CIP catalogue record for this book is available from the
British Library.

Every reasonable effort has been made to trace
copyright-holders of material reproduced in this book,
but if any have been inadvertently overlooked the
publishers would be glad to hear from them.

Printed in the UK
10 9 8 7 6 5 4 3 2 1

Contents

CONTENTS

Introduction

> '*I am Franky from Germany and I search for a well-built young Boy between 18 and 30 years old to be slaughtered and then consumed … come to me, I will butcher you and eat your delicious flesh.*' *Website forum 'Wanted' ad, early 2001.*

Late in 2002, police in Germany received a tip-off from a web-surfer that 'Franky', a subscriber to the 'Cannibal Café' and other websites aimed at cannibalism fetishists – clinically called 'vorarephiliacs' – was seeking a volunteer who would allow himself to be killed and eaten. In affiliated chat rooms he was making online boasts of having done this once already and, as proof, had posted a photograph of himself butchering a body in what appeared to be a purpose-built slaughter room.

By December, 'Franky' had been identified as Armin Meiwes, aged forty-two, the sole occupant of Wüstefeld Manor in Amstetten, a sprawling black-and-white mansion with thirty-six rooms which dated back to before the thirteenth century. When officers arrived at the house, they were shown around by Meiwes himself and noted that Meiwes had preserved his mother's bedroom with her dressing-table still displaying her personal items, adding a frisson of Hitchcock's *Psycho* to their guided tour. Later newspaper reports were to state that Meiwes sometimes liked to wear his mother's clothes, speak in her high-pitched voice and that he had constructed a shrine to her, complete with a plastic mannequin doll which he put to bed each night.

Meiwes was extremely helpful to the police. When arrested, he admitted to being 'Franky' and also readily confessed to having killed and eaten a man who had responded to his original 2001 internet appeal, offering detailed descriptions. He led the officers to various sites in the house, including a torture room containing meathooks on the walls, a cage which he had constructed and a bed with restraining ropes; there was an oversized barbecue pit and a burial-place in the garden containing body parts. Meiwes's victim was Bernd Jurgen Armando Brandes, a software engineer from Berlin, who had been killed at the house in March 2001 – almost two years previously. Meiwes's startling claim was that Brandes had been a willing victim whose fantasy he was fulfilling. Brandes's fantasy was to have his penis cut off prior to death and to then eat it. Meiwes had obliged him in this.

As part of the arrest, the officers also took away some videotapes, later describing Meiwes's collection of sadistic and cannibalistic pornography as 'encyclopaedic', embracing 'every perversion imaginable' – on one CD alone there were 3,000 pictures of agonised torture victims. But among the films were some made by Meiwes to record what had happened with Brandes, including the failed attempt of the two men to eat the severed penis after Meiwes had fried it – they found it too tough, he explained. There were records of his butchering of Brandes's body and the freezing of portion-sized pieces of it for his future consumption. Meiwes calculated that he had eaten more than forty pounds of Brandes's flesh during the eighteen months since his death. Now, with the freezer empty, Meiwes was searching for his next victim via the most recent computer website advertisements which had led the police to him. Despite their horror and disgust, the judicial authorities did, at least, expect that securing a conviction would be a quick and straightforward affair thanks to Meiwes's openness in confessing his actions. How mistaken they were.

Meiwes's view – and his later defence against a murder charge – was that he had committed no crime. To his mind, he had not achieved his cannibalism fantasy by unfairly seizing a helpless stranger to murder, but rather he had gone about it in a sensible, businesslike way at the beginning of 2001, placing the very polite internet advertisement inviting someone to be his next meal, much in the manner of a lonely-hearts ad. And, astonishingly, the dinner invitation proved irresistible to more than four hundred vorarephiliacs who responded. The extra lure of emailed photographs of Meiwes's 'slaughter room' complete with a metal table set up for draining victims' blood proved too much for some: several individuals went to Wüstefeld Manor and allowed themselves to be hung upside down on hooks or wrapped in cling film by Meiwes. One of them, a hotel worker from London, would later tell the criminal trial that he was chained to a bed while Meiwes used a marker pen on his body to denote different cuts of meat for later butchering. However, like the other fantasists who visited Meiwes, he changed his mind about being killed and left the house without any objection from a disappointed Meiwes. Then, in February 2001, bisexual Bernd Brandes, aged forty-three, responded. 'I'm your meat,' he said. 'I offer myself to you and will let you dine from my live body. Not butchery, dining!'

As he confided to Meiwes that he nursed a lifelong desire to feel the extreme pain of having his penis bitten or cut off, Meiwes realised that Brandes could be the date of his dreams.

* * * *

The following chapters provide a history of the perpetrators of 'anthropophagy': literally, that means 'to consume humans'. Cannibalism is the crime which probably shocks and disgusts people more than any other. Yet along with the antipathy and horror, cannibalism and vampirism also exude a simultaneous fascination. Why is that? Could there be something in our psychological make-up which harks back to the primitive past which we all share? And in our twenty-first-century 'civilised' world, how many are there living among us who have the capacity to slither back into that bestial nature evidenced by the case histories in this book? For it is undeniable that cannibalism runs like a blood-red thread through the tapestry of mankind's history: man has always been carnivorous and in ancient days he was unconcerned about whether the prey he dragged back to his cave had four legs or two. What horrifies is that society's taboos of more recent centuries fail to keep those old, savage desires in check among some; they desire blood; they wish to kill and consume their victims. And in our world of intellectual progress and sophistication, it is even more shocking to discover just how widespread this attraction to the most degenerate and violent instincts of animal evolution is. Armin Meiwes, for example, claimed there were more than 800 cannibals in Germany at the time he came to trial in 2006 – and no one argued with this figure.

It is a wretched irony that the internet – the summit of scientific triumph realised by the combined imaginative genius of mathematicians, physicians, engineers, astronomers, computer and space scientists – has been appropriated by those whose depraved cravings constitute evolution's polar opposite. Paedophiles, pornographers, stalkers, sadists, cannibals … whatever any defective individual's predatory inclinations might be, they have been provided with a cyber-universe where, with only a couple of clicks, debauched desires can be fulfilled and even shared with other misfits, degenerates and criminals, thereby offering mutual or group validation of their particular sexual aberration. For those who know how to find them, there are grossly pernicious 'secret' sites in cyberspace which do not appear in Google searches. These hidden sites are only accessible via 'deep net' Tor networks – complex nodal connections which conceal a person's IP (Internet Protocol) address, thereby providing visitors with near anonymity in the real world – or as these users call it, 'Meatspace'.

Some of the earlier material contained in my first edition of *Cannibal Killers* in 1993 also appears in this book, albeit abbreviated. In those days, the internet was in its infancy and its use was limited. In those days, the extremity of horror experienced by cinema audiences who watched the Oscar-winning *The Silence of the Lambs* (1991) would, in some rare individuals, have aroused excited empathy with the film's protagonist, Hannibal Lecter. In those days, those people would have believed themselves to be solitary in their perverted sickness; they would have known how abnormal their desires were. In those days, ashamed, they would have kept them hidden.

The internet has changed all that.

Overpowering Instinct

'The mere memory of Man as I knew him had been swept out of existence. Instead were these frail creatures who had forgotten their high ancestry, and the white Things of which I went in terror. Then I thought of the Great Fear that was between the two species and, for the first time, with a sudden shiver, came the clear knowledge of what the meat I had seen might be. Yet it was too horrible! ... Clearly at some time in the Long-Ago of human decay the Morlocks' food had run short ... I tried to look at the thing in a scientific spirit. After all, they were less human and more remote than our cannibal ancestors of three or four thousand years ago ... Why should I trouble myself? These Eloi were mere fatted cattle, which the ant-like Morlocks preserved and preyed upon'

H. G. Wells, *The Time Machine*

They brought the severed heads in first. On golden platters. Frozen in death, the faces of the young slave girls were still fresh and beautiful, the almond eyes lifeless. The men's mouths watered to think how sweet and tender their flesh would be when, in just a few minutes, it was served to them, the honoured guests. Week after week, hundreds, probably thousands, of guests banqueting at the court of Shih Hu, who ruled the Huns of northern China between AD 334 and

AD 349, savoured the delicacy of a young harem girl, killed and cooked to excite their palates. Part of the preprandial ritual was this passing round of the platter – similar, perhaps, to the manner in which we might now go to a fish restaurant and choose a live lobster to be cooked for us. There is no record of any guest recoiling from this human feast. And until the early nineteenth century, restaurants serving human flesh were common in China.

But why? How could a succession of families in China – a land that was, in many ways, a cultivated and ordered society – sit down to dine upon another human being? How could the guests at Shih Hu's banquet enjoy the flesh of those doomed girls whose misfortune was that they looked good enough to eat? It was, of course, an awesome demonstration of power – slaves were the stock of noble families, no more than their cattle. But more importantly, and more simply, they liked the taste. When all the moral arguments are set aside, these are the reasons we now eat animals: we have the unchallenged power to do so, and we enjoy the taste.

In extremis, how likely is it that, like the Morlocks – one branch of H. G. Wells's imagined humanity of the future in *The Time Machine* – we might cast conscience aside and the crouching predator in our primitive past might arise? For although we now consider that it is not ethically agreeable for us to eat others of our own kind, archaeologists and anthropologists have uncovered plenty of evidence to show that as soon as man was able to walk upright, he indulged freely in carnivorous and cannibalistic activity. The reasons were various: over the centuries, cannibalism was resorted to in times of famine or as the preferred form of protein. It was practised for magical, mystical or religious reasons. It was a form of revenge against enemies.

And finally, then, just as now, there would likely be a scattering of deviant individuals who obtained sexual gratification from acts of sadism and cannibalism. To try and comprehend the reasoning of this last small section, it is perhaps necessary to investigate the strength of the compelling subconscious power exerted by the reasoning of the former groups, set within the customs of their time and culture.

* * * *

CULTURAL CANNIBALISM
In Britain, archaeological discoveries indicate that Britain's Stone-Age population was cannibalistic – one such finding came in 1987 during a Cheddar Cave dig in Somerset[1] – and there are reports of the practice in England and Ireland during the famine of the seventh century and in Scotland three hundred years later for the same reason. In fact, it seems clear that there are few places in the world untouched by cannibalism until comparatively recently. Any investigation into recorded history reveals that throughout the centuries our ancestors have invented all manner of ways in which to attack and inflict the most cruel hurts upon their fellow humans, seemingly without conscience – and that includes eating them.

Mention has already been made of the fourth-century Chinese emperors' predilection for eating their slave girls, but proof that cannibalism still flourished in the Far East came from Marco Polo a thousand years later when he returned to Italy with horror stories from China and Tibet. Nineteenth- and twentieth-century missionaries and explorers – the fortunate ones – furnished us with much of our information about tribal cannibalism in countries like Africa. When it came to ultimate demonstrations of power, man's inhumanity to all other animals including our own species knew no bounds: in parts of Africa, slaves were paraded for sale in the marketplace and, just as

H. G. Wells's Eloi were used as cattle by the Morlocks, they were fattened for food. Enemies slain in battle were also eaten, as were family members who died of natural causes. Adulterous women faced the same fate. Tribes which raised cattle, such as the Zulus, were not cannibals, but people-eating tribes could often be recognised by their teeth, which they would file to sharp points. During the Second World War there were several reports of near-starving Japanese detention-camp soldiers selecting prisoners of war to kill and then eating parts of their bodies. In the second half of the twentieth century, tyrannical African leaders Idi Amin and Emperor Bokassa were both found guilty of eating their human captives.

In one South American tribe, slave-women were impregnated in order that their captors could eat their babies. On other occasions, conscious victims had limbs removed and were made to watch while they were cooked and eaten. Sometimes, to underline the contempt felt for them, they were invited to take part in the meal. In Fiji, human flesh was craved in preference to animal flesh. It was prized so highly that it even had a name – 'puaka balava', meaning 'long pig'. Here a man exercised such dominion over his wife that if he so wished, he could kill and eat her without fear of reprisals. In Papua New Guinea, cannibalism may have endured until comparatively recently – Japanese soldiers were said to have been captured and eaten during the Second World War. And the dark suspicion that anthropophagy may still persist within societies who dwell in far-flung and hidden reaches of the world was confirmed in July 2012, when twenty-nine members of a cannibal cult were arrested in Papua New Guinea after they had eaten at least seven people (four men and three women) whom they believed to be sorcerers.

Primitive superstition is also the excuse made for the slaughter in Tanzania of more than eighty albino people since 2000, including children and babies seized from their mothers or kidnapped. Albino people have long been ostracised and feared as supernatural in Tanzania, but witch doctors are prepared to pay £50,000 ($75,000) for a complete corpse, according to the Red Cross. This is because their body parts are believed to confer power, good luck and wealth, whether by being ingested or being turned into grisly 'magic charms'. Tanzania's President, Jaya Kikwete has denounced the killings as an 'evil' which has shamed his country and in 2015 more than two hundred witch doctors and healers were arrested. One hundred and thirty-three were charged with murder and in March 2016 the death-sentences began to be passed: nineteen were sentenced to death for their crimes then, the same penalty would follow for others found to be guilty. But during that year, a surge of similar killings of albinos for their skin and body parts was revealed in Malawi, fuelled by a belief, said an Amnesty International spokesperson 'that bones of people with albinism contain gold'.

Elsewhere in Africa, paranormal sacrificial beliefs still persist: in January 2020, a Nigerian court heard the admission of twenty-three-year-old Owolabi Adeeko that he and his mother, Bola Adeeko, assisted by their village pastor and self-proclaimed 'prophet' Segun Philip, had killed Owolabi's girlfriend Favour Oladele, a final-year sociology student at the University of Lagos. The trio intended using her body parts in a 'money ritual' – making magical concoctions to sell to others in a get-rich-quick scheme. They removed the girl's head, heart, breasts and other organs for the concoction, which the mother and son consumed, 'for spiritual cleansing'. Owolabi said afterwards that the family had not become rich and he was now facing the death penalty. 'I think the money ritual did not work,' he said.

According to historical legend, the most infamous British cannibal was Sawney Bean, who, with his wife – 'a woman as viciously inclined as himself', according to chronicler John Nicholson – dwelt with their numerous offspring in a cave close to the sea in Galloway, Scotland, during the sixteenth century. He abandoned his trade as a hedger and ditcher and opted instead to prey upon people. The family lived by highway robbery: ambushing, killing and then eating passers-by. Body parts which they were unable to eat at once were pickled in brine or hung in their cave. They had no obvious sexual or mystical motives for their actions; they robbed the people of their bodies in the same way that they robbed them of their possessions – which they then, presumably, sold in the Edinburgh region. Over a period of twenty-five years it was estimated that Bean and his family, which ultimately extended to forty-six men and women who knew no other diet or way of life – proof that 'culture is king' – had killed and eaten more than a thousand people. Because nobody survived their attacks, local people were oblivious to their existence.

It was only when the Bean family became careless and began tossing surplus body parts into the sea that the authorities started to ask questions and residents became fear-struck. Even then, the perpetrators of such vile deeds could not be traced. Realisation only dawned fully when, during the Bean family's attack on a man and his wife, whom they killed, another group of travellers arrived to fight them off. With a battalion of armed men and bloodhounds, the cannibals' family cave was discovered. The soldiers were horrified to see parts of human bodies hanging up to cure or being cooked over a fire. The family were taken to Leith where, without trial, they were executed, using the obscene methods of the time – by having limbs cut off before being burned to death. There are those – like writer Ronald Holmes – who believe that Sawney Bean did not really exist, but was merely the stuff of myth, a demonic bogey-man figure like the vampire or the werewolf – 'a primeval presence from the dark past of the human mind,' he says. However, the tale has been well documented in its claim to be factual and it must be noted that unlike the previously-mentioned mythological night monsters, there are no magical or even devilish dimensions assigned to Sawney Bean.

It is risky, too, to believe that because a person's crimes are so unspeakably shocking as to defy the laws of humanity, they could not possibly have taken place in reality. One has only to look at historical sadists like Vlad the Impaler (1431–1476), who cruelly relished the murder of thousands in the most bloody of ways – and is also said to have provided Bram Stoker with his inspiration for the novel *Dracula* – or the sixteenth-century Hungarian Countess Elizabeth Bathory, a distant relative of Vlad, who bathed in and drank the blood of hundreds of virgin girls because she believed it would keep her youthful, to find purveyors of barbarity far beyond the bounds of human compassion. Even now, in the twenty-first century, we still witness the perpetration of the most primitive atrocities against the innocent by brutal dictatorships around the world and by terrorist groups in Syria, Iraq and other Middle Eastern countries, so why should a one-off monster like Sawney Bean not belong in history's chamber of real-life horrors? Half a century after the Bean family's reign of terror and, curiously enough, in exactly the same part of Scotland, Nichol Brown was executed for killing and eating his wife. During his trial it became evident that flesh-eating was not an unusual event for him. It was revealed that one night, in his local inn in Leith, he declared to his drinking companions that he would go to the gibbet whereon hung the body of Norman Ross, a criminal who had been hanged a week earlier, and he would bring back a piece of the body and consume it in front of them. He went away and returned with a lump of flesh from the dead man's thigh, cooked it on the fire and ate it, fulfilling his promise as they watched.

In desperate circumstances, man has always shown a readiness to eat whatever protein was available in order to save his own life. In the nineteenth century, a few prominent cases of this 'expedience' cannibalism arose in the Western world, although during the court cases which followed the American incidents there were doubts raised about the manner in which victims died. In 1846, Lewis Keseberg, a German by birth, was, with his wife and two children, among the Donner Party, a group of California-bound settlers led by George Donner through the Sierra Nevada Mountains. Appalling weather conditions forced them to slaughter their animals and then fighting broke out between the members of the party. Some people died of cold and starvation and the dead bodies were eaten by others.

It was then that alleged murders began, including one incident when Keseberg took a small boy to bed with him one night and presented his body to the others in the morning for butchering. The others were convinced Keseberg had murdered the child. Some of the travellers, including the Donners, had split off from the main wagon train and it was these few, including Keseberg, who were left behind after repeated rescue attempts had saved the forty-five remaining living people out of an eighty-nine-strong party. But when the final rescue party arrived to take the Donners to safety, only Keseberg remained in the carnage-littered camp, looking fat and well, lying beside a simmering pot containing the liver and lungs of a human being. The liver belonged to Mrs Donner, he told the horrified rescuers, adding, 'She was the best I have ever tasted.' They were suspicious because only weeks earlier Mrs Donner had appeared healthy and nowhere near death, but Keseberg said she, the last survivor apart from himself, had died naturally. Keseberg was regarded as a murdering cannibal by his fellow men, but at his trial he claimed that like the other members of the party, he had only resorted to cannibalism as an act of despair. He was freed by the court and within a few years he found a new career ... running a steak house.

Thirty-odd years later, Alfred Packer did not have such a lucky escape. In 1873, Packer was a gold prospector who ignored the bad-weather warnings from indigenous Americans at an outpost and insisted on guiding a party of five from Salt Lake into the San Juan Mountains; he ended up eating them. He had been paid well by the men, but weeks later he arrived back alone, saying the others had abandoned him. Suspicion was aroused because Packer looked very corpulent for someone who claimed to have been struggling in the snow in adverse conditions. In addition, he was laden with money, guns and knives which had belonged to the other members of the party. When the bodies of the five missing men were eventually found, four had had their skulls crushed, apparently while they slept, and the fifth had been shot. Four had been totally stripped of flesh and the other partially so. When he eventually came to trial ten years later, Packer was judged to be guilty of murder and sentenced to forty years' hard labour, but he was actually released after seventeen. During the sentencing of Packer, Judge Melville Gerry made an infamous remark which has since entered the annals of American history: 'There were only seven Democrats in Hinsdale County, and you ate five of them, you depraved Republican son of a bitch.'

During the same period in the nineteenth century, England had its own tale of cannibalism to occupy the horrified masses. In 1884, Captain Thomas Dudley and Edwin Stephens were two of four survivors of a shipwreck which happened hundreds of miles to the west of Africa.

They took to a dinghy with only two tins of turnips to sustain them and after three weeks adrift with no food or water, Dudley decided that one of them must die to save the others. Seventeen-year-old cabin boy Richard Parker – 'the weakest, the youngest, the most unresisting,' declared the judge – was killed by Dudley and the men stayed alive by feeding on the boy. When they were rescued four days later Dudley freely admitted this, claiming as his defence 'the pressure of necessity' because the crew were in extremis. He and Stephens were sentenced to death, but this was later commuted to six months' imprisonment.

A century on, in 1972, a passenger aeroplane travelling from Argentina to Chile crashed at an altitude of 23,000 feet in the Andes mountains, the most hostile of territories where, with sub-zero temperatures, edible vegetation is absent. Several of the passengers perished in the crash or soon afterwards so that of the forty-five passengers, thirty-two found themselves stranded in an alien terrain, with no radio, food or hope of immediate rescue. That hope faded even more with the passing weeks and as the pangs of hunger became unbearable, the survivors were left with only one option if they wished to remain alive: to overcome their revulsion and eat the flesh of their deceased fellow passengers. Some of them could not bring themselves to do it and refused. They died. Others stayed alive for seventy days by eating the flesh raw to preserve its nutritive value. When they were finally rescued, only sixteen survivors remained. The story was told dramatically in the 1993 film *Alive!*

But the 'reasons' for using humans as food were not always to do with obtaining nutrition for survival. Instances of cannibalism as revenge are sprinkled throughout history even until comparatively recent times. For instance, John Johnson was a trapper who lived in the mountains of Montana in the United States in the 1880s and maintained a private war with the Crow Indians, who had murdered his

Native American wife and child. Whenever he came upon a Crow camp, he would attack it single-handedly, kill the Indians, butcher their corpses and, for some inexplicable reason, eat only their livers. He was known, unsurprisingly, as Liver-Eating Johnson and far from being ostracised for this horrid practice, later became a sheriff in Coulson, Montana, maintaining law and order for several years before vanishing into the mountains again.

Blood-drinking and flesh-eating customs in history are multi-dimensional and there was more than just sating the appetite or a thirst for revenge in the activities of some tribal cultures, such as those in Africa or Australia. Among these tribes there was a powerful belief that by eating humans or drinking their blood one transferred their finer qualities to oneself. To eat a slain enemy was not only an act of revenge; it also enabled one to absorb his strength and courage, thus becoming a tribute to the enemy warrior. Slaughter was not always necessary: to eat deceased relatives was to honour them and to devour a dead elder enabled the absorption of the aged one's ancestral wisdom. Australian aborigines believed that if a child ate his dead father he would inherit the father's hunting skills. And as reported earlier, mystical beliefs still prevail elsewhere in the world. Albinos are targeted in Malawi and Tanzania, but the notion that cannibalising others, whether actually or symbolically, will enable communication with wish-granting spirits is common to many religions.

* * * *

BLOOD AND SPIRIT: 'THE BLOOD IS THE LIFE'
Beyond its biological value, blood was believed by our ancestors to contain mystical energies – strength, spiritual essence, life itself. The superstitions attached to blood were evidenced by the initiation ceremonies undergone

by young aboriginal men who had to drink human blood for the sacred powers it bestowed upon them. In eastern Prussia, an executed person's blood was considered lucky and in other parts of Europe such fresh blood was thought to protect against illness. The belief in several cultures was that drinking the blood of a dead person whom one suspects might return to haunt the living – perhaps as a vampire – protects against such an event. This view is alleged still to exist among some native Canadian tribes. The symbolic importance of blood in the developed world continues: barely a century has passed since bleeding with leeches was considered to be a medical cure for many ills, including lunacy. And in present-day Britain, those individuals who take pleasure in the blood-letting rituals of hunting foxes and deer might pause to consider the primitive significance of 'blooding' a child during this 'sport' – that is, smearing the blood of the eviscerated deer upon his head – during his first hunt.

Over the centuries, as *Homo sapiens* evolved and his imagination developed, mystical beliefs came to dominate his life. Arrogantly, he awarded himself 'god-given' spiritual qualities and advantages which he arbitrarily deemed were not present in other species. The gods which he created were, of course, sympathetic to his aggressive interests and offered him clear justifications as to why he should continue to do as he had always done, including torturing, killing, inflicting unbearable pain upon other human beings, drinking their blood and eating their flesh. With this divine rubber stamp, humans continued to indulge their brutal, cannibalistic desires. Cruelty and slaughter, therefore, found their place as part of blood-drinking and flesh-eating rituals and of human sacrifice, all of which became central to many tribes' belief systems. In order to assure the fertility of their land and their people, many cultures appeased their gods with the blood of their weakest members.

In Crete, the people were said to fertilise Mother Earth with the blood of their victims, and similar blood rituals could be found elsewhere. The Aztecs of Mexico, for instance, worshipped so many blood-thirsting deities that barely a week went by without some helpless infant, young man or woman or captured prisoner being sacrificed by the priests. For the sun- or moon-god to bring fertility to the Aztec crops necessitated the removal of a live victim's heart, whereupon it was held aloft, still beating. The corpse was then distributed to the crowd and, with heavy symbolism and solemnity, rather than the people needing to satiate their hunger, it was cut up and eaten. Such customs were hard to break, even when European explorers came into contact with the Aztecs and other related peoples. There were still reports of such ceremonies as recently as 1838.

The North American Indians' ancient belief in a host of gods and spirits also involved cannibalism. Known for the richness of their legends, Native Americans understood that a cannibalistic spirit was able to take over a person's body, enabling him to eat human flesh, either from slain or captured enemies or from dead relatives. Over time in contact with other cultures, the literal interpretations of their beliefs were dispensed with, although they continued to be acted out symbolically during ritual dances. In Lapland, symbolic ceremonies surrounding death included naming a reindeer after the dead person (choosing an animal of a similar age and sex to the deceased), then ceremonially killing and eating it.

Lest twenty-first-century readers begin to feel superior about such atavistic impulses, perhaps a glance is required at the major religions which prevail in the world today and their roots in either fact or myth. The Judaic tradition described in the Old Testament tells believers that God gave man dominion over all the animals to devour as we pleased. Blood-sacrifice and ritual played a major part in the religious lives of people during Biblical times and many pages of the Old Testament contain stories outlining God's instructions to followers on the exact and bloody methods to be used associated with differing animals when making these sacrifices. In Genesis 22, Abraham is said to have been called upon by God to sacrifice his adored only son Isaac in a similar manner. Isaac was only saved by an eleventh-hour reprieve from the Lord, who then told Abraham that he had only asked him to do this terrible act as a demonstration of faith. The assumed spiritual and mystical essence of blood was of great importance then and the vestiges of such belief remain today within the Jewish faith – and indeed, within other faiths – where, although meaning and requirements may have changed over the ages, blood is still believed to contain specific qualities. Notably, Jehovah's Witnesses refuse blood transfusions because of their literal interpretation of Biblical passages such as 'Only flesh with its soul – its blood – you must not eat' (Genesis 9: 3–4). They do not, however, denounce meat-eating. Orthodox Jews and devout members of certain other religions like Islam continue to eat only the meat of animals which have been slaughtered in a certain way which drains them of blood.

By the time the New Testament was written, the emphasis on literal sacrifice – human or otherwise – was becoming redundant. But as with many major religions, at Christianity's heart is the principle of the noble sacrifice of its central figure. Although Jesus of Nazareth may have preached of a new, benevolent God who commanded the finer human values of compassion, kindness and non-violence, nevertheless he was bloodily sacrificed in primitive tradition. And it was this ancient primal custom of human sacrifice which he highlighted symbolically when he dined with his disciples at the Last Supper. Offering them bread, he urged: 'Take, eat; this is my body which is given for you,' and with the wine, he said: 'This is the new testament in my blood, which is shed for you' (Luke 22). This ceremony with its mystical allusions of blood being a symbol of life still prevails today in the Christian church's service of Holy Communion. In fact, the Roman Catholic teaching since 1215, when Pope Innocent III ordered a new Catholic dogma, is that 'transubstantiation' takes place – that is, that upon ingestion the bread and wine actually turns into Christ's body and blood, rather than being a mere symbolic substitute. What better illustration of our unconscious preoccupation with 'magical thinking' – something which we may like to think belongs in our primitive ancestry, but is, in fact, still very much a part of life for large numbers of us.

The black arts remain an area where blood sacrifice persists, both of animals and, if we are to believe the claims, also of humans. Satanists glorify their unholy master by offering blood, it is said. Drinking of blood or its symbolic substitute forms a large part of cult activities in a scarcely more sophisticated way than the tribal rituals practised by pagan cultures. Incidentally, equally important during black magic ceremonies is sexual activity, and a similar inextricable linking of blood and sex in the imagination forms a combination which is crucial to the thinking of most of the murderers to be discussed in this book. The blood-sex link is also powerful for countless other serial killers and violent rapists who may be, but usually are not, Satanists. While we view their criminal activity as perverted and obscene, believing it to be far removed from normal sexuality, one can, perhaps, begin to perceive the unconscious depths wherein the roots of their perversions lie and it is perhaps unsurprising that the Devil was blamed for such criminality during the ignorant years of the Middle Ages – although, as the witch hunts of the sixteenth and seventeenth centuries evidenced, the truly guilty were very few in comparison to the number of innocent victims of the Church's persecution.

It is well known that the early purveyors of Christianity achieved their remarkable success partly by superimposing Christian festivals and feast days upon existing pagan celebrations. Therefore, Christmas was determined as the twenty-fifth of December, not because Christ was born on that actual day but because this was the traditional Winter Solstice. Despite – or more likely because of – the monopoly which Christianity held upon societal belief, fear of paganism and devilish dabblings was rife. This superstitious tendency lasted long beyond the appalling chapter in European history when thousands of pitiful individuals – mainly elderly women – were tortured, burned or murdered most cruelly by the panicked authorities on the grounds that they were witches. It was not necessary to commit any offence to be denounced, tortured and slaughtered as a witch and the scale of the massacres was horrifying. In Germany at least 100,000 people were executed as witches, simply on the say-so of someone else – a person who might equally have been tortured to extract names. Death, finally, was by burning alive. Indeed, the German authorities at Neisse in Silesia anticipated the Nazis by three hundred years by constructing an oven, in which were roasted more than a thousand people in the space of nine years, including children of between two and four years. So in an age when Satan invaded everyone's terrified sensibilities, it seems logical that when an individual really did behave in such an abominable and sickening way as to be beyond human comprehension, people fell back upon the Devil and his works to provide an explanation.

★ ★ ★ ★

OF VAMPIRES AND WEREWOLVES

Even accounting for the advances in global communication, it is undeniable that the incidence of serial killers, a large percentage of whom are sexual sadists, increased over centuries to an all-time high in the 1990s, for reasons which will be addressed later. But that is not to say that such disturbed criminals are solely a modern phenomenon. In 1573 at Dole, France, Gilles Garnier, a recluse who confessed to killing numerous children – their bodies were found mutilated and half-eaten – may have been one of the earliest recorded serial killers. An explanation for his deeds was demanded and, predictably, the Devil's sorcery came to the fore. Garnier admitted that he was a *loup garou*, a werewolf, a condition he said he had acquired through witchcraft after meeting a phantom who taught him how to change at will into a wolf by rubbing an ointment over his body (a common method, according to legend). After killing a child of twelve – by tearing her to pieces with his teeth and his wolf's paws, he said in his confession – he ate parts of her body, then cut a joint to take home for his wife, Apolline. He killed and ate three other children in a similar way and admitted that he had the same unnatural inclinations even when he was in his normal, human state rather than in werewolf mode. His punishment was to be burned alive. One cannot be sure whether or not Garnier was actually guilty since he was doubtless tortured cruelly to produce a confession – or whether he truly did believe himself to be a werewolf, for the incident occurred when European werewolf hysteria was at its peak.

Fifteen years later, in Bedburg, Germany, Peter Stump (also called Stubbe in some accounts) was executed in the most vicious manner after admitting a twenty-five-year spree of cannibal killings, the barbarity of which turned him into a fearsome folk legend. Again, he confessed that the Devil had taught him the art of metamorphosis and had given him a form-changing wolf's skin which he wore when he pursued young women and children. But when he caught his victims, he said he shifted back into his human shape while he raped and murdered them with terrible cruelty. During the first five years after he had made his pact with the Devil, Stump said he had murdered thirteen people, including two pregnant women whose unborn babies he admitted tearing from their mothers' bodies to devour their hearts 'panting hot and raw'. He also killed countless animals, he said, but what caused the greatest shock was his admission that he had killed and eaten his small son, whose mother, Beell, was Stump's own daughter with whom he had an incestuous relationship. He told with relish how he had found the boy's brains to be 'most savoury and delicious'.

The people of Bedburg and neighbouring villages were afraid to go out alone during this twenty-five-year period, claiming to have discovered bloody limbs of men, women and children littering the fields. When Stump was eventually executed, so were his daughter and his mistress, who were judged to have been accessories to murder. As with Garnier, the torture methods used at this period in history were such that one cannot be certain whether Stump was really under the delusion that he was a wolf when he slaughtered and devoured his victims. Werewolfery was second to witchcraft in the Middle Ages, zealously regarded as a Devilish canker in society which had to be rooted out and confessions were extracted from 'werewolves' – both male and female – in the same abominable way that they were wrenched from those accused of witchcraft. Stump's death was no less horrid than the pains he had inflicted upon his victims: he was tied to a wheel, had lumps of flesh torn out of him with red-hot pincers and his limbs were broken with a wooden hatchet before he was beheaded and his decapitated body burned.

Such barbarity on the part of the authorities always casts doubt upon the confessions of the accused, but what cannot be disputed is that someone committed the crimes; the mutilated bodies bore testimony to the fact that there were sadistic cannibal killers then, as now. The Garnier and Stump cases, together with other similar ones, added authenticity to the werewolf legend to those who sought it, but over a one-hundred-year period a staggering 30,000 cases of 'werewolfery' were recorded in France alone – and it would seem obvious that at a time when the world's population was much smaller, the incidence of so many unhinged individuals defies belief. In fact, even though the twentieth-century Western world surpassed itself not only in the number of sadistic cannibal killers, they were few in number when compared to such claims during the age of werewolf hysteria hundreds of years earlier.

Interestingly, werewolves and vampires complement each other in that they are both mythical blood-drinking and flesh-eating creatures which were called upon during those times to provide colourful descriptions when particular predatory crimes were committed, providing a mystical 'explanation' for murders so horrible that they could not be countenanced. The enduring myth of the werewolf – a human who changes shape on the night of the full moon[2] – continued for a surprisingly long time to be brought forth to explain the deviant behaviour of individuals.

In 1849, Parisians were relieved to hear of the capture of the 'beast' which had been breaking into graves of women and small girls in cemeteries and tearing the bodies asunder, then rolling in the bloody fragments. The culprit was a junior infantry officer called Sergeant Bertrand and his description of the compulsion which took hold of him prior to committing these outrages bears similarity to those of the 'werewolves' of earlier times. Someone with cannibalistic homicidal urges may hallucinate enough to convince himself he is a vicious animal, then venture into the night to satisfy his primeval bloodlust, transferring the blame onto his alter ego, the wolf. In the perpetrator's eyes, this makes it the crime of the wolf and transforms the shameful dimension of man-eat-man cannibalism into the more acceptable wolf-eat-man killing.

Among indigenous Canadian people, the spirit of the werewolf – or Wendigo – was a persistent legend. It was believed that the Wendigo could possess a person and induce him to perform unspeakable acts, and in 1879 a Cree Indian named Katist Chen, who was also known as Swift Runner, claimed to have been influenced by the Wendigo when he murdered and ate his mother, wife, brother and six children during a hunting expedition the previous year. His earlier claim that the family had starved to death was dismissed and he was found guilty of murder. Later he confessed the Wendigo story to a priest and said that the spirit had visited him in his cell and tortured him to make him confess. Only this way, Swift Runner said, could he banish the spirit. He was hanged, notably being the first man executed by the Royal Canadian Mounted Police.

Reports of lycanthropy continue even today, although in enlightened Western society it is now considered a clinical delusional disorder. Sufferers – as with Gilles Garnier and Peter Stump, perhaps – believe themselves to be transformed into wolves and act accordingly, howling, unleashing bestial sexual attacks upon helpless victims and eating nothing but raw, bloody meat. Other sufferers, who are among at least eighteen recorded cases in Britain and France during the last quarter of the twentieth century, may believe themselves to be other animals like cats and dogs – and in one case, a thirty-five-year-old man thought he was a gerbil for three days. Robert Louis Stevenson's well-known *Dr Jekyll and Mr Hyde*, published in 1886, drew upon this sort of delusional illness and also used it to illustrate man's innate desire for aggression.

Fearsome legends develop in all manner of ways: in 1985, Dr David Dolphin, a Canadian chemist at the University of British Columbia in Vancouver, suggested there was a real physical disorder which might have contributed to werewolf and vampire legends during an age when scientific ignorance made people look for magical answers to inexplicable phenomena. Dr Dolphin described to the American Association for the Advancement of Science the physical symptoms of porphyria. This is a genetic condition which strikes one in 200,000 – which means there are around three hundred potential cases in Britain today – and it results in a lack of heme, which is produced in the liver, to help red blood cells carry haemoglobin. King George III of England was a sufferer and it has been suggested that the ailment also afflicted artist Vincent van Gogh and his siblings, in particular his brother Theo. Sufferers are so photosensitive that they can be disfigured by sunlight and may become intermittently frenzied and uncontrolled. When exposed to light the upper lip may recede and the skin crack, causing bleeding and the teeth to appear more prominent. Horrific skin lesions can appear on the face, again causing loss of blood.

The patient can crave blood and a major treatment for some porphyrias is an injection of heme, but during a time in history before such medical knowledge was available, the symptoms could have been relieved by the drinking of blood – and because of the aversion to sunlight, physicians would keep sufferers secluded during the day. Porphyria is but one reason why the legends of werewolves and vampires might have prevailed; one also has to consider the powerful cultural determinants such as preoccupation with the magical quality of blood and ingrained beliefs about creation and prolongation of life. And there is also that other overwhelming biological instinct, sex. The werewolf of legend had a fondness for tender flesh and warm, flowing blood, but he was quite prepared to devour the already-dead, unlike his fellow monster of myth, the vampire, whose prey had to be living. But they both had an inclination to sexually attack victims. It is fascinating that in modern fiction – and by modern, I mean little more than the last hundred years – while the werewolf is still regarded as a violent, fearsome brute, the vampire has acquired a seductive, sensual magnetism which owes much to Bram Stoker's infamous 'undead' creation who has been incarnated in more films than any other character – Dracula.

Before the nineteenth century, mythical vampires were regarded as charmless creatures who possessed the bodies of buried corpses. Red-faced, bloated and swollen like leeches with the blood they had consumed, they were said to be discovered when bodies were exhumed. In fact, there is a logical answer to this appearance of a cadaver: a physical rather than a supernatural explanation, consistent with a decomposing corpse which swells as the intestinal micro-organisms produce methane gas. The vampire's skin was said to be taut like the skin of a drum because of this bloating; the ancient Slavic view was that the vampire had no bones, but was merely a blood-filled sack – which one might think would seem to render the monster immobile, but for the fact that he was facilitated in his ghastly endeavours by the Devil's powers. But compare this image with that of more contemporary fiction: the tall, dark, slender aristocrat in his black cloak, whose pronounced canine teeth serve their primitive purpose (the teeth of legendary vampires before this time were unremarkable).

A sexual dimension was certainly present in vampires of folklore – they were said to be sexually rapacious and those suspected vampires who were exhumed and found to have erections (again, a common occurrence as bloated corpses begin the process of decomposition) fed this fable. But until the nineteenth century the vampire was not believed to use powers of seduction in order to achieve his predatory ends; only during this period did the bloodlust of the fictional vampire became irrevocably entwined with primitive sexuality through the rather obvious symbolism used, not necessarily consciously, by a sexually-frustrated Stoker among others. Accepting that myth has always exerted a hold on past and present beliefs, it is perhaps unsurprising that a libidinous Count Dracula tapped a rich vein of fascination in human beings which has resulted in a remarkable fictional evolution, especially in movies and on television where the figure of the vampire obliged to live forever has proved compelling. Anne Rice's novel of 1976, *Interview with the Vampire* – followed by the film of the same name, starring Tom Cruise and Brad Pitt – was one of the first to present bloodlust explicitly as uncontrollable sexual hunger, and this metaphor, inspiring fear, sympathy and in some cases arousal, says much about the primitive instincts which linger beneath the organised surface of our lives.

What is even more fascinating is the manner in which writers of fiction began to 'normalise' the vampire as the twentieth century passed into the twenty-first, creating empathy with the monster, even in works aimed at children. The writer Darren Shan produced a successful series of 'young adult' vampire novels, beginning with *Cirque du Freak* in 2000, in which the child protagonist experiences loneliness and alienation from all the people he loves after suffering a bite from a vampire and having to reconcile himself to an everlasting future as one of the undead. Later films such as those in the *Twilight* series and *Let the Right One In* (both released in 2008) and

TV series exemplified by *Being Human* and *True Blood* (both launched in 2008) and *The Vampire Diaries* (2009) not only invited the viewer to feel compassion and even affection for the vampires who live alongside humans and struggle like addicted junkies to conquer their appetites while condemned to everlasting life, but they also marked a further movement of the goalposts of long-held myth, permitting these individuals, for instance, to defy their earlier fictional pattern of behaviour: they were able to go out during daylight hours, see their reflections in mirrors and survive on the blood of animals or blood stored in blood banks, rather than that of humans.

On the UK's BBC TV, this trend was amusingly satirised in sketches by comedians Alexander Armstrong and Ben Miller playing foppish traditional vampires who express confused despair at such new modern rules of vampirism, and, like old men reminiscing, yearn for their own golden era when they were clear about what was 'normal' for a vampire and what was not. At least such modern distortions of the old blood-fuelled rules did not apply to the group of undead housemates negotiating the modern world in the 2014 comedy movie *What We Do in the Shadows* – followed by the three 2019–2021 TV series of the same name – but viewers were still intended to like and empathise with them. This was like *Friends*, but with added teeth, bats and buckets of blood.

★　★　★　★

SEXUAL DEVIANCE
The maintenance of a myth relies on a slight substratum of fact such as the appetite of the legendary vampire, which lies in our history and our subconscious. However, regardless of contemporary fictional representations of evolved vampires, in the real world of non-myth 'normal' sexuality

does not involve ingesting one's partner's blood. There are, though, a minority of people who do regard blood-sucking as an erotic experience. Vampirism is documented as deviant sexual behaviour by researchers such as Krafft-Ebing and although usually found in association with other psychiatric disorders, some evidence suggests that as a clinical entity on its own, it may be commoner that we imagine, especially when allied to criminal behaviour. Strictly speaking, the term 'vampirism' means the ingestion of fresh blood but clinically it can also refer to – and occur alongside – necrophilia (sex with a dead body) and necrophagia (consumption of dead human flesh). Vampirism – biting and ingesting blood – occurs in individuals operating at a primitive developmental level and is seen 'not infrequently' in association with serious sexual offending.

In November 2021, there was widespread disbelief and horror in the United Kingdom after the arrest of David Fuller from Kent, who pleaded guilty not only to murdering two women thirty-five years earlier, but to having sexually abused scores of corpses in the mortuaries of the hospitals where he had been working as an electrician. Sixty-seven years old at the end of 2020 when an innovative DNA breakthrough revealed his 1987 murders, Fuller's computers provided detectives with even more sickening evidence which marked him as Britain's most prolific sex offender: he had filmed and photographed himself sexually abusing the bodies of an 'unprecedented' number of women and girls whom he had removed from mortuary refrigerators. There were at least seventy-eight such identifiable victims among Fuller's hard drive collection of four-million images of sexual abuse, many of these downloaded from the internet. Fuller's victims ranged in age from under-eighteens to women over eighty-five. Among the multiple charges which Fuller admitted were thirty-three counts of sexually penetrating corpses. 'No British court has ever seen abuse on this scale against the dead before,' said a spokesman for the Crown Prosecution Service.

In the present day, we consider ourselves an advanced species, putting a premium on finer emotions like love, compassion and protection of the weak. We call this 'humanity' and are shaken and devastated when individuals like Fuller break the ascribed rules of 'civilisation' and plummet to its lowest ebb. In the late-nineteenth century, Europeans were equally shocked by killers like the still unidentified Jack the Ripper, who not only murdered five women in London, ritually disemboweling them, but also took the kidney of one victim and wrote to the police, saying it tasted 'nise' [sic]. During the same period, in Europe, twenty-nine-year-old 'French Ripper' Joseph Vacher went to the guillotine after confessing to slaughtering eleven women and youths in south-east France – strangling, stabbing, raping, mutilating, castrating and disembowelling them, as well as inflicting terrible injuries with his teeth. Across the Atlantic, in 1897, German-born Adolph Luetgert, a Chicago butcher, murdered his wife and used her flesh in sausages which he sold to his customers. The story traumatised America and, like the British and French killers, the name of Luetgert entered the annals of that country's history of horror.

But the twentieth century was to see more, not fewer, cannibal killers emerge.

* * * *

In the Soviet Union, a century on from Vacher and Jack the Ripper, Andrei Chikatilo (see Chapter Nine) operated using exactly the same methods and his dreadful toll was fifty-five victims – the worst individual sadistic serial killer the modern world had known when he came to trial in 1992, even taking into account his fellow Russian, Nikolai Dzhumagaliev, whose white metal false teeth had earned him the name 'Metal Fang' in the media. Institutionalized in 1980 for his crimes, Dzhumagaliev had killed at least seven women – he claimed there were scores more – and he had served their flesh to friends at parties. He was exposed by two of his guests, who discovered a severed head and intestines inside his refrigerator. Mystifyingly, 'Metal Fang' was released in 2001 and by that time, another Russian, Alexander Spesivtsev had challenged Chikatilo's sickening record. Dubbed 'The Cannibal of Siberia', Spesivtsev killed and consumed at least nineteen street-children and women but was suspected of some eighty murders in total. He was captured in 1996 after a plumber who had entered his empty apartment to repair a broken pipe at the request of neighbours, discovered blood-spattered walls, human flesh in the kitchen, a decapitated and mutilated body in the bath, and a horribly injured woman, who was still alive. She died in hospital a day later, having given evidence to the police. In 1999, judged insane by a Russian court, Spesivtsev was committed to a psychiatric hospital. His mother, Lyudmila Spesivtsev, was imprisoned for thirteen years as an accomplice.

In 1976, in the heavily industrial Ruhr region of West Germany, Joachim Kroll, a brown-eyed, balding little man of forty-three, admitted having killed more than a dozen people, some as young as three years old, over the previous twenty years. But the police believed the figure was much higher. Kroll could not remember them all, for he had a poor memory and lost interest in his victims after he had killed, raped, mutilated and, in the majority of cases, cooked and eaten the flesh from their bodies. Kroll, who was a lavatory attendant, was not judged to have the above-average intelligence which psychiatrists sometimes associate with sadistic serial killers. On the contrary, he was labelled as mentally deficient by the authorities owing to his lack of schooling and inability to read. There was also his odd behaviour when arrested: he displayed an apparent unconcern about his crimes, a readiness to co-operate and a naive belief that after confessing he would be allowed to go back home – perhaps, he speculated, after a medical operation to render him harmless to the opposite sex.

As with the majority of sadistic killers, Kroll had never had a successful relationship with a woman. Many of his targeted victims were small girls and he kept a large collection of children's dollies as bait. Several little girls went for walks hand-in-hand with 'Uncle Joachim', clutching one of his dolls. Almost all of them were unharmed, possibly because Kroll was forbidden by his tenancy regulations to take them up to his room (which did not stop him from frequently trying to do so), but more likely because he knew that the children's parents were aware of the whereabouts of their infants; they regarded Kroll as kindly and trustworthy. However, his final murder victim was four-year-old Monika Kettner, a little blonde girl who lived a few doors away from his apartment and whom he had plucked from the nearby children's playground and smuggled into his room. She was the only local child to have been murdered by Kroll, a discovery made by police who were called to the apartment block by his neighbours. Little Monika's remains – including a complete set of internal organs – were blocking up a shared toilet on the landing. The rest of the child was discovered by police to be boiling in a stew on Kroll's stove and neatly wrapped in pieces in the refrigerator and deep-freeze.

Kroll usually looked farther afield for his prey, travelling on public transport across his region to indiscriminate places. His first sadistic killing (he confessed to the police) was in Walstedde in 1955 when he was twenty-two years old, the victim being nineteen-year-old Irmgard Strehl. This was followed many months later by the murder of another young woman, Klara Tesmer, using an identical modus operandi – but this time a hundred miles away in Rheinhausen. The third killing, he remembered, was that of sixteen-year-old Manuela Knodt in Bredeney to the east, a half-hour trip by train from his hometown. This apparent randomness of location caused confusion and averted suspicion. The police in each town perceived no links between the killings and, tragically, a Rheinhausen man, Heinrich Ott, who was arrested and charged with Klara's killing and several other sex murders in the region over the preceding few years, hanged himself while awaiting trial. In retrospect we may wonder whether Kroll was responsible for at least some of those unsolved murders – and for subsequent others which Kroll, under arrest, claimed had slipped his memory.

Over the years, Kroll was greatly aided by the blunders of the German police. After two separate murders of girls aged twelve and thirteen in the Bruckhausen region in 1962, officers began to come to unthinkable conclusions: flesh had been removed from the buttocks and thighs of both the children and each of the neighbouring police forces acknowledged with horror that the man they sought was a cannibalistic killer. Unfortunately, they did not share this view with each other and make the connection. Thus it was that yet two more innocent men in adjacent areas were arrested for the two murders. Despite their denials, one man was convicted and received a twelve-year prison sentence and the other, Walter Quicker, on whom the police lacked any evidence, was nevertheless ostracised by his community upon his release and, in his misery, committed suicide.

Again, in 1966, Adolf Schickel, the fiancé of twenty-year-old Ursula Rohling who had been a Kroll victim, was questioned by police for weeks but although they believed him guilty, they had no proof and reluctantly they set him free. The story became a tragic parallel to that of Walter Quicker: ostracised by his former friends and neighbours who also branded him as guilty, Schickel was driven out of the town and less than four months after his fiancée's death, he drowned himself in a river. And yet another case: after Kroll's killing of a thirteen-year-old girl in a town close to Grossenbaum in 1970, Peter Schay was punished by the community, if not the law. He had been charged but cleared of the murder because there was no concrete evidence to convict. Nevertheless he was cruelly taunted by his neighbours as a 'murderer'.

It would be another six years before Kroll's confession absolved all these unfortunate men of the crimes they were believed to have committed. Kroll was given a life sentence and a place in history as the perpetrator of the longest series of sadistic murders which had ever been known in Germany, a country which has always had a high rate of sex murders. Throughout the twenty-year manhunt, though, the police emerged with little credit, readily attributing Kroll's rapes and murders to other people. Not only had innocent men in the Ruhr region killed themselves or been wrongly sentenced, but when Kroll was finally captured, police suspicions extended to only a handful of victims. Kroll supplied confessions to the remainder, often by remarking casually: 'I think I murdered someone in that town.' Police then matched up the unsolved crimes with Kroll's recollections as to when, where and how the murders had happened. It is truly astonishing that a region less than fifty miles long by twenty miles wide could be littered with the corpses of Kroll's victims and yet Kroll could escape detection for decades.

On the other side of the world, similar stories became known. Dean Baker confessed to a Californian patrolman in 1970: 'I have a problem: I'm a cannibal.' Whereupon he pulled from his pocket a man's severed fingers and admitted to killing someone and eating his heart raw. In New York, history teacher Albert Fentress had invited an eighteen-year-old boy into his house, then shot him, cut up his body and ate parts of it. He was committed to a mental institution indefinitely in 1979. Four years later, Michael Woodmansee was jailed for killing and cannibalising a young boy in Rhode Island. He was set free in 2011 after serving twenty-eight years of a forty-year sentence. Further south, in Rio, Marcelo Costa de Andrade was arrested in December 1991 and confessed that during the previous eight months he had killed fourteen boys aged from six to thirteen, and drunk their blood 'to become young and pretty like them'. In 2007 in Mexico City, José Luis Calva was sentenced to eighty-four years for killing and eating his girlfriend, although circumstantial evidence linked him to eight other murders. Calva committed suicide in jail a few months later.

Europe has also seen cannibalistic crimes during the same *fin de siècle* period: German Walter Krone went to jail for seven years in 1980 for eating parts of a girl who had died in a street accident and in Turkey the 'Cannibal of Ankara' Özgür Dengiz murdered three men in 2007, including a computer engineer who had angered him by suggesting that he could not afford to buy a laptop he was looking at. When fresh human meat was found in his apartment Dengiz declared: 'I love to eat human flesh. It makes me ecstatic.' In London, in 1992, Mark Heggie, aged twenty-three, drank the blood of his victim after trying to kill her, telling detectives he often drank animals' blood and had obtained work in abattoirs to satisfy his craving. He was sent to a mental hospital. The cannibalistic murder in 1998 of Julie Paterson, a thirty-one-year-old mother of four from Darlington in the north-east of England, set off an extraordinary chain of events. The killer, David

Harker, admitted the crime, boasting to friends: 'I've killed a girl called Julie,' and later telling a psychiatrist that he dismembered her before cooking her flesh with pasta and cheese, but refusing to reveal the whereabouts of her corpse. By chance a torso was found in a binbag in an overgrown garden – but other body parts have never been recovered. Harker bragged that he had killed two people previously and, pleading diminished responsibility to the manslaughter charge, he was imprisoned for life. One of the psychiatrists who interviewed him concluded that he was 'evil'. There is a postscript to this story, however: Julie's death left her partner Alan Taylor a broken man who became obsessed with avenging himself on Harker. In 2006, Taylor was an unemployed alcoholic living in a hostel when he strangled a fellow tenant to death. He was hoping that his thirteen-year sentence would be served at Darlington Jail – the prison where Harker was – and some said this was part of his murder-revenge plan all along. But Taylor was sent to a different prison. Three months later he hanged himself in his cell.

Bradford, Yorkshire – also in the north of England – was the location of three of the thirteen murders committed by 'Yorkshire Ripper' Peter Sutcliffe, during the late 1970s. In 2010, Bradford was once again the focus of murder enquiries when Stephen Griffiths admitted killing three women there using a crossbow, then eating parts of them, both raw and cooked. Griffiths was a part-time Ph.D. student who was studying criminology. In court, he gave his name as 'the Crossbow Cannibal' – which was his MySpace 'handle'. By 2020, Griffiths had made six suicide attempts while serving a life sentence in Wakefield Prison, a jail known as 'Monster Mansion' because of the high number of murderers and rapists held there.

It seems that whatever the century, few parts of Great Britain remain free of this most heinous of crimes and in South Wales during November 2014, another crazed cannibal claimed a victim. Twenty-two-year-old Cerys Yemm was killed by Matthew Williams – whom she had just met – after going back with him to his room in a bail hostel for newly-released prisoners near Newport. The police, responding to an emergency call, found Cerys near death and lying in a pool of blood while Williams was reported to be eating his victim alive, tearing at her face and eyes with his teeth. The thirty-four-year-old killer was tasered by the officers and subsequently died: Williams had a history of drugs and violence offences and had only two weeks earlier been released from prison after serving half of a sentence for a violent attack on a former girlfriend. He had been high on drugs at the time of the attack on Cerys. In April 2017, an inquest jury passed a verdict of Cerys's unlawful killing by Williams.

In 2004, South Korea was stunned by the crimes of thirty-four-year-old Yoo Young-chul, who was declared the country's worst serial murderer. He confessed to killing twenty people between 2003 and 2004 – mostly prostitutes and wealthy men – decapitating, mutilating and eating the raw livers of at least eleven of them. 'Women shouldn't be sluts and the rich should know what they've done,' the unrepentant Young-chul told the media by way of explanation for his crimes. He was sentenced to death in Seoul in 2005, the first such sentence handed out since 1997. South Korea is one of only three established, developed democracies which still retains the death penalty (the others are Japan and the USA) and at the time of Young-chul's crimes the South Korean government was engaged in debate regarding its abolition, which in 2020 is still ongoing. Meanwhile, Young-chul remains on death row.

Although much rarer, there have been female cannibal-killers, too: twenty-six-year-old Anna Zimmermann from

Mönchengladbach, Germany, who in 1981 murdered her lover, cut his body into pan-sized steaks and, after saving them in the freezer together with a finger, an ear and his penis, fed him to her two children, who were aged six and four – something she had previously done with the family pets. And Australian Tracey Wigginton, who stabbed to death a man she met at a Brisbane dance in 1989 and, according to the friends who were with her at the time, supposedly did it in order to drink his blood in the belief that she was a vampire. Two psychiatrists testified their belief that Wigginton suffered from dissociative identity ('multiple personality') disorder, but she was imprisoned for life and finally released on parole in 2012.

Eighty-year-old grandmother Sofya Mikhailovna was dubbed the 'Russian Sweeney Todd' when, in October 2019, the ingredients were revealed for the meals and sweetmeats which she had made for her neighbours in Khabarovsk. They were unaware that the meat-in-aspic dishes that she gave them, or the jellied sweets she handed to local children, had been created from the flesh of her victims, including that of her lodger, whose dismembered body parts were found in her fridge after she was arrested. The police suspected Mikhailovna of at least another seven murders spanning fifteen years; among her victims was an eight-year-old girl who had earned the woman's wrath because she was noisy and rude to her. The child's severed head was found in 2005 and prosecutors said that forensic evidence in Mikhailovna's apartment linked her to the girl's murder.

Such females are the exception and in the chapters which follow – focusing on murder cases within the last hundred years where such cannibalistic perversions play a fundamental role – the culprits are almost exclusively males who are held in the grip of a sexual compulsion. For, having looked at dietary need, nutritional desperation, magic, religion and cultural factors as motives for cannibalism and blood-drinking, here is the final reason, the only one truly in operation today: sexual desire originating from the sort of primal instincts which I have described. Bloodlust is a motivating factor, but the incidents in the following chapters bear no resemblance to those in fictions such as *Dracula*, in which a victim falls helplessly beneath the vampire's voluptuous spell, willingly surrenders to his desires and then experiences something akin to orgasm during the vampire's 'love bite'. The real victims are torn apart and brutally savaged in a way which would have more in common with the mythical werewolf than the vampire. We are looking here at the lowest, most heinous point on an imaginary scale of sexual behaviour. And could it, perhaps, compare with man's evolution? Man's forebears emerged carnivorous from the slimy swamp, passed through aeons of blood-filled ritual ruled by primal instincts like cannibalism and blood-drinking, and now, in the twenty-first century, we imagine we have reached the pinnacle of evolutionary accomplishment. As this book illustrates, some of us clearly have not, for those same primeval instincts drive the individuals who now turn to cyberspace to share their most depraved desires with others who are similarly inclined.

What does this tell us about the state of humanity in our generation? We live in an age when, across the globe, appalling violence is still an active currency. In the Middle Ages the powerful were sanctimoniously slaughtering 'witches', but as events in recent history prove, the human ability to abandon enlightened principles and indulge in unspeakable cruelty – even genocide – still needs little prompting. For all the horror with which we look back upon the millions of lives destroyed over the last century in modern witch hunts perpetrated by nations against each other, or against ethnic or religious minorities or political opponents, similar events still persist in the 2020s, made possible by regiments of apparently sane people who are easily induced to wipe out thousands of their own species. And in the comfortable West where values such as democracy, freedom and human rights are a source of pride, this generation at the wave-front of history has a record number of serial killers either in prison or on the loose, and there are more instances of sadistic attacks and murders of the helpless, sometimes for no reason other than for 'kicks'.

A greater proportion of 'civilised' Westerners are excited by the scent of terror and blood than we may wish to admit, and fetishists abound. Psychiatrists now have a name for the unusual psychiatric condition (or paraphilia) whereby an individual is sexually aroused by the erotic fantasy of eating or being eaten by another being: vorarephilia, a word taken from the Latin *vorare* meaning 'to swallow or devour' and the Ancient Greek *philia*: 'to love'. A 2014 study by James Cantor and Amy Lykins indicates that not infrequently vorarephilia occurs alongside other deviant desires such as bondage, humiliation and sadomasochism, pregnancy fetishes, the fantasy of being swallowed alive, coprophilia, sexual attraction to unrealistically disproportionately-sized people (and in some instances of being eaten by such a person and then expelled in their faeces) and sexual arousal associated with eating human flesh.

Putting to one side a tendency to fantasise and fetishise – which is unique to our species – sexual cannibalism is primarily to be found among the much lower orders of living creatures like insects and arachnids – it is well-known that the female praying mantis and certain female spiders often eat their suitors during mating. I wonder just how far removed the nature of *Homo sapiens* is from the atavistic impulses which control other lower species as well as our own evolving ancestors – or, indeed, from those murderers in our midst whose sexuality can only operate at such a primordial, carnivorous level? What happens in these warped individuals to stir their dreadful instincts? Here's a question: is our revulsion to cannibalism a kind of acquired response, rather than a 'natural' one? On the evidence of man's ever-present capacity for inhumanity, could we all become heartless killers – and even revert to cannibalism – given the right set of circumstances?

And H. G. Wells's *The Time Machine*: was that time-travel story forward through the years really a comment on man's future? Or was it perhaps about man's subconscious impulses?

Cruelty Amid Chaos

'If you were to destroy in mankind the belief in immortality, not only love but every living force maintaining the life of the world would at once be dried up. Moreover, nothing then would be immoral, everything would be permissible, even cannibalism'

Fyodor Dostoyevsky, *The Brothers Karamazov*

Cannibal killers are few and far between. While the number of criminal homicides peaked towards the end of the twentieth century it declined thereafter, apart from the occasional sharp spike on the graph in recent years, which then subsided. The homicide figure is still alarming, however: in 2019 there were almost sixteen thousand murders in the United States alone. Statistics show that the incidence of serial murders also began to decline sharply from nearly a thousand internationally in the 1990s to a quarter of that number during the last decade. Nevertheless there have been more serial killings over the last hundred years than ever before in civilisation's history. Among those, the crime which, because of its primitive bestiality, evokes the ultimate revulsion in the overwhelming majority of us is, thankfully, uncommon. How curious, then, that a comparatively small country like Germany has produced an unrepresentative number of cannibalistic murderers, with four of the most infamous of these operating during the 1920s – between the two world wars.

After the Great War of 1914–18, anarchy reigned in Germany. Law and order had collapsed, there was a profusion of thieves and confidence tricksters – and the rest of the people got by as best they could. Article 231 of the 1919 Treaty of Versailles, known as the 'War Guilt clause', ordered Germany to take the blame for starting the war and 'causing all the loss and damage', demanding that it disarmed, made territorial concessions and paid reparations to certain other countries amounting to £6.6 billion. A century on, this sum is equivalent to £284 billion or $442 billion. Forced to sign the treaty and obey its demands, Germany's economy went into free fall and the country entered a period of chaos. There was an atmosphere of godlessness. Streams of refugees roamed the cities looking for jobs, begging on the streets and sleeping on pavements. Sections of society – socialists, communists, Jews – began to be scapegoated as having questionable loyalty to the country. A backwards glance at the way Nazism was able to flourish and gain primacy over the next decade invites speculation about what exactly was happening to human nature in German society during this time, which predisposed an overwhelming number of its people to tolerate – and take part in – the atrocities which lay in store. One evolutionary answer immediately springs to mind. When the viability of any species or group hits rock bottom, the law of the jungle dictates the survival of the fittest. But that does not necessarily mean the survival of the best.

Into this desperate society one morning in 1918 walked a newly-liberated Fritz Haarmann; the prison gates slammed shut behind him and he breathed the fresh air of freedom once more. Recognising Hanover as being riddled with crooks and villains who exploited those weaker than themselves, Haarmann felt at home. He liked the world he now found himself in. He had not seen military service for he had been serving a five-year jail term for fraud and theft, the most recent in a long history of imprisonments imposed as punishment for stealing, picking pockets or indecently assaulting small children. He was thirty-nine in 1918 and had little to show for his life, having spent it as an itinerant hawker and thief, devoted to his mother who had been incapacitated after his birth and remained a lifelong invalid, but filled with hatred for his father, an embittered railway worker with the revealing nickname of Sulky Olle. Fritz's father had beaten him and made his childhood desperately unhappy. As Fritz grew older it became apparent that his IQ was lower than average and he showed signs of the uncontrolled violence which was to make him one of the worst mass murderers of all time. With what turns out in hindsight to have been commendable astuteness, Fritz's father had tried to have him committed permanently to an institution when he sensed the potential dangerousness of the boy, but doctors declared Fritz safe and refused Herr Haarmann's request. Had they thought otherwise, a great many deaths would have been averted.

As a child, Fritz used to enjoy dressing up in the clothes of his three sisters – they had drifted into prostitution when they were comparatively young – and as a teenager he was sent to a mental institution for a spell after attacking small children. He escaped to join the army, but was soon dismissed as an 'undesirable' and it was then that he devoted himself to a career of theft and sex attacks. A fleshy man with superficial charm, he was blatantly homosexual and made his mark on the criminal underworld, where he was well liked but considered to be rather stupid, if harmless. He would have been rather less popular had his associates realised he was also a police informer, for this was yet another string to Haarmann's bow. The police approved of him because of his 'it's a fair cop' attitude: he never resisted arrest, appeared to enjoy the discipline of jail life and joked with them as they pulled him in. He was nicknamed 'Detective' by the Hanover police because he told them of so many planned crimes and plots; he was even paid a small salary and given a badge – something which provided excellent cover for him to commit his own dreadful crimes. Moving among the swindlers at the market in Hanover, Haarmann began gravitating to the nearby railway station, where wretched refugees arrived from all over the country to huddle around stoves in the station's waiting area and beg from passers-by. Among them were scores of homeless youths, some not even teenagers, most of whom were runaways, many being nameless, therefore untraceable. Over the next five years these boys proved easy prey for Haarmann, literally. A smiling Haarmann would flash his police badge and invite a youth to accompany him home. Coupled with his charm and apparent sympathy for their plight, the promise of a good meal tempted these lost and hungry youngsters to return with him to his apartment as easily as the witch persuaded Hansel and Gretel to enter her gingerbread cottage. And Haarmann had exactly the same thing in mind.

The apartment which he shared from 1919 with his young lover, twenty-year-old Hans Grans, was in Hanover's ghetto area, on the third floor of a crumbling block overlooking the River Leine. After bringing the youths home, Haarmann would seduce or attack them, use them for his own sexual gratification, and then kill them by tearing their throats out with his teeth, after which he would drink their blood and indulge in necrophiliac activities. Then he would drag the victim's body up to his attic, where the walls were crimson with encrusted blood. There, sometimes helped by Grans, he would dismember the body and slice it up, transferring the pieces of flesh to buckets. Then Haarmann donned his other vile identity: that of market meat-trader. Taking his buckets of human flesh, he sold it, along with second-hand clothes, at his stall in Hanover's marketplace, telling the hungry German citizens that it was horsemeat. The clothes of his victims also found their way on to his stall. His black-market meat business was highly successful – after all, his prices were lower than anyone else's – and the police, who needed spies like Haarmann to enable them to monitor underworld corruption, turned a blind eye to the illegal trading activities of their paid nark.

Haarmann's first victim among the starving and penniless boys who fell prey to his bribery and charm was seventeen-year-old Friedel Roth, who disappeared in 1918 after being seen with Haarmann. The police investigation led them to Haarmann's door, but their enquiries were half-hearted; Haarmann was, after all, very useful to them. Many years later, when he was finally caught, Haarmann bragged that when police visited his room, 'the head of the boy was lying wrapped in newspaper behind the oven'. When Haarmann met the psychopathic Hans Grans (who, curiously enough, was a runaway who escaped the lost boys' usual fate) the slim, elegant youth was to incite him to further outrages. Grans, a librarian's son, was Haarmann's social superior and tormented Haarmann with sarcastic remarks and insults. He selected victims and ordered their murder, often simply because he wanted their clothes. Haarmann sold clothes from victims only days after having killed them. On one occasion, Grans was identified as wearing a suit that only a few days earlier had been seen on a boy at the railway station.

Haarmann's neighbours were oblivious to what was going on, although they were later to recall that they often saw a large number of young men entering the apartment, but never saw them leaving. They heard chopping noises through the walls but thought nothing of it; after all, this man was a butcher so it was only to be expected that he chopped up carcasses. Even when one neighbour bumped into Haarmann in the hall when he was carrying a bucket of blood downstairs, she suspected nothing. Another, meeting Haarmann after he had been butchering a body in his attic, asked him cheekily, 'Am I going to get a bit?' Haarmann merely laughed and promised her some meat next time. Occasionally he would supply meat to people in the other apartments. His main problem – disposing of the skulls and bones of his victims – was somewhat solved by giving the bones to the neighbours, who would make soup with them, believing them to be from animals. But eventually, people began to harbour suspicions. These bones were too white, they murmured. What sort of animal did they come from? Haarmann stopped handing the bones out and tossed them, with the skulls, into the river which flowed close by. One customer who bought some meat from Haarmann's market stall was worried enough to go and ask the police what it was. She was told it was pork.

If the police really did suspect the true nature of Haarmann's activities – and perhaps one can understand why such a terrible idea never entered their heads – it was in their interest to ignore it. Time and again, parents in search of their lost sons found the trail of clues led to Haarmann, who had been the last person with whom their sons had been seen; time and again the police declared themselves satisfied that he was innocent, with no connection to the youths' disappearances. By 1923, Haarmann had become of great value to the police and was under their protection. He was helping them to recruit people for a secret organisation which wanted to combat French occupation of the Ruhr and he had even joined forces with a prestigious police official to run a detective agency. But thankfully the newspapers were under no obligation to protect a killer or draw a veil over police corruption. It was they who eventually pressured the authorities into taking some action by highlighting the number of youths who arrived in Hanover and then instantly disappeared. One newspaper suggested the figure could have been as high as 600 in one year. With publicity, the very name 'Hanover' began to induce a chill and rumours began to circulate that there were such things as werewolves after all – and that one was at large in the town, eating the children. The police pooh-poohed such suggestions and dismissed them as hysteria. Then, a skull was washed ashore beside the River Leine.

It was May 1924 and the frightened public began harassing the authorities and demanding action. A second skull – a small one – was discovered a few days later, and more were found in the months to come, together with sacks full of human remains. Dredgers were brought in to dig in the riverbed: more than five hundred human bones were found. The horrified citizens of Hanover were defying their own disbelief and putting two and two together. Haarmann was their prime suspect. Knowing public opinion was against him, the chief of police had no alternative but to have his valued informer watched. At the end of June 1924 in Hanover railway station Haarmann tried to pick up a boy who then called the police, accusing Haarmann of having sexually interfered with him. Haarmann was arrested and, with him in custody, officers went to search his apartment. They found the bloodstained room, together with piles of clothes, but, when confronted, Haarmann protested. He was a butcher, he said, and a clothes trader. What did they expect to find? To the police officers, blood was blood and offered few forensic clues, even as regards the mammal from whence it had come. In 1924, DNA fingerprinting lay sixty years in the future and even the research evidence on blood types was not to be disclosed for another six years.

It was the mother of a missing boy reporting that her son's coat was being worn by one of Haarmann's neighbours, which prompted the killer's full confession. He instantly implicated Grans in the murders. At the trial in December 1924, Haarmann, now forty-five, and Grans, twenty-five, were charged with the murder of twenty-seven teenage boys, but this was believed to be an underestimate. One policeman believed that during the previous year or so, Haarmann and Grans had been killing two boys a week. When asked how many youths he had murdered, Haarmann shrugged carelessly and replied, 'It might have been thirty, it might have been forty. I really can't remember the exact number,' and this ghoulish contempt was evident throughout the trial. Famous now, he regarded the courtroom as his stage. Although Grans remained silent throughout, Haarmann behaved like a callous showman, admitting his guilt, showing no remorse but instead making vulgar asides to Grans. Despite there being heartbroken relatives of his victims in court, he interrupted proceedings at will, often making jocular remarks and claiming that he was a selective killer, choosing only to kill good-looking boys and denying three of the charges. One parent whose son was missing showed a picture to the court and Haarmann objected indignantly, cruelly saying, 'I have my tastes, after all. Such an ugly creature as, according to his photographs, your son must have been, I would never have taken to ... Poor stuff like him there's plenty ... Such a youngster was much beneath my notice.' One distraught mother broke down while testifying and Haarmann, finding this tiresome, interrupted to ask the judges if he could smoke a cigar. Amazingly, he was given permission.

The newspapers, which had been so instrumental in bringing Haarmann to justice, were revolted at the way he behaved and did not conceal it. One report described the pitiful scenes: 'as a poor father or mother would recognise some fragment or other of the clothing or belongings of their murdered son ... And with the quivering nostrils of a hound snuffling his prey, as if he were scenting rather than seeing the things displayed, did he admit at once that he knew them.' People in court paled when Haarmann was asked how he killed his victims and he replied without emotion, 'I bit them through their throats.' He became furious when it seemed to him that Hans Grans might be found innocent. 'Grans should tell you how shabbily he has treated me,' he protested. 'I did the murders – for that work he is too young.' But he told how Grans knocked on the attic door after he had just finished dismembering one body, and said, on entering, 'Where is the suit?' Cold and unmoved, Grans remained unnervingly silent, which the crowds in court found equally horrifying.

Haarmann was anxious not to be found insane and sent to a mental hospital, instead pleading with the court to behead him in public, on the spot where he had plied his evil trade. 'I want to be executed in the marketplace,' he demanded excitedly. 'And on my tombstone must be put this inscription: "Here lies Mass Murderer Haarmann". On my birthday Hans Grans must come and lay a wreath upon it.' On the last day of the trial he shouted at the court: 'Do you think I enjoy killing people? I was ill for eight days after the first time. Condemn me to death ... I am not mad. It is true I often get into a state when I do not know what I am doing, but that is not madness ... I will not petition for mercy, nor will I appeal. I just want to pass one more merry evening in my cell with coffee, hard cheese and cigars, after which I will curse my father and go to my execution as if it were a wedding.'

Two psychiatrists declared that Haarmann was mentally sound. He was found guilty of twenty-four murders and beheaded. Grans was sentenced to life imprisonment but was released after twelve years, to walk the streets once more.

★ ★ ★ ★

Haarmann was proof that given the right social conditions, a killer who is careful and cautious can escape detection for years. Between-the-wars Germany with its catastrophic hyperinflation and mass unemployment evidently provided the right climate in which the usual restraints of civilisation were removed, allowing perverts and psychopaths to flourish. Just as history has told how primitive peoples who have practised cannibalism and brutishness abandon it when touched by civilisation, the reverse evidently applies. With poverty rife in Germany at this period, survival and self-interest were the dominant motivators, so maybe it is no surprise that 'dog eat dog' became a byword. And it seems in many cases, people ate people, too.

Haarmann had two cannibal contemporaries. George Grossmann, like Haarmann, butchered an unknown number of people during the years after the First World War. Unlike Haarmann, his primary urge for killing was said to be fuelled by mercenary greed rather than sexual deviance, although one might doubt the truth of this, for even the most avaricious villain would blanch at Grossmann's method of getting rich illegally. The modus operandi was startlingly similar to Haarmann's. A pedlar, he hung around Berlin's railway station and picked out women who were particularly plump. He took them home, killed them and chopped up their bodies into cuts of meat to sell to the hungry people of Berlin. With inflation running so high that armfuls of money were needed to buy even a loaf of bread (at one point the German mark stood at nineteen million to the British pound), Grossmann's cut-price joints proved popular and highly lucrative. He lived in a Berlin rooming-house and, in 1921, tenants in adjoining rooms reported hearing sounds of a struggle coming from his room. When police burst in, they found the trussed-up corpse of a girl on the bed, waiting to be butchered by Grossmann. Grossmann hanged himself in jail.

Meanwhile, in Münsterberg, Silesia (now Ziębice, Poland), Karl Denke was running a boarding-house, offering free accommodation for the many homeless tramps who passed through the city during the dire years between 1918 and 1924. They should have known there was no such thing as a free lunch. If one mark of a maniac is a glib exterior and the ability to charm one's associates, then Denke, like so many other psychopathic killers, displayed it. He was known as 'Papa' among his neighbours and tenants and was regarded as a God-fearing, law-abiding man. Every Sunday, he went to church, where he played the organ, and his kindness to the homeless was admired.

But as a landlord, he had his tenants at his mercy – and since many were vagrants about whom no one asked any questions, they made easy prey for Denke. Between 1921 and 1924 he killed at least thirty strangers, male and female, in order to eat their flesh, bit by bit. Then, as a chilling postscript to his abhorrent activities, he methodically entered in a ledger the victims' names, weight, date of arrival at the boarding-house and date of death, before pickling parts of the bodies in brine to eat later. Just before Christmas 1924, his crimes were discovered. A man who lived on the storey above Denke heard terrible screams from the lower floor and rushed downstairs to find a young man bleeding profusely from a wound on the back of his head, caused by a hatchet. The man, who was one of Denke's tenants, soon lost consciousness, but before doing so, managed to say that Denke had attacked him from behind. The police, thinking it was a routine assault case, were staggered to find pots of bones and the pickled remains of thirty bodies in Denke's flat. Denke admitted his crime and said he had eaten nothing but human flesh for three years. Soon after his arrest in 1924 Denke committed suicide by hanging himself with his braces in his prison cell.

But if these quietly cunning cannibal killers escaped justice for so long, the infamous Peter Kürten, who was also busy instilling terror into the folk of Düsseldorf at around this time, outlasted them, managing to avoid detection for seventeen years, from 1913, when he committed his first murder, to 1930. Kürten was inspired by his own madness, rather than anything as mundane as financial expedience during an economic slump. His insanity was portrayed by Peter Lorre in Fritz Lang's 1931 movie about Kürten's crimes, *M*.

The 'Düsseldorf Vampire', as he came to be known, was born in 1883, one of thirteen children in a family steeped in crime and violence. His brothers all served jail sentences for theft and his father and grandfather were both alcoholics. His father was cruel and violent to both his wife and his children. He would take his violent sexual impulses out on his wife by having brutal intercourse with her as the children watched her pain and indignity, and he regularly raped his daughter during her childhood and beyond. Kürten followed his example and raped the girl, too.

When he was a child of only nine years, Kürten was additionally drawn into the sordid world of yet another individual who would aid his conditioning into the future of blood and violence which he was to enjoy. The man was the local council's dog- and rat-catcher who had a penchant for torturing animals; part of his sickness was to do it while the young Kürten watched. Kürten found the sight of suffering animals stimulating, and since the rat-catcher also committed sexual acts as part of his attacks, yet again the coupling of sex and sadism reinforced the child Peter's sexual predilections. Kürten soon graduated to committing his own acts of torture, stabbing sheep and other docile farm animals. He found the sight of blood particularly stimulating and often tore the heads off swans to enable him to drink their blood, a taste he never outgrew; when he was an adult and murdered many people, he often indulged in brutal sadism and necrophilia, sometimes drinking the blood of the corpses.

At the age of sixteen, he met an older woman whose masochistic tendencies complemented his sadistic desires. During sex, she would enjoy being half-strangled and beaten and she even drew her daughter – who was the same age as Kürten – into their sexual acts. But despite their apparent carnal compatability, the relationship failed. Soon after this, Kürten attacked a girl in a wood and left her for dead, but she survived. Then came an attack on another girl, whom he tried to strangle, for which he was arrested and sent to prison for a derisory four years. Altogether, Kürten spent twenty-seven years in prison out of the forty-seven years of his life, during which time he contented himself by fantasising about performing sadistic acts upon the helpless, or killing schoolchildren by giving them chocolate laced with arsenic. He also obtained sexual pleasure from imagining setting fire to buildings, causing the people inside to perish and upon release he began to act out his fantasies for real. Fortunately, no one died during the fires which he started, but his sadism claimed many victims. Several women and children who were attacked escaped over the years, but many more were slaughtered.

His violence first exploded into murder in 1913 when he broke into a tavern and killed the ten-year-old daughter of the innkeeper as she lay asleep in bed. Kürten recalled the killing in detail at his trial, showing no emotion other than enjoyment at the recollection. 'I discovered the child asleep. Her head was facing the window. I seized it with my left hand and strangled her for about a minute and a half. The child woke up and struggled but lost consciousness ... I had a small but sharp pocket knife with me and I held the child's head and cut her throat. I heard the blood spurt and drip on the mat beside the bed ... The whole thing lasted about three minutes.' The day after the murder, Kürten went to a café opposite the inn to drink a glass of beer, to read about the murder in the newspaper and to listen to shocked locals discussing the crime. 'All this amount of horror and indignation did me good,' he said.

Called up to the army, Kürten deserted the following day – presumably the sight of blood and death only held appeal when he was not at personal risk. He ended up in jail once more for arson offences and volunteered to work in the prison hospital to enable him to lay out prisoners who had died. Kürten's appearance belied his bloodlust. He was a fastidious, charming, smartly-groomed, well-spoken man with impeccable manners, able easily to persuade his victims to walk with him in a park, or otherwise meet him alone. Children, too, warmed to him and trusted him, which made his grisly acts that much easier to perform – and lends them an added dimension of abomination. In fact, he appeared to be a gentle man to all who knew him – or thought they knew him – including his wife, whom he married in 1921 in Altenburg and to whom he was always kind and loving. When Kürten finally confessed his crimes to her, she would not at first believe him.

Within his marriage, Kürten appeared to try to suppress his sadistic instincts, restricting himself to fantasy and exciting himself by reading about Jack the Ripper, who had caused a frenzy of fear in London a few decades previously. He even took a normal job as a moulder in a factory and became an active trade union member – although he did take mistresses with whom his sexual activities became increasingly violent. He enjoyed beating and half-strangling his sexual partners. But a few years after his marriage he went back to Düsseldorf because he had started a new job. 'The sunset was blood-red on my return to Düsseldorf,' he told a psychiatrist many years later. 'I considered this to be an omen symbolic of my destiny.' It was 1925 and from indulging in occasional opportunistic bloodletting, he began to commit more and more crimes of arson and sexual violence, building up to a campaign of murder so intense that from February 1929 the city was in a state of terror for a full sixteen months until Kürten was caught. Indeed, it was an irony that Kürten's wife was so afraid of the 'Düsseldorf Vampire' that her husband had to accompany her when she came home late at night from the restaurant where she worked.

Men, women and children were stabbed and horribly mutilated in frenzied attacks, their bodies sometimes tossed into the river. Kürten cunningly varied the style of his attacks in order to confuse the police: sometimes his victims were stabbed, sometimes strangled, sometimes bludgeoned to death. All the police knew for sure was that many, many crimes had been committed by someone who enjoyed drinking the blood of his victims. On occasions he returned to the graves of those he had killed and dug up the bodies. Once, when he did this, he had intended to crucify the corpse, but then abandoned the idea. 'I caressed the dead body ... experiencing the tenderest emotions that, as a living woman, she had failed to arouse in me earlier,' he was to confess later. As Kürten's defence lawyer said at his trial when trying to encourage the jury to proclaim Kürten insane: 'He unites nearly all perversions in one person ... he killed men, women, children and animals, killed anything he found.' And in addition to the murders, there were other attacks in which the victims, miraculously, escaped.

His last murder victim was a five-year-old girl, Gertrude Albermann, whom he slaughtered with a thin-bladed knife, slashing thirty-six wounds on the child's body – yet he was captured by chance after he inexplicably let a potential victim go. Meeting twenty-year-old Maria Budlik in May 1930, he took her back to his flat for coffee and then offered to walk her home. On the way he dragged her into a wooded area and began to strangle her and to try to rape her. Suddenly, he stopped and demanded, 'Do you remember where I live, in case you ever need my help?' Smartly, Maria lied, saying she did not remember – which doubtless saved her life. Kürten escorted her to her tram and she returned to her dwelling, whereupon she contacted the police and led them to Kürten. When Kürten knew that the police were on his trail, he told his wife the truth about his Jekyll-and-Hyde life, urging her to tell the police he had confessed to her, so she could claim the reward which was being offered for his capture. She did so.

At his trial in 1931, he admitted to sixty-eight crimes, pleading guilty to nine charges of murder and seven of attempted murder. Held in an escape-proof cage, Kürten confessed his crimes in detail, admitting to being a sex maniac, rapist, sadist, arsonist, murderer ... and vampire. Clearly deriving pleasure from the recollections, he described his crimes in depth – even down to his sexual attacks on animals – and admitted drinking blood from the cut throats, hands and other wounds of both his male and female victims. Calmly he told of his repetitive dreams of sex, death and blood, his obsession with Jack the Ripper and of his desire that one day he would deserve a place in a waxworks 'Chamber of Horrors'. He blamed his childhood and his spells in prison for twisting his mind and turning him into a killer – and he also blamed his victims for 'asking for it'. 'I do feel that I must make one statement: some of my victims made things very easy for me. Man-hunting on the part of women today has taken on such forms that ...' Kürten began pompously to say, before the judge's disgust exploded and, outraged, he silenced the killer. Kürten was found guilty and sentenced to death by guillotine. As the day dawned, Kürten's perverted obsession with blood took on a new twist. He asked his psychiatrist, curiously: 'After my head has been chopped off, will I still be able to hear, at least for a moment, the sound of my own blood gushing from my neck?' He added, 'That would be the pleasure to end all pleasures.'

A Cannibal in New York

> *'There is no better way to know death than to link it with some licentious image'*
>
> Marquis de Sade

It is a widely-held belief that sex-pests are harmless inadequates. When a woman encounters a 'flasher' in the park, discovers someone has stolen her underwear from the washing-line, hears of a Peeping Tom in the neighbourhood or picks up the telephone to hear a stranger whispering obscenities, she knows that her fear is irrational. After all, haven't we been told that these nuisances are no more than that: sad individuals whose feebleness and undoubted impotence with women means they are pursuing a fantasy outlet rather than dealing with reality? Isn't the best advice simply to ignore these perverts and they'll go away?

Psychiatrist Robert P. Brittain in his 1970 classic essay 'The Sadistic Murderer' sounded a note of caution about such complacency. When sadistic murderers are finally caught, he revealed, those with criminal histories have usually committed sex offences of a non-violent nature, such as those listed above. 'It does not follow that all who commit such acts are potentially sexual murderers and many may only be social nuisances; it does follow, however, that such offenders should be examined most carefully because a proportion, however small, are potentially very dangerous,' Dr Brittain wrote. Those in authority who deal with perverts of the obscene-phone-call variety should, by rights, be aware of research such as Dr Brittain's and there ought to be careful monitoring of the offender in case he is one of the few whose crimes escalate into worse offences. But they are seldom taken very seriously even these days. So, ninety years ago, what chance was there that the New York authorities would guess that the apparently trivial offence for which Albert Fish had been arrested concealed crimes which were so monstrous as to be incomprehensible to most people?

Fish, a harmless-looking, frail old man with grey wispy hair, was arrested in December 1930 for writing obscene letters to lonely widows who had placed advertisements in personal columns of newspapers and magazines, or who had lodged their names with marriage agencies. The letters had been sent over a period of years and his requests to the women were explicit, couched in the most disgusting terms; in essence he wanted the women to beat him or join with him in whipping boys. He was taken to the psychiatric ward of the Bellevue Hospital where psychiatry division director Dr Menas Gregory, after consultation with his assistant, reported Fish to be 'abnormal – a psychopathic personality, with evidence of early senile change, but not insane or a mental defective.' Despite a history of masochistic sexual perversion from early on in his life, Fish's behaviour was judged to be 'quiet and co-operative, orderly and normal' and he was released. Unknown to them, this man – 'sane', 'orderly' and 'normal' – had, two years previously, abducted and killed a twelve-year-old child in a frenzy of sexual ecstasy, cut her into pieces, put the pieces into a stew with vegetables and eaten her.

That May in 1928, the thin, respectable-looking elderly man who had called at the home of Edward and Delia Budd in New York had called himself Frank Howard. His shoes were brightly polished, his hat had a silk lining and his shirt had wing-collars. 'He looked like a decent man,' Edward Budd was later to recall. The man was responding, he said, to a newspaper advertisement which the Budds' eldest son, eighteen-year-old Edward Jr, had placed, seeking summer-vacation work. He claimed to have a farm on Long Island and to be in need of extra help. An arrangement was made for 'Mr Howard' to collect Edward the following week and take him to see the farm. The Budds, being open-hearted people, invited him to come early so he could have dinner with them. And that was how he met little Grace, their second-youngest daughter. When 'Frank Howard' suggested helpfully that he could deliver Grace to a children's party, the Budds raised no objection and off they went, the old man and the little girl hand-in-hand, like a trusting Little Red Riding Hood walking away with the Wolf towards the subway station. Grace was wearing her confirmation dress. 'She looked real sweet in her grey coat and hat,' Edward Budd told reporters six years later. 'She was real happy. We didn't see anything wrong. We said she should go, and come home early. We never did see her again.'

Is it nature or nurture which turns a man into something worse than a beast? A popular view among those who study the formation of personality is that environment moulds a person, for better or worse; in a sense, this might be seen to absolve someone of blame for their later actions. To suggest that some people might simply be born bad, their brains containing 'a fluke, an accident of internal wiring' – as writers Christine McGuire and Carla Norton said of another American sadist, Cameron Hooker, in their 1991 book *Perfect Victim* – can draw many a frown from social psychologists. Superficially it might seem that Hamilton Albert Fish's disturbed background bore some responsibility for his aberrant behaviour.

Born in 1870 in Washington, DC into a respectable family, his father died when he was five and of necessity his mother went out to work, placing Albert in an orphanage. That misfortune – according to Fish – was to blame for his later abominable crimes. Cruel treatment was meted out to the children. 'I saw so many boys whipped it ruined my mind,' he was to say later. From being an apparently contented child, Albert became a stammering wreck. He wet the bed until he was eleven and frequently ran away – 'every Saturday' he claimed. But later investigations also uncovered disorders of the mind within Fish's immediate family – which included his parents' siblings. No fewer than seven of them suffered from psychoses or had psychopathic personalities. A couple of them died in mental institutions, another was an alcoholic and others were looked upon as 'completely crazy'. Even Fish's mother was regarded with suspicion by neighbours, who reported that she was delusional and heard voices. Fish was later to claim that it was his own older brother who had sparked his childhood interest in anthropophagy by telling him gruesome tales of cannibalism in the Far East. This was hardly *The Waltons*, then (referring to the eponymous TV series about the struggles of a respectable and loving but impecunious American family during the Great Depression years). And significantly, among the subsequent discoveries made by psychiatrists, it was revealed that when one of Fish's teachers spanked children on their bare bottoms, whereas the other pupils cried, Albert Fish enjoyed it. He was only five years old at the time. Pinpointing the cause of Fish's twisted mind is, therefore, tricky: blaming it all upon childhood circumstance might be foolhardy.

Fish became a painter and decorator and eventually married – a marriage which resulted in six children. After twenty years his wife ran away with their lodger, leaving the children behind, and it was at this point that Fish apparently snapped completely, although his wife later said of her marriage to Fish: 'He was crazy.' However, the abandoned husband raised the children alone, the youngest being three years old at the time, and apparently never harmed them physically. At Fish's later trial his daughter, Mrs Gertrude DeMarco, by then in her thirties, recalled how her father had insisted on prayers before every meal, frequently read the Bible and regularly attended church. As far as she could remember, Fish had never struck any of the children, she said, but he did involve them freely in his masochistic practices. Not content with self-flagellation, he encouraged his children and their friends to beat him on the buttocks using a paddle studded with inch-and-a-half nails, which he had made himself. He indulged in other, equally bizarre behaviour, climbing to the top of a hill near their home in Westchester County, New York, and baying at the moon naked, screaming: 'I am Christ! I am Christ!' Obsessed with flesh-eating, he served raw meat to his children on nights when the moon was full and collected newspaper articles on cannibalism, which he carried around with him until they turned into yellowed crumbs in his pockets.

Fish became a drifter, travelling through America, settling briefly to work as a house-painter and then moving on. During his sojourns he would write his obscene letters to lonely women ... and he would attack children, having an especial fondness for little boys. He claimed to have attacked at least a hundred – 'I have had children in every state,' he bragged when he was finally arrested for Grace Budd's murder – and the authorities suspected the one hundred figure was an underestimate.

He was believed to have killed at least fifteen children. He would tie them up, beat them and torture them cruelly, usually refraining from gagging them because he liked to hear their terrible screams. He frequently attempted to castrate the small boys – and, according to his own admissions, sometimes succeeded. Frequently he would abduct racial-minority children; he discovered that during an era of rampant racism, law-enforcers did not look for missing black children as assiduously as they looked for white children.

Fish was the archetypal bogeyman of whom parents warn their children: he tempted them with sweets or stories of parties, he led them away from safety, strangled them, and on occasions chopped them up and fed on their flesh and blood. Psychiatrist Dr Frederick Wertham said after his first interview when Fish was in custody for the Budd murder: 'He looked like a meek and innocuous little old man, gentle and benevolent, friendly and polite … If you wanted someone to entrust your children to, he would be the one you would choose.'

There was a full moon on the night of Sunday June 3, 1928, the ill-fated date when Fish had returned to the Budds' house for dinner. Some days previously, he had visited a pawn-shop in Manhattan and bought a cleaver, a saw and a butcher's knife. On the day of his visit he had wrapped the weapons in a brown paper parcel and asked a news vendor to look after the package for him. Later, with Grace by his side, he picked up the parcel and it rested between them on the train to Greenburgh in Westchester County – that was where his sister lived, he explained. As they were getting off the train, Grace hesitated and ran back inside the carriage. She returned with his parcel, handed it to him with a bright smile and took his hand again as they walked to a broken-down house with a timeworn sign declaring it to be Wisteria Cottage. It backed onto a wood and Fish suggested that Grace go and pick some flowers while he checked to see where his sister was.

Once he was inside, Fish went into one of the upstairs rooms overlooking the wood, laid out his sharpened weapons – his 'implements of Hell', as he was later to call them – stripped naked and called to Grace from the window. She came into the house and when she saw his scrawny, white, bare flesh, she screamed: 'I'll tell Mama!' Sweating and excited, Fish pounced on the terrified child and strangled her as she struggled violently. Then in a frenzy, he hacked the small body into numerous pieces, placed the head in an outside toilet, dressed again and left the blood-soaked room, taking with him some parts of Grace's body wrapped in a cloth. Once home, he cooked the pieces of flesh with vegetables and ate the stew. For nine days, he made return visits to Wisteria Cottage and returned with more body parts to eat. As he devoured them – or even when he merely imagined devouring them – he would experience exquisite sexual pleasure. At the end of nine days he collected into a bundle what remained of little Grace Budd and threw the bundle over a wall at the back of the house. Then, as Grace's distraught parents were beginning their life-sentence of anguish, hoping against hope that their daughter was still alive, 'Frank Howard' moved on again.

Why was he not caught? In his life he was caught – many times – but he was always released. There were frequent arrests and questionings by police over the corruption of minors, but Fish served brief sentences, the longest being sixteen months for larceny when he stole money from a store. His offences were not considered to be serious and although he was kept in psychiatric hospitals for short periods in 1930 and 1931, he was freed as 'not insane' and, after the obscene letters charge, he was put on probation for a mere six months. In the end, Fish sealed his own fate with his sadist's desire to inflict even more pain on the Budd family. The slender hope they nursed that their little Grace was still alive somewhere was snuffed out when, six years after her disappearance, an unsigned letter arrived from Fish.

He began the letter by telling of 'a friend' who, as a deck-hand, was stranded in China in 1894 at a time of famine:

'So great was the suffering among the very poor that all children under 12 were sent to the butchers [sic] to be cut up and sold for food in order to keep others from starving ... You could go in any shop and ask for steak ... Part of a naked body of a boy or girl would be brought out and just what you wanted cut from it. A boy or girls [sic] behind which is the sweetest part of the body and sold as veal cutlet brought the highest price.'

After this nauseating beginning, Fish continued by saying that his 'friend' returned to the USA with a taste for human flesh and captured two small boys whom he spanked 'to make their meat fresh and tender', then killed and ate them. 'I made up my mind to taste [human flesh],' he wrote and revealed that when Grace had sat on his lap and kissed him at dinner 'I made up my mind to eat her.' Fish then salaciously detailed what had happened in Wisteria Cottage, including Grace's desperate cries and unspeakable fear, knowing that each word would be like a scalpel-blade in her wretched parents' breasts. Finally, he ended the obscene letter by saying that he had not attacked Grace sexually: 'It took me 9 days to eat her entire body. I did not fuck her tho [sic] I could of had I wished to [sic]. She died a virgin.' This was a lie, he later confessed to a psychiatrist.

The police went to work on the letter right away, discovering that a monogram design on the envelope led back to a Manhattan company and their investigations then led them to a New York rooming-house where Fish lived.

As some detectives interrogated him, others went through his belongings and found a bunch of faded newspaper clippings bound together, every one of them about Fritz Haarmann, the 'Hanover Vampire' who, as the previous chapter outlined, had abducted young men in the early 1920s, killed them and sold their flesh in the marketplace. Meanwhile Edward Budd had arrived at the police station and instantly identified 'Frank Howard'. Fish told his terrible story with obvious relish and Grace's remains were found at Wisteria Cottage.

Fish confessed to murdering a man in 1910, to mutilating and torturing to death a mentally-handicapped boy in New York in 1919 and doing the same to another boy in Washington the same year. He admitted killing and eating four-year-old William Gaffney in 1927, and five-year-old Francis McDonal in 1934. The police suspected him of many more murders, but began the process of charging him with the killing of Grace Budd. Then they handed him over to the medical professionals. The psychiatrists were flabbergasted as Fish revealed one perversion after another as providing a lifelong source of enjoyment.

Sado-masochism was only a starting-point: an X-ray revealed twenty-nine needles embedded in his body – some of them enormous needles which are used to repair canvas – and almost all of them lodged in his pelvic-perineal area around the rectum and near the bladder. They had been inserted through the skin rather than swallowed, and it was estimated that many of the needles had been in his body for years, judging by their erosion patterns. Fish freely admitted that he had stuck needles into his body near the genitals for many years, usually pulling them out again. 'I put them up under the spine,' he said. 'I put one in the scrotum too, but I couldn't stand the pain.' The twenty-nine needles were those which had been put in too far to remove. Chillingly, Fish said he also enjoyed inserting needles into the bodies of children.

'There was no known perversion that he did not practise and practise frequently,' said Dr Frederick Wertham, who made a detailed study of Fish and listed eighteen of the sexual perversions in which he indulged. As well as sado-masochism these included exhibitionism, coprophagia (eating of faeces), undinism (sexual acts involving urination), fetishism (abnormal preference for a non-genital part of the body such as buttocks, or for inanimate objects) and cannibalism. One of Fish's pleasures was to soak cotton-wool in alcohol, insert it into his anus and set fire to it. Wertham proclaimed Fish to be a man of intelligence and cunning, the truth of whose stories could not always be separated from fantasy, but in time he judged himself able to separate fact from fancy and it was to Wertham that Fish revealed the details of Grace Budd's death and the sexual thrill he experienced when eating parts of her body, or when he thought about the murder and the subsequent cannibalism. He took enormous pleasure in describing to the psychiatrist how he cooked and ate a child. 'He spoke in a matter-of-fact way, like a housewife describing her favourite methods of cooking,' said Wertham.

Religious mania can be added to the catalogue of Fish's deviations. In jail awaiting trial, he regularly fell to his knees in prayer, and in keeping with his children's stories of their naked father in the moonlight shrieking 'I am Christ!', Fish told Wertham that God had ordered him to commit his vile acts on children. Paedophiles often tend to present themselves as rigidly religious and moralistic, as testified by Fish's daughter when she recalled her childhood, but not many claim to have heard voices from angels. Fish professed to have heard words like 'stripes' – which, he explained, was a heavenly order to lash the children. He would quote and misquote the Bible to support his deeds.

'Happy is he that taketh Thy little ones and dasheth their heads against the stones,' he would say, or 'Blessed is the man who correcteth his son in whom he delighteth with stripes, for great shall be his reward.' Claiming to be convinced that God wanted him to castrate little boys, he compared himself to Abraham offering his son Isaac as a sacrifice. On other occasions he saw himself as God making a sacrifice, just as Jesus was sacrificed.

Harnessing religion to justify one's wickedness is nothing new. From the heresy trials of the Middle Ages to the present day when people commit the most sickening atrocities upon each other in the name of one religion or another, human beings have always enjoyed having an excuse to sate their appetites for cruelty. As philosopher Blaise Pascal noted: 'Men never do evil so completely and cheerfully as when they do it from religious conviction.' Hallucinatory 'voices from God' sometimes occur in cases of paranoid schizophrenia – for example with Herbert Mullin, who offered his doctors a bizarre logic for his having killed thirteen people in Santa Cruz during the four months up to February 1973. Under the delusion that God required a certain number of human 'sacrifices' every year, Mullin concluded that earthquakes, such as those along the San Andreas fault in San Francisco, only occurred during periods when the murder rate was low. 'Murder decreases the number of natural disasters and the extent of the devastation of these disasters,' he concluded. In order to protect America against the great earthquake, Mullin asserted, he randomly killed as many people as possible. And since there were no major earthquakes in 1973, this was proof to him that he had fulfilled his mission. Forty years later, in 2013, Jorge Beltrao Negromonte offered a similar 'reason' to a Brazilian court before he was sentenced to twenty-three years' imprisonment. The court heard how, aided by his wife and his mistress, the fifty-four-year-old former university professor butchered three young women, then cooked and ate their flesh in stews and pies, selling them on the street and even feeding some to the infant of one of the victims. Negromonte ran a religious sect called 'The Cartel' and declared his belief that murder and cannibalism was necessary for 'population control' of uneducated people. By fulfilling this 'divine' calling – and inspired by a book of satanic rituals – he told the court that his soul and those of his co-murderers would be purified.

This biblical thread reverberates in Albert Fish's comparison of himself to Abraham sacrificing his son. It finds another echo in an incident which took place many decades later but in a less developed culture than that of New York. In August 1973 a thirty-year-old man was tried at a court in Goilala, Papua New Guinea, for the murder of his own baby son. A man of limited education and intelligence, there was a history of mental disorder within the family and he had been raised in a land with a primitive belief system which had historically encompassed violence and cannibalism, to be indulged in as a necessity when food was scarce, to avenge enemies, or for magical reasons, such as to enable one to absorb the virtues of others. In 1973, though, none of these ancient beliefs applied – and certainly not to the man in the dock, who had attended well to what Christian missionaries, who were extremely active in Papua New Guinea, had told him. He devoutly read many religious books including the Bible and he was particularly taken with the stories which focused upon sacrifice. Calmly and earnestly, he told the court that he had wanted to help his people and reached a conclusion on how to do this. He stated:

'I decided to kill my child. After I had made up my mind, I fasted for five days. I then took my little boy into the bush and came to the place where I had decided to kill him. When I came to the spot, I prepared a small place for the child to sit and I spread a lap-lap [a waistcloth] on the ground for him, then I began to dig a grave. After that was finished, I struck him twice on the forehead with my axe. I then took my knife and cut him in the stomach and upward toward the chest and through the bone. I then took his heart out. I chopped it up and ate some of it. I also made some cuts in my own body and mixed some of my son's blood with this. Then I put the body in the grave. I had brought some glue and petrol with me which I mixed with the remaining cut slices of my son's heart. I tried to boil it but was not successful. I had hoped that the steam and the rest of the mixture would go up to God and he would then send me the power in my dreams to do the right things for my people. The people's heads would also become clear, and they would then do the necessary things to bring about the white man's way of life. God would send many goods to the people and we would find money. Then I lay down in the grave and slept with my dead son. No dream came the first night. On the second, I dreamed that I saw a light go up to heaven. I then covered the grave and returned to my village.'

The psychiatrist who reported this case, Dr B. G. Burton-Bradley, concluded that the man displayed 'marked autistic thinking and was in a delusional state prior to the act'. He found evidence of schizophrenia and warned of the dangers inherent in unthinkingly teaching religion – which is frequently interlaced with symbolism – to a people whose own history might influence their present thinking and create misunderstanding in someone who is mentally unstable and might try, as this man did, to emulate certain aspects of biblical teaching.

Dr Wertham did not claim that Albert Fish was influenced by cultural, cannibalistic roots when the murder trial began in March 1935, but he did regard Fish to be insane. The prosecutor, Elbert T. Gallagher, insisted otherwise, saying: 'He is not defective mentally ... he has complete orientation as to his immediate surroundings ... there is no mental deterioration, but ... he is known medically as a sex pervert or a sex psychopath ... his acts were abnormal ... he knew it was wrong ... he is legally sane and responsible for his acts.'

Fish's attorney, James Dempsey, opined that Fish had a Jekyll-and-Hyde personality, with one side of his character sweet and gentle and the other side monstrous. He refused to put Fish on the witness stand, saying that he did not believe an insane man should testify. 'The story of this man's life is one of unspeakable horror ... it would disgust and nauseate you,' he said.

Dr Wertham said he believed Fish to be 'basically a homosexual' and a paedophile: 'Women were just a substitute.' He told the jury that the old man read all he could about violence and torture and revealed that as far back as twenty-five years previously, Fish had tried – and failed – to castrate a teenage boy he picked up in St Louis. He had cut the youth's buttocks with a razor-blade and drunk his blood, but had refrained from killing him, giving him money instead. When Fish had arrived at the Budd house, it had been his intention to take Edward Budd away and castrate him, but on seeing what a strong and powerful youth he was, he thought better of it and selected weaker, more defenceless prey. Dr Wertham told of how Fish had inserted roses into his penis, and would then eat the roses. He spoke of Fish's marriage and declared that Fish's wife was interested to some extent in his sexual perversions. 'His relations with her were entirely abnormal,' the doctor stated – which was borne out by the woman herself, who had told reporters after Fish was arrested: 'The old skunk, I knew something like this would happen.'

Fish was undoubtedly insane, declared Dr Wertham, but four other psychiatrists were brought into court to disagree with him about Fish's sanity. One of them was Dr Menas S. Gregory who, as head of the Bellevue Hospital, had not exactly covered himself in glory by having released Fish four years previously with the verdict that he was 'abnormal – a psychopathic personality, with evidence of early senile change, but not insane' and displaying 'normal' behaviour. He persisted in this view, stating that many of the assorted perversions enjoyed by Fish were not uncommon. When asked if he considered a man who indulged in such pursuits to be 'all right' he replied: 'Not perfectly all right, but socially all right. There are men high up socially and financially who unfortunately suffer that way. They know right from wrong. They are successful people.'

The jury found Fish guilty and the death penalty was mandatory. Fish was dispatched to Sing Sing Prison to await his punishment. He did not show fear; quite the contrary. 'What a thrill it will be if I have to die in the electric chair!' he sighed. 'It will be the supreme thrill – the only one I haven't tried.' When the moment came in January 1936, he sat in the electric chair and eagerly helped the executioner to fix the electrodes to his legs, smiling as other electrodes were placed on his head. According to onlookers' claims, he did not die instantly. As 3,000 volts shot through Fish, the needles which were still embedded in his body short-circuited the electric chair. It was not until a second charge of electricity seared through Fish and a haze of blue smoke rose from the slumped body that he was declared dead.

The Kiss of the Vampire

'He took out a small jewelled knife and put the point to my finger. A drop of blood came forth. I would have cried out, but something in his expression kept me still. "That is the first colour to remember,"' he told me.

Norman Mailer, *Ancient Evenings*

JOHN GEORGE HAIGH

Mrs Olive Durand-Deacon had a business plan. It was 1949 and post-war woman was rediscovering glamour, with role-models like Rita Hayworth and Betty Grable offering a cinematic ideal. Noting a public preoccupation with ornamental beauty, sixty-nine-year-old Mrs Durand-Deacon was certain there was a market for artificial fingernails and, as she told her best friend Constance Lane, the project excited her. The elegant widow, who had been left £40,000 by her late husband, decided to confide her enterprising plan to the handsome young man who was a fellow-resident at the Onslow Court Hotel in South Kensington, London. John George Haigh was interested. Just by coincidence, he told her pleasantly, he was a director of a company in Crawley, called Hurstlea Products. Why didn't they go there together and see if the managing director would be interested in Mrs Durand-

Deacon's idea? The lady eagerly agreed ... and that was the last that Mrs Lane, ever heard from her.

After a short time, Mrs Lane became worried. She knew of Mr Haigh's arrangement to take her friend to Crawley and contacted him to ask him if he had any clue about her whereabouts now. Haigh was terribly concerned. He told Mrs Lane that it was true he had planned to drive Mrs Durand-Deacon to see his boss, but when she failed to turn up for the appointment he had gone alone. 'We should inform the police,' he said, looking anxious, and the two of them did just that. Haigh couldn't have been more helpful, which was an extraordinary way to behave, for he must have guessed that the police would check out both his story and his life. It took them a very short time to discover that he was not a director of Hurstlea Products, although he worked for them on occasions, but that he did have a criminal record, having been imprisoned on fraud and forgery charges three times since 1935. He took a vain pride in his ability as a master-forger but, unknown to the police, during his periods of freedom he had been committing other, graver crimes.

Investigations led the police to Crawley, where they discovered the Hurstlea Products connection. Haigh had the use of a Hurstlea warehouse in return for the work he was supposed to be doing for the company. When the police forced their way into the warehouse they made a chilling discovery: a tank large enough to contain a human being, gallons of acid, a rubber apron and gloves ... and a great deal of blood on the walls.

One of the policemen spotted a scrap of paper flapping upon the ground; it was a dry-cleaning receipt for a Persian lamb coat from a cleaner's at nearby Horsham. Following this trail turned up their next clue: jewellery which had belonged to Mrs Durand-Deacon had been sold in Horsham by a man answering John Haigh's description.

They pulled Haigh in. To their surprise, Haigh confessed almost immediately and regaled the officers with a colourful description of how he had killed Mrs Durand-Deacon and disposed of her body. 'She was inveigled by me into going to Crawley in view of her interest in artificial fingernails,' he said and continued:

'Having taken her into the storeroom, I shot her in the back of the head while she was examining some materials. Then I went out to the car and fetched a drinking glass and made an incision – I think with a penknife – in the side of her throat. I collected a glass of blood, which I drank. I removed her coat and jewellery (rings, necklace, earrings and crucifix) and put her in the forty-five-gallon tank. Before I put her handbag in the tank, I took from it about thirty shillings and a fountain pen. I then filled the tank with sulphuric acid by means of a stirrup pump. I then left it to react.'

Mrs Durand-Deacon weighed two hundred pounds and the effort of getting her body into the tank had exhausted Haigh. While recovering his strength, Haigh mentioned as an afterthought, he went to the local tea-shop. 'I should have said that, in between having her in the tank and pumping in the acid, I went round to the Ancient Prior's for a cup of tea,' he said in the confession which was later read out in court. It took several days for the body to break down in the acid, which necessitated a few visits to Crawley by Haigh, he reported.

And why, asked the police officers, did he commit this atrocity? He had a thirst for blood, he explained, and as the shocked officers prepared to leave, appalled yet satisfied with the confession they had obtained so easily, he asked if they wanted to know about the other murders he had committed. They listened with growing incredulity.

The first murder was in 1944 (said Haigh) and the victim was Haigh's friend and occasional employer, a young man called Donald McSwann who ran a slot-machine arcade in the city. Haigh sometimes worked for McSwann as a mechanic and had invited him to lodge with him so that McSwann could avoid the call-up (obligatory war-time military service). McSwann was afraid of dying, but as events turned out, he should have taken his chances with the British Army fighting the Germans in Europe. At least that way he would have known who his enemy was. The moment he walked into Haigh's basement workshop followed by the man he thought was his friend, his destiny was decided.

Did Haigh have any motive for killing McSwann when he smashed an iron bar over the hapless youth's head? ... Apart from a desire to drink his blood? Haigh said he did not. He told the police that after biting into the jugular vein on McSwann's neck, he feasted with pleasure. But after satisfying his appetite, Haigh looked at the bloodstained body lying on his basement floor and wondered what to do next. It wasn't that he felt any remorse for snuffing out a young man's life so brutally; on the contrary, he was merely plagued with the problem of having a dead body on his hands. For a whole day he mulled over how he could dispose of McSwann's body. Then, he told the police with a triumphant smile, he hit upon the solution: he would cut up the body and dissolve it with sulphuric acid. After completing his task, he poured the sludgy mess, a bucketful at a time, down a manhole in the basement, which was connected to the London sewage system. Then he calmly took over the running of McSwann's pinball arcade and no one asked any questions.

But Haigh was soon beset by a tiresome problem. McSwann's wealthy parents kept writing to their son and sooner or later Haigh knew that they would become suspicious if there was no reply. This was where Haigh's forgery skills became invaluable. He kept Mr and Mrs

McSwann away from his door for a whole year by telling them their son was hiding out in Scotland until the end of the war. He even travelled up to Scotland every week to post forged letters to them 'from their son'.

The war in Europe ended when Adolf Hitler committed suicide in May 1945 and within a matter of weeks the McSwanns received a letter from 'Donald', inviting them to visit him at the home of his friend John Haigh. It was July 1945, almost a year after McSwann's death, when Haigh bludgeoned McSwann's parents to death and disposed of their bodies using the same method which had been so successful after he had killed his friend, their son. Then, using forged documents, he helped himself to the McSwann estate, which included five houses plus an additional fortune which he transferred to his own name.

Incredibly, the crimes remained undetected and Haigh was delighted with his own cleverness, but the enormous stolen fortune was not destined to last. Haigh was a gambler and this, together with some bad investments and a hedonistic lifestyle, meant the cash quickly dwindled. By 1948 he was casting around for another wealthy victim. A young married couple, Dr Archie Henderson and his wife Rosalie, presented themselves. He invited them to look at his new workshop in Crawley. They met the same fate as Haigh's previous victims. When a snag occurred in the form of Rosalie Henderson's brother inquiring after the whereabouts of the couple, Haigh managed to convince him not only that the couple had left the country to go to South Africa, but that Dr Henderson had borrowed £2,500 from him and had pledged to Haigh that if the money was not repaid within two months, he would give Haigh his house and his car. There were three other murders, Haigh confessed, but they were just casual strangers, killed to enable him to drink their blood, because the need had come upon him.

He neither knew their names, nor cared, he said, flipping his hand in disdain.

Haigh told his stories with such obvious relish that the police began to wonder whether he was speaking the truth or whether the tales represented the overactive imagination of a madman, because the supposed murders he spoke of were so bizarre. How could Haigh have avoided detection for so many years, they wondered? Could they really believe his stories of blood-drinking?

Of course the police were not naïve when it came to the abnormal desires of criminals. In the psychiatric literature could be found accounts of others who had experienced the same deviant thirst for blood. For instance, there was the man who had been a stretcher-bearer during the 1914–18 war, who had enjoyed feeling the blood of the wounded drench his clothes. He had told his psychiatrist that he would wear his underclothing stiffened by the dried blood for a long time afterwards. He was a hypochondriac and his habit was to go to slaughter-houses to drink a glass of warm blood as a therapeutic measure. He had previously murdered a woman, cut up and eviscerated her and cannibalised her body. Recollecting this gave him such sexual satisfaction that he would attain an orgasm.

But Haigh was claiming no such sexual motive. His bloodlust was fired, he said, after he had a recurring dream of walking in a forest of crucifixes which turned into green trees, dripping blood. One tree would assume the shape of a man who held a bowl in which he would collect blood from one of the other trees and offer it to Haigh, but would then move away when Haigh tried to take it. Only after Haigh began killing, he said, did the man come within reach and in his dream Haigh was able to drink the blood, just as he drank the blood of his victims in real life. In total he had killed nine people, he claimed, and in each case he had cut open their necks to drink a cupful of blood from each, to quench 'the desire that demanded fulfilment.' He said he would drink 'for three to five minutes, after which I felt better.' After regaling the policemen with these tales of bloody reality and nightmare, Haigh smiled a wolfish smile. 'Of course, you can never prove it,' he told them. 'There's no evidence.' This was true: there was no trace of the victims' bodies – if indeed victims had existed; Haigh's confession was so fantastic that some officers wondered whether it was entirely fuelled by fantasy. Forensic experts dispatched to Crawley found the spot outside the warehouse where Haigh emptied the acid tank. An undissolved bone, a gallstone, a red plastic bag which was the property of Mrs Durand-Deacon and an almost complete set of dentures were discovered, which, the widow's dentist confirmed, did indeed belong to the lady.

Haigh's case bewildered the lawyers too. In six of the nine cases of self-confessed murder, a ready motive was Haigh's greed for money or for acquiring the property of the deceased by fraudulent means. Mrs Durand-Deacon actually had little money, but Haigh was not to know that – and he was certainly hard-up; a cheque he had given to the manageress of the Onslow Court Hotel had bounced.

The killing of total strangers who yielded him nothing other than their life-blood was a little more difficult to explain in terms of a sane man with a greed-motive. Before Haigh's case came to court he was questioned by psychiatrists who could find nothing in his family background to explain any of his crimes, whether it was the fraud offences or the murders, with their suggested aberrant behaviour. Haigh was an only child of middle-class, God-fearing parents who were members of the Plymouth Brethren and demanded strict conformity from their son. As a schoolboy he was an organist and chorister at Wakefield Cathedral and displayed good character until he was twenty-five, when he served the first of his prison sentences. Could the excessive exposure to religion have caused his abnormality? Could he have been rebelling against the suffocating piety of the circumstances of his childhood? It's a consideration. However, there are many other children raised by strict religious parents, and there are parents who treat their offspring in far worse ways than demanding that they attend church regularly, but only a tiny proportion of such children turn into ferocious killers.

Also, Haigh's childhood nature did not tally with the psychological profile of the cold-hearted man he had become. It was said that he had been a generous boy, made friends easily and was kindly, adoring animals and hating cruelty and violence. Yet, he revealed, even as a very small child he liked blood and would lick scratches or cut himself to suck his own blood. His dreams were filled with images of injured and bleeding people and he was fascinated by the Church's Holy Communion, in which supplicants were obliged to imagine they were drinking the blood of Christ. He even dreamed of the bleeding figure of Christ and the crucifixion, sometimes imagining that blood came from the cross, spilling out over the altar in the cathedral.

He said that it was a dream in 1944, when he was thirty-five, which prompted his first murder. Earlier in the day he had accidentally injured his head and blood had dripped into his mouth. That night he dreamed that his mouth was 'full of blood, which revived the old taste' and he knew he would have to drink some blood to satiate himself. Before each of the killings he would have the series of dreams about the forest of crucifixes dripping blood. They would begin during the week and end on a Friday which, as psychologists have since noted, was the day of the Crucifixion.

'Being led by an irresistible urge, I was not given to the discovery of the distress this might cause to myself and others,' he said, thinking of his parents, to whom he felt bonds of affection all his life. Indeed, he had good friends who remained to support him even after his conviction. A marriage at twenty-five had broken down and Haigh had no apparent interest in sex thereafter. No one had suspected he was capable of such heinous crimes.

No, this was not the psychodynamic profile of someone who could be guilty of the actions to which he had confessed, decided psychiatrists. His identity seemed inconstant and to reconcile this, it was suggested that Haigh had a Multiple Personality Disorder (now referred to as Dissociative Identity Disorder) – the most serious and complex of all the psychoses. How else could a gentle child become a skilled swindler and then suddenly change his criminal tack and become a killer and a 'vampire'? This psychiatric proposition opened the door to an 'insanity' plea, which Haigh readily made through his lawyers. He was dubbed 'The Vampire Killer' by British newspapers, but the judge and jury refused to accept this as evidence of insanity. Haigh knew he was doing wrong, they decided, therefore he was sane and guilty. It took them a mere seventeen minutes to find him guilty and sentence him to death by hanging. Apparently undismayed by the failure of his insanity plea and evincing the same cheerful countenance as he did during his court appearances, Haigh, it seemed, was not afraid to die. He asked for a rehearsal of the hanging before the event, in case 'anything went wrong on the day', and even bequeathed some of his clothes to Madame Tussaud's waxworks museum so his wax model would look at its best in the Chamber of Horrors.

Insane? Since Haigh's death there has been much controversy in psychiatric circles about Haigh's mental state and whether or not he was faking his abnormality. But psychiatrists R. E. Hemphill and T. Zabow made a study of 'clinical vampirism' in 1983 and concluded that Haigh was indeed a vampirist. Noting that vampirism has been reported in medical literature for more than a century, they classified this rare condition as not only the sucking of, or craving for, blood, but also an abnormal interest in death or the dead. The condition cannot be placed in any pigeonhole of psychosis, they say, because: 'It is not a primary symptom of any other psychiatric or psychopathic disorder, and its specific motive distinguishes it from other blood-related aberrations. The condition is not likely to be discovered except in criminal cases ... Some of our patients who carry out self-mutilation cut themselves in order to suck blood ... Vampirism, although specifically psychopathic, is not necessarily associated with general or violent psychopathic disorder and, conceivably, might occur in persons not recognised as abnormal, for example, Haigh.'

The essential characteristic of the vampire – both in myth and in reality – has always been that he drinks blood 'specifically to satisfy a need'. Haigh easily fits this model, say the psychiatrists. He ingested his own and others' blood, and after taking a cupful achieved 'a warm, relaxed feeling, with calm and a disappearance of the craving.' Additionally, he was attracted by death and spent time with his decomposing victims. His identity was changeable. The two psychiatrists went on to say: 'Haigh appeared to develop satisfactorily to adulthood; he fluctuated thereafter, and the fastidious, socially acceptable young man cannot be recognised in the callous, revolting murderer ... Vampirism and psychopathy developed in spite of favourable influence and no possible causes for either were discovered.'

Hemphill and Zabow concluded that vampirism is a clinical entity on its own, not necessarily associated with other disorders such as sadomasochism, where a desire for cruelty or self-punishment is a primary aim. But, they warn, 'Vampirism is thus a possible cause of unpredicted repeated murder which is likely to be overlooked. The vampirist may show no obvious signs of mental disorder. It is a disturbing thought that a pleasant person, like Haigh, unsuspected, may be a vampirist liable to a periodic craving for blood.'

Or was he? It has not gone unnoticed that the only assertion of Haigh's vampirism came voluntarily from Haigh himself. Herschel Prins, a British professor of clinical criminology, challenged Hemphill and Zabow's assertion that Haigh was a vampirist. 'Haigh attempted to simulate insanity,' reports Prins. 'Part of this simulation was to claim to have drunk the blood of his victims and to have drunk his own urine.' Such a view is perhaps validated by the trial prosecution's disclosure that Haigh had quizzed a policeman about the chance of ultimate release from Broadmoor Hospital (one of Britain's major psychiatric institutions for dangerous killers who are considered to be clinically insane). That piece of evidence helped to convince the jury that Haigh's insanity plea should be discounted.

As regards vampirism being a separate clinical entity, while acknowledging Hemphill and Zabow's suggestion that the phenomenon may be more common than has hitherto been supposed, Professor Prins points out that vampiristic activity 'is not infrequently seen in association with serious sexual offending where biting and perhaps the ingestion of blood may be a fairly common phenomena' and, noting that it takes place in people functioning at a very primitive mental and emotional level, he is unsurprised that it is 'not infrequently' associated with schizoid, schizophrenic or the 'borderline' disorders. However, most clinicians who have explored the vampirism phenomenon relate it to sexuality of one form or another: that the practice satisfies oral-sadistic needs, for instance. Hemphill and Zabow were at pains to point out that Haigh was uninterested in sex, 'and blood evoked no sexual feeling, in contrast with a very rare form of sadomasochism in which drinking a partner's blood is said to cause sexual arousal and orgasm.'

Haigh's explanation, given just before his execution in August 1949, was that he was 'impelled to kill by wild blood demons, the spirit inside me commanded me to kill.' And in a book about the Haigh trial, Lord Dunboyne wrote: 'No other reported case (which is) traceable seems to suggest that a murderer drank the blood of the murdered as an end in itself, unassociated with any sexual perversion.'

★ ★ ★ ★

RICHARD TRENTON CHASE

But barely thirty years after Haigh's execution – in January 1979 – the trial began in Sacramento, California, of another man who initially seemed readily to fulfil Lord Dunboyne's criteria. His reason for drinking human blood was, he said, 'therapeutic.' He believed that he was dying and his only cure was to drink blood, which was why he had slaughtered six people, including a twenty-two-month-old baby, had cut open bodies, scooped out containers of blood and taken it home with him to drink.

Richard Trenton Chase said at the murder trial that he had begun drinking blood after watching medical shows on television. He started with birds, then moved on to rabbits, dogs and cows before he graduated to killing humans. Which explained why there were so many missing dogs and cats in Sacramento County in the late 1970s – and provided an answer for Chase's neighbours, who had often puzzled about the number of puppies and cats he carried into his apartment which were never seen again. Then the

day came, just after Christmas 1977, when Chase took his
.22 handgun and went after people instead.

His first victim was Ambrose Griffin, a fifty-one-year-old
engineer who was casually gunned down as he carried the
groceries into his house from his car. He died in hospital.
Two days earlier one of his near-neighbours had been
rather luckier. Dorothy Polenske had been in her kitchen
when she heard a pop, the kitchen window shattered and
she felt something pass through her hair. Police later found
a .22 calibre bullet embedded in a shelf. It was from the
same gun which was to kill Ambrose Griffin.

Almost a month later, Chase struck again – and this
time he was to satisfy his longing for blood. The victim
was Teresa Wallin, twenty-two years old and three months
pregnant. She had been carrying a sack of rubbish to the
front door when it opened and Richard Chase, standing
there, fired three shots into her. Then, picking up an empty
yogurt carton from the rubbish-sack, he dragged her to
the bedroom where he tore into her body with a knife and
dragged out the intestines. As the pathologist was to later
report, the killer 'tampered with' the viscera by carefully
displacing the kidneys and 'explored the innards of the
deceased.'

When the police, led by Lt Ray Biondi, turned up to
survey the horror, they saw that Teresa's underclothes
had been pulled down around her ankles, but in a book
he wrote about the case,[3] Lt Biondi said that did not
necessarily mean she had been sexually assaulted. 'Some
sexually deviant killers, I knew, pulled down clothing and
elaborately positioned bodies so that their victims would
be found in such humiliating poses,' he noted – and his
assumption was correct in this case. There was no evidence
of sexual assault. In fact, it is interesting to note that
although some authorities might interpret murder using
a firearm as being Freudian sexual symbolism – replacing

penetration and ejaculation with the penetration of a bullet from that eternal phallic symbol, the gun – this method is notably rare in sexually-inspired serial killings. The sexual motive usually demands that the murder involves violent physical contact, which is how such killers obtain satisfaction and which stimulates their feeling of power.

Other discoveries at the murder-scene where Teresa Wallin's torn body lay, bewildered the police. A crumpled yogurt container, smeared with blood inside and out, lay beside the body. On the wooden floor alongside were 'bloody, ringlet-shaped stains,' Lt. Biondi reported. 'I had never seen anything like them and couldn't imagine what the ringlets were.' That was because the answer defied imagination. Four days later those ring-shaped bloodstains would be recalled with a chill of horror by Lt Biondi and other homicide officers.

On that day, Richard Chase had called at the home of Evelyn Miroth, a thirty-eight-year-old single mother who had two sons aged thirteen and six years old. On 27 January 1978 she was baby-sitting David, the twenty-two-month-old baby of her friend Karen Ferreira. If the policemen had been shocked by the scene of carnage at the Wallin home, the sight that met them at Evelyn's house was enough to move some of them to tears. Evelyn's body, naked except for a necklace, was on the bed, attacked in exactly the same way that Teresa had been, but with extra mutilations. One eye had been carefully gouged out by severing the muscles around the eyeball, and a butcher's knife and a carving knife lay bloody at her side. A family friend, Daniel Meredith, lay on the living-room floor with a bullet in his head; he had been shot at point-blank range. On the other side of Evelyn's bed was the small body of her six-year-old son Jason, also shot in the head. Jason was dressed in his best clothes, ready to go out on a day-trip with neighbours. The pathologist arrived at the scene and, examining Evelyn Miroth's body, noted that there appeared to have been little bleeding. Unlike the Wallin murder, there was evidence of sexual assault: the woman was later discovered to have been sodomised and also penetrated anally with a knife. As with the Wallin murder, there was an unusual clue. 'There is a series of rings in the carpet next to her body' the pathologist reported – and he guessed they were made by human blood contained in a bucket or pan. The pathologist's later post-mortem report was compared to the results of the autopsy on Teresa Wallin. In both cases, the same organs had been cut and pulled from the abdomens of the victims. This, said the pathologist, would 'facilitate getting at blood in the abdominal cavity.' His guess was correct: Chase had used a vessel for that very purpose, to enable him to take the blood home with him.

But there was even worse to come. The police found baby David Ferreira's cot – empty, but with a bullet-hole in the blood-soaked pillow. The baby's body was nowhere to be found. Richard Chase had taken that away with him, too. To what end, the investigators could not bring themselves to imagine. Could their killer really be so depraved as to snatch babies from their cribs and prey upon them, like a wild beast? Using the tactics which have been proclaimed successful by the FBI's Behavioural Science Unit at Quantico and made famous by such films as *The Silence of the Lambs*, Lt Biondi and his men set about trying to formulate a psychological profile of their murderer, using any clues as to his behaviour and personality which could be found at the scenes of the crimes. They concluded he was a white male in his twenties, probably schizophrenic, a loner and unmarried, probably unemployed (the murders took place in the daytime) with limited social skills, and that he had recently been released from a mental institution. 'In short, we had profiled a weirdo,' said Biondi. But profiling alone does not catch a murderer; that is the laborious, and infinitely more dangerous, work of police officers. The hunt for the 'weirdo' was stepped up.

Richard Chase was twenty-eight and had been in and out of psychiatric hospitals for years. In one he earned the nickname 'Dracula' from fellow-patients because he used to kill birds and drink their blood and his preoccupation with blood meant he talked only about killing animals. More than once in the past he had been found naked in a Nevada field covered with the blood of a cow he had slaughtered. But the doctors did not consider him to be dangerous and he was repeatedly released, usually into the care of his mother Beatrice.

Where did the roots of Chase's perversion lie? His early childhood had been unusually happy, giving no hint of the monster he was to become, but at the age of ten he began killing cats in the neighbourhood and burying their bodies in the garden. His teenage years were overtly normal, but although popular, Richard proved to be impotent with girls, which was a source of great trauma to him: so much so that at eighteen he went to see a psychiatrist to talk about this problem. Chase left home and began acting irrationally, becoming obsessed with his health. He told people his stomach was turned around the wrong way and that his heart often stopped beating. Once, he believed he had had a heart attack and called the emergency services. He told the doctor that his heart and kidneys had stopped working, his pulmonary artery had been stolen and his blood had stopped flowing. He said he had a hernia and that his entire body was numb. Medical examinations showed there was nothing physically wrong with Chase, but doctors diagnosed chronic paranoid schizophrenia and kept him in the psychiatric ward for three days. Then, declaring him not to be dangerous, they discharged him.

Over the years, Chase sought medical help again and again as his behaviour became more extreme. Sometimes he claimed his mother was trying to poison him and he threw meals on the floor when she had prepared them. He convinced her she should buy an oxygen tent and then claimed she was controlling his mind. He moved in with his father and, unknown to Mr Chase, he began buying rabbits and butchering them, drinking their blood 'to help his weak heart'. However, because he had stopped complaining about physical illness his father thought he was recovering. Then his son became sick. It was caused, said Richard, by having consumed a rabbit that had eaten battery acid, which had now 'seeped through' the walls of his stomach. Again he was admitted to a mental hospital and again he was judged to be a paranoid schizophrenic. Again, they released him after a short time, the psychiatrist saying he had developed 'good socialisation' and a 'realistic view of his problems'. That was the year before Richard Chase began shooting people and drinking their blood.

Buying the gun had been easy. In California, the only requirement for gun ownership was a driving licence and a signature declaring that one had never been convicted of a felony, never been a mental patient or never been judged to be dangerous because of a mental disorder. Buying a weapon over the counter in the only developed country in the world where guns vastly outnumber citizens is still as straightforward as that, which explains why gun homicides in the United States are a common cause of death, matching the number of people who die in car crashes – figures which are continually increasing, year-on-year until the present day. According to the National Highway Traffic Safety Administration (NHTSA) even with the travel restrictions imposed during the 2020–2021 Covid-19 pandemic, American roads got even more dangerous: during the first three months of 2021, NHTSA estimated that 8,730 people had died in motor vehicle traffic crashes, an increase of 10.5 per cent on the 7,900 fatalities in the same time period a year earlier. Gun deaths followed the same upward trend.[4]

Between 2008 and 2017, at least 342,439 people were shot to death in the United States. Gun deaths reached an all-time high in 2021 when between January and September, according to the Gun Violence Archive, in addition to the tens of thousands of non-fatal shootings, the death-toll from non-suicide incidents was 14,516 – the deadliest year of gun violence in two decades (there are actually twice as many gun suicides). This figure was 1,300 higher than in 2020, a year when a record twenty-three million firearms had been purchased; in itself this was a sixty-five per cent increase on 2019's gun purchase figures. The Gun Violence Archive also noted that during the same January to September 2021 period the USA experienced almost five hundred 'mass shootings', which they define as the killing of four or more people, but not including robberies or domestic shootings.[5] The United States now own almost fifty per cent of all worldwide civilian-held firearms – the highest rate on the planet. Not including the military or police, almost four hundred million weapons are currently held in a population of around 330 million; that is, 120 firearms for every one hundred residents (including children), and the number continues to increase.

Even more stark is the fact that sixty-three per cent of American households do not possess a single gun, meaning that all this weaponry is owned by only thirty-seven per cent of the households. In 2013 President Barack Obama, amid much opposition from the USA's powerful National Rifle Association gun lobby (which also represents gun manufacturers), used his executive authority to tighten firearms regulation to prevent mentally-ill people such as Richard Chase from buying weapons – but this was only adopted by twenty-two of the fifty-two states. In 2017 the newly-elected president, Donald Trump, announced the overturning of Obama's rule to keep guns out of the hands of mentally-ill people. And in the autumn of 2021, as the number of Americans who had died from the Coronavirus pandemic passed 700,000, the Republican Governor of Texas, Greg Abbott, scrapped many public protections regarding the buying and possession of a gun, including introducing an 'open carry' permission and allowing young people to buy guns from the age of eighteen. At that point in 2021, there had been more than a thousand firearm killings in Texas, representing seventy-six per cent of all homicides in the state.[6]

Small wonder that law-abiding American citizens sleep restlessly in their beds, when men like Richard Chase are still able to purchase a gun as easily as they might hire a car. And in the 1970s, Chase, after shooting up the puppies and kittens he had acquired through the small-ad columns of newspapers, moved on to bigger things. This was what Ambrose Griffin's life had represented for Chase: he had just been 'target practice'. The police captured him within days after a former school friend reported a chance meeting she had had with Chase. She had been shocked at his odd behaviour and at how skinny and dirty-looking he had become. Her response to a 'wanted' poster led to Chase's arrest. In his pocket was Daniel Meredith's wallet, together with pictures of Evelyn and Jason Miroth. Chase denied everything, except the killing of some puppies. He said he cut up one dog with a machete 'because it was mean'. (Chase was later to express regret about killing cats and dogs, although this remorse did not extend to the people he had murdered, even after his eventual admission of guilt.) His confidence only shook on one occasion. When the nurse at the police station took a blood sample from him, his terror was so great that he had to be held down.

Meanwhile, Chase's apartment was being taken apart. The first thing the police noticed as they opened the door was the terrible smell which invaded their nostrils. The sight that met their eyes was even more nauseating. Everything was bloodstained, from the walls and floors to an unwashed plate and drinking tumbler. On the wall were pictures of human anatomy and among Chase's books were various medical volumes about the internal organs of the body, psychological data and health topics. The U-bend traps under the drains in the sinks and bath were found to contain blood and tissue, which was later identified as human brain matter. Bits of bone were found scattered around the kitchen and a filthy, bloodstained electric blender emitted a foul stench. Of baby David Ferreira there was no sign. Chase was adamant in his denials. Then, for some reason, he decided to confess to a cellmate as he was held in custody. The other prisoner was serving a sentence for repeated drunken driving – and he was revolted at what Chase had to say. 'I don't remember how I drank the blood. I just sucked it,' Chase told him.

He went on to say: 'I had to do it. I have blood poisoning and I need blood. I was tired of hunting and killing animals so I could drink their blood. I thought about it for several weeks and decided I would kill humans for their blood.'

Chase told the other man details about the murders which tallied with what the police knew, and added that he had shot the baby because it was screaming. 'I took it home, where I drank some of its blood. When I was through with it I took the body out and placed it in the garbage.' There was more that Chase did not reveal. Two months later, when the police eventually found the baby's decapitated body, they discovered the infant had been shot and repeatedly stabbed. Chase had also cut open the child's skull and removed the brain.

Primitive rituals made much of drinking blood to maintain health or cure the sick, so was there the faint possibility that Chase did need blood as a nutrient? In view of his mental state, no there was not, but as outlined in an earlier chapter, Canadian chemist Professor David Dolphin identified the genetic condition of porphyria which, he surmised, could have given rise to the vampire myth because of its diminishing effect upon the production of heme, the red pigment in the blood. In a less medically-enlightened age, to ingest large quantities of blood would have alleviated symptoms; therefore, contends Professor Dolphin, blood-drinking 'vampires' may well have been victims of porphyria. Even the folklore concerning garlic used as a 'weapon' against vampires has a scientific explanation: one of the constituents of garlic – dialkyl disulphide – may contribute to the destruction of heme in the body. 'This suggests that garlic might increase the severity of an attack of porphyria ... Can you imagine a more powerful "talisman" against vampires than this?' asks Professor Dolphin.

Perhaps John George Haigh's defence lawyers might have been fascinated by the idea of porphyria in 1949, but despite Richard Chase's pale, undernourished appearance, such a notion would not have gained the sympathy of Ronald W. Tochterman, the assistant chief deputy district attorney who conducted the prosecution of Richard Chase in Santa Cruz in 1979, and who had no doubt that vampirism was very much linked to sexuality. His research showed that some sexual sadists claimed therapeutic justification for their ingestion of blood merely to conceal their sexual predilection for mutilating and – literally – erotic bloodthirstiness. It even has a name: haemostodipsia. Those with this condition desire blood both during sex and at other times, when the act of blood-drinking or watching the flow of blood offers them their sole means of sexual gratification.

One psychiatrist concluded that Chase was not schizophrenic but had a 'paranoid antisocial personality' with 'a well-developed sense of right and wrong'. Chase told another psychiatrist how he had collected animals' blood in a cup to drink, but admitted that it had not helped his illness. He said he enjoyed watching operations on television and found the sight of a heart pumping blood to be fascinating. He thought that drinking human blood would be 'therapeutic'. The psychiatrist reported to the court: 'He (Chase) believed that drinking blood was a possible solution to save him from certain death.' But, he added, 'he understood that he was killing people and that it was wrong to kill people.'

Chase was judged to be sane and, therefore, culpable for his crimes. He was capable of choosing not to kill people, said the psychiatrists. In a US state where, for such culpability, the death penalty applies, Chase's defence was that of insanity. He did not deny the crimes and admitted shooting baby David Ferreira, taking his body away and decapitating the corpse to drink his blood, but said he 'thought the baby was something else.' Although the FBI's Behavioural Science Unit cites Chase as a classic example of a disorganised offender, Mr Tochterman drew attention to his capability for carrying out his crimes, evidenced by planning ahead for his activities, performing his deeds with care and then evading detection. He always wore rubber gloves for his bloody work, he attacked particular organs, and, in the case of Teresa Wallin, after his craving was satiated, he washed his hands and the knife, returning it to the rack in the kitchen. The lawyer related other ghastly murder details, including those concerning little David Ferreira – 'Murders,' said Mr Tochtermann, 'which were caused by Chase's sheer sexual sadism motivated by a literal blood lust.' The trial took four months, at the end of which the jury declared Chase to be sane and guilty of six counts of first-degree murder. His pleas for mercy were discounted.

'You have to be the most naïve optimist, a Pollyanna ten times over, to believe that Mr Chase has the possibility to be a decent human being. He is a dangerous person ... a time bomb,' Tochterman said. Later, as he reflected on the case, Lt Biondi put it more baldly: 'He was crazy as a loon – but he did have the choice to kill or not to kill. The FBI consider him a classic example of a disorganised killer, but he was cagey enough to get away from each scene without being caught.'

Chase was sentenced to die in the gas chamber, but he chose instead to commit suicide in the San Quentin Penitentiary where he was being held, on Boxing Day 1980, by taking an overdose of the pills he had been prescribed for depression.

Do Mothers Make Monsters?

They fuck you up, your mum and dad.
They may not mean to, but they do.
They fill you with the faults they had
And add some extra, just for you.

Philip Larkin, 'This Be The Verse'

What would be the result of crossing Norman Bates, mother-obsessed murderer from the movie *Psycho*, with 'Buffalo Bill', the serial killer of women who removed sections of his victims' skin to fashion his own suit in the horror-flick *The Silence of the Lambs*? Throw a little of Hannibal Lecter – the sinister anti-hero of the latter film and book – into this foul brew of disturbed humanity, and you have Edward Gein. Ghoulish Gein is thought to bear the dubious distinction of inspiring the creation of at least two screen monsters, even without taking his cannibalistic tendencies into account. But unlike some of the other killers discussed in this book, Gein was no glib charmer with a superficial normality. Neither was he one of those Jekyll-and-Hydes whose crimes, when they come to light, cause enormous public amazement because the revealed killer had presented such a well-balanced facade to the world. On the contrary, Ed Gein was not really like that at all.

A strange, eccentric little man with pale, guarded eyes and a reserved manner, Gein was not given to idle chit-chat with his neighbours. People in rural Plainfield, Wisconsin, USA, would later admit that, in retrospect, he always had been a weirdo. But no one could possibly have imagined just how very weird he was until the day in November 1957 when the police arrived at his farmhouse making enquiries about the disappearance of Bernice Worden, the mother of a local store owner ... and made discoveries so unspeakable that some of the investigating officers felt their stomachs heave.

No one could ever have guessed the private depravity of someone who had lived within this small 700-strong community all his life; someone who had run the 160-acre family farm on the outskirts of Plainfield alongside the overpowering presence of his mother and his only brother Henry, until they both died, leaving him completely alone. Someone who, thanks to federal subsidies, did not need to farm his land any longer so abandoned it, and with so much extra time on his hands, took to doing odd jobs for residents of the township to earn a little cash and to alleviate his loneliness. Someone who was living off the fat of the land in more ways than one. But, of course, no one in the vicinity really knew Ed Gein at all, even though he had always lived among them. His mother had seen to that.

Gein was born in 1906 and he and his brother were completely dominated by their possessive, man-hating mother Augusta, who preached hell-fire scriptures at her sons but hated her alcoholic husband George so much that she used to kneel in her children's presence and pray that her husband would die soon. Saying she feared that her boys' morality would be sullied by contact with the outside world, the austere and unloving woman kept them isolated and refused to allow them to make friends, all the while quoting from the Bible. All men are sinners, she warned – but in particular she was suspicious of other women, and advised both boys against getting involved with girls. Women are scheming and cunning, she would tell her sons and she took pains to ensure that any relationship which looked like developing for them – with people of either sex – was brought to a sharp end.

In 1940, Augusta's prayers were answered and George Gein passed away. When old Mrs Gein died of a cerebral haemorrhage five years later after being nursed for a year by her sons, Henry and Ed were bereft. They came to depend upon each other just as they had once depended on their mother. When Henry died in a forest fire, Ed was left alone in the enormous farmhouse set amid land which stretched as far as his glacial eyes could see. He began to act oddly. First he sealed up his mother's bedroom, the drawing-room and five more upstairs rooms, living in only one room and the kitchen. Then he began buying books and magazines about human anatomy and spent hours poring over them. He became fascinated by the atrocities committed by Nazis during the Second World War. In particular he devoured information about the concentration-camp medical experiments performed on Jews and became fixated upon corpses.

Soon, second-hand experiences of cadavers were not enough and Gein began robbing graves to fulfil his necrophiliac needs. In this he was helped by an elderly, simple-minded associate called Gus. He convinced Gus that he needed the bodies for 'experiments' and the couple would sneak into far-flung Wisconsin cemeteries to steal complete corpses. On other occasions Gein took only the body parts which particularly interested him. Gus helped Gein to store the bodies in a shed at the back of his farmhouse and, it seemed, never asked questions of Gein, nor spoke of the crimes to anyone else.

Later, Gein was to declare that he had believed himself to be a transsexual and that reading about the gender re-assignment operation of Christine Jorgenson in the early 1950s – the first such sensational story to make headlines in the USA – had made his desire to become a woman even more urgent. Possibly, this desire was part of a warped emotional legacy from a mother who had swamped his own male personality. But, he later explained, this was why he wanted to study female reproductive organs. Gein would dissect the bodies and keep some parts – heads, sex organs, livers, hearts and intestines. He would eat the dead flesh of the corpses and make household ornaments and decorations from body parts. Painstakingly, he sewed himself a belt out of carved-off nipples and he upholstered a chair with human skin. A table was propped up by human shin-bones. A tom-tom drum was created out of a coffee-tin with human skin stretched across it and half a human skull became a soup bowl. The four posts on Gein's bed were topped with skulls and a human head hung in his house in the way most people would position an attractive plant. On the walls were nine death-masks – the skinned faces of women – and he made decorative bracelets out of human skin.

In his study of sadistic murderers, Robert P. Brittain notes that such a killer might hide in his house a mask, cloak or sinister objects such as 'a hood of the Ku Klux Klan type ... a child's doll, a life-sized model of a woman ... or ... the place itself might be made to represent an execution chamber.' In Gein's case, this was no representation: by the time he was caught, it was an execution chamber. Dr Brittain remarks that some sex-killers may also be transvestites, although their predilections are somewhat different from the usual desires of regular transvestites, but even he, hardened as he was from studying sadistic killers, might have raised an eyebrow at the transvestite measures which Gein took to satisfy his perversion, including making himself a mask from a woman's face and a waistcoat out of female skin, complete with breasts. He would skin bodies and wear the skin as if it were a shawl, or fashion it into leggings. The female sex organs which he had hacked out of corpses and from the bodies of those he subsequently murdered, were toys to him: he would play with and fondle these rotting pieces of tissue, saying later that this gave him 'inexplicable thrills', and he even filled a pair of women's knickers with excised female genitalia, which he would then put on. Crazed Gein would, on certain nights, dress up in his macabre costume and dance around by the light of the moon or admire himself in a full-length mirror. This ghoulish behaviour stimulated him because, claim Jack Levin and James Alan Fox in their book *Mass Murder*, it enabled Gein 'to recreate the form and presence of his dead mother.'

But as happens with sadistic murderers, it became necessary for Gein's fantasies to intrude upon reality in a more lethal way. When his accomplice Gus became too old to farm his land and moved into an old people's home, Gein decided it was too much trouble – and too much hard work – to dig up corpses on his own. It was but a short, conscience-free step for Gein to move from acquiring already-dead bodies for his 'experiments' to acquiring live ones ... and then swiftly rendering them dead.

In the middle of a snowstorm on one winter night in 1954, Gein waited outside Hogan's Tavern, a bar in the nearby town of Pine Grove, until all the customers had gone. Then he walked up to the saloon-keeper, Mary Hogan, a tough and dominant fifty-one-year-old woman who bore a striking resemblance to Gein's mother, calmly placed the muzzle of his gun against her head and shot her dead with a single bullet. He hauled her body outside and strapped it to a sledge he had brought with him. It took him many hours to drag the sledge home through the snow.

How many other victims did Gein claim in a similar way? There were the scattered remains of an estimated fifteen bodies found at Gein's house when he was eventually arrested, but Gein could not remember how many murders he had done. He did, however, remember eating the flesh of both the disinterred cadavers and his murder-victims and he was able to recall, with undisguised pleasure and no sense of shame, the times when he would prance naked around his kitchen or bedroom, cavorting with his gruesome mementos. This disclosure suggested that he did not perceive such acts as abnormal. The police believed – but could not prove – that he was responsible for the disappearance of several missing local females over the decade preceding 1957, the year of Gein's arrest, including an eight-year-old who had disappeared on her way home from school one day in 1947 and a fifteen-year-old girl who went missing while babysitting one day in 1953. Her bloodstained clothes were discovered later, but again, there was no body to be found.

Gein's activities were brought to an end after the murder of his next, and last, known victim. Like Mary Hogan, she was a middle-aged woman similar in looks to Ed Gein's dead mother. On the morning of 16 November 1957, the deer-hunting season began in the county, providing the cue for the men of Plainfield to don their warm jackets, boots and deerstalker hats and, leaving their womenfolk behind in the town, take off into the wild yonder for a spot of bloody slaughter. Ed Gein had something similar in mind when he wandered into town that day. In Frank Worden's hardware store he found Frank's mother Bernice minding the shop, as Gein had known she would be when he had heard Frank talking about the deer-hunting trip earlier in the week. He used the pretext of wanting to buy some anti-freeze and while an unsuspecting Mrs Worden wrote out the sales-slip, Gein casually took a .22 rifle from a rack on the wall and shot her once in the head at point-blank range. Then calmly locking up the shop and putting the cash-register under one arm, he dragged Mrs Worden's lifeless body out the back way, put her into her own delivery van and drove to a forest where he had left his own car. He transferred the body to his car and drove away fast; home to his house of death.

During that day several locals saw Gein. One man called on him to apologise about shooting a deer on Gein's land. Gein was busy working on his car and waved aside the apology. Later, two teenage neighbours called to ask Gein to run them into town and he emerged from his house with his hands red with blood. He told them he was dressing a deer, but broke off to give the youngsters a lift and was rewarded with an invitation to stay to supper with one of the families. He accepted. Meanwhile, the men who had gone on the hunting trip were arriving back in town.

When Frank Worden returned from his day's sport, he found the store deserted, the cash-register missing and a pool of blood on the floor, with a trail leading to where his delivery truck had been parked that morning. The truck was gone and a neighbour told him he had seen it shoot out of town that morning. Frank's nagging feeling of sickness grew as he remembered that his mother had had no deliveries to make. But something was tugging at his memory ... what was it? Frank, who was deputy sheriff of Plainfield, suddenly remembered: Ed Gein had ordered some anti-freeze and had told him he would be calling at the store to collect it that day. Frank raced back into the store: on the counter was the half-written receipt for anti-freeze.

He immediately told the sheriff of his suspicions and the police set off for Gein's home. Meanwhile, other officers had found Gein having supper at a nearby home and began to question him. Could he account for his movements that day?

'Somebody framed me,' declared Gein immediately.

'Framed you for what?' the policemen asked him.

'About Mrs Worden,' Gein replied.

'What about her?' asked the officers.

'Well, she's dead, ain't she?' said Gein.

Gein was securely locked in a police cell as the sheriff's men descended on his isolated farmhouse. Since there was no electricity, the place was in darkness, so, using flashlights, they began searching. What they found in the barn repelled them. Mrs Worden's headless body was hanging upside-down from a pulley attached to a block and tackle and hoisted to the ceiling. The corpse had been gutted and hung in just the way, said one of the policemen on the case, that a deer might have been trussed up. With her head cut off at the shoulders, Gein had slit the skin on the back of her ankles and through the cut tendons he had inserted a three-and-a-half-foot-long wooden rod, by which she was suspended.

Could the police make a more gruesome discovery? Well yes, they could, and did. Mrs Worden's head was found with two hooks in the ears, ready for hanging on the wall. The house was filthy, littered with old newspapers and the rotting remains of meals. As if stuck in a time warp, it appeared to have been untouched by any clean-up effort since the death of Gein's mother twelve years previously. The remains of Mary Hogan were found in a house which resembled an abbatoir. In the basement human body parts hung from hooks on the walls and the floor was thick with dried blood and tissue. In the kitchen, four human noses were found in a cup and a pair of human lips dangled from a string like a grisly mobile toy. Decorating the walls were ten female heads, all sawn off above the eyebrows, some with traces of lipstick on the cold, rigid lips. The refrigerator contained frozen pieces of human meat. A heart – Mrs Worden's – was in a pan on the stove. And there was an armchair ... with *real arms*!

When the sheriff returned to town with his men, they were at first too traumatised to tell what they had found, but gradually they began to reveal the full, unbelievable horror of the Gein house. Gein was unperturbed and at first denied everything. Then he began talking and confessed about his macabre cannibalistic practices together with the two murders. There were probably more murders, he said, but his memory did not serve him well. Bizarrely, Gein was most angry at the accusation that he had stolen the cash register containing forty-one dollars from the Worden shop. This was not the case, he raged; he only took the cash register to find out how it worked – for the same reasons of curiosity that had caused him to dig up and eviscerate the dead bodies. 'I'm no robber!' he protested ... Although when it came to stealing corpses, this was another matter. He freely admitted his grave-robbing activities and said that his practice was to note when there was a funeral in town and go that night to the graveyard to dig up the body. They were always the bodies of women and he always left the grave 'in apple-pie order', he declared with some pride.

'I had a compulsion to do it,' he admitted. 'It all started after my mother died in 1945. I felt I wanted to change my sex and become a woman. I used to skin the bodies and wear the skin. I'd make a mask from the face, then I felt I was really like the woman I wanted to be. I liked to wear women's hair, too. I'd wear a scalp like a wig. I enjoyed cutting up bodies and sorting out the inside parts.' When police checked out those graves which Gein remembered robbing they found them to be empty. The people of Plainfield were horrified when news of their lonely neighbour's crimes and obsessions began to spread.

Okay, they said, so Ed Gein was always a little strange – becoming even odder after his mother's death – and you might warn your children to give him a wide berth, but no normal person could ever have begun to imagine the vileness of his acts. Many shuddered with sickened disgust to remember that Gein had sometimes given them gifts of 'venison', and after Gein was taken away, his farm, which was due to be auctioned, was set on fire and burned to the ground. No culprit was ever found by the town's police.

The psychiatric report on Gein concluded that he had schizophrenia. He told the psychiatrists that as a child he had watched his mother killing a pig, cutting open its stomach and eviscerating it with her bare and bloody hands, and when Gein eventually appeared in court charged with the murders of Mary Hogan and Bernice Worden, his plea of 'guilty but insane' was backed up by the doctors. Gein was sent to the state mental hospital for an indefinite time. His repeated requests for parole were turned down (the last was in 1974) and one of American history's most revolting cannibal killers died ten years later, still in captivity in the psychiatric ward at Mendota, aged seventy-eight. He was buried in Plainfield cemetery, next to his mother.

In their 1985 book, *Mass Murder*, James Fox and Jack Levin claim that Gein, although little known outside Wisconsin, came to the attention of Hollywood's horror film industry. Long after he had been incarcerated for life, *The Texas Chainsaw Massacre* film was released. Fox and Levin identified in the film 'numerous elements reminiscent of Gein'. Another movie called *Deranged* bore an even closer resemblance to Gein's activities, with a serial killer at one point dressing in the skin of one of his female victims. But when Fox and Levin wrote their book, the closest celluloid parallel to Ed Gein was Norman Bates, the psychotic motel owner in Alfred Hitchcock's classic film *Psycho*, adapted from the novel by Robert Bloch. It was the chiller of its era, with the late Anthony Perkins giving a mind-numbing performance as a man who was so obsessed with his dead mother that he held conversations with her, dressed up as her when carrying out his murders, and kept her dead body in a rocking-chair in the cellar – complete with wig – in an effort to bring her back to life. This portrayal, say Levin and Fox, equated with Gein's use of female body parts in an attempt to 'symbolise and resurrect' his mother, conversing with her and, as with the Norman Bates characterisation, there was a struggle with 'strict moral constraints that had been enforced by their dominating and sickly mothers.' Another writer, Brian Marriner, suggests the opposite, concluding that Gein did not want to replace his mother but that his mutilation of dead female bodies was a 'symbolic form of revenge on his cold and unloving mother.' He points out that both Mary Hogan and Bernice Worden resembled Augusta Gein: ' … middle-aged, overweight and dominant. Was he killing his mother over and over again?'

In 1991 Hollywood rendered yet another predator who appears to have been based upon Gein. Thomas Harris wrote the novel *The Silence of the Lambs* in 1988 as a sequel to *Red Dragon*. The principal character in both books is Dr Hannibal Lecter, a psychopathic psychiatrist who cannibalises his victims. In the Oscar-winning film version of *The Silence of the Lambs*, Lecter (played with sinister charm by Anthony Hopkins) is in an escape-proof psychiatric institution, but his help is sought by the FBI, who are trying to capture a serial killer nicknamed Buffalo Bill. The killer's 'trademark' is that he flays his victims' torsos. As the story progresses we learn that Buffalo Bill is a twisted transvestite who is tailoring his own female outfit, sewing the pieces of skin together to make a complete woman's skin. At one point a naked Buffalo Bill, with his male genitals strapped down between his legs, prances and pouts in front of a mirror, clearly convinced he looks like a woman. The parallel with Ed Gein, dancing in the moonlight wearing his 'suit' of women's skins is too obvious to be coincidental.

Are mothers at the heart of such grotesque perversions? The 'Monstrous Maternal' is a literary and psychological trope which figures as far back as the Greek myths. Powerful but un-nurturing, rejecting and cruel or suffocating and dominant – such women are portrayed metaphorically as 'cannibalistic', sucking the life and independent spirit from their offspring and in the process are often blamed for creating monsters. In the next chapter we may speculate on this further, with yet another cannibal killer.

'Few and evil have the days
of the years of my life been'

Genesis 47:9

> *'I will kill thee/And love thee after'*
> *Othello*, Act V, Scene 2
> *'If I kiss her, I would have to kill her first'*
>
> Edmund Kemper, at the age of seven

Going on appearances, Ed Gein and Ed Kemper could not have been more different. While Gein was small and insignificant in stature, Kemper was unusually tall – six feet nine inches – and powerfully built, weighing twenty stone. Ed Gein was certainly a crazed monster, but as to the minutiae of sexual sadism, his prime motivator was his necrophilia, rather than Kemper's preference, which was torturing, observing the suffering and fear of his victims and avenging himself on women in a world in which he felt he was an outsider. Finally, the two men's lives and lifestyles bore little relation to one another in other ways: Kemper's family were city-based, in Santa Cruz, California, whereas the Gein family led a life of isolation in small-town Plainfield and until Gein's arrest, at the age of fifty, no one had any inkling of the secret disturbances of his mind. But there were plenty of early indications that Kemper was dangerously abnormal, for his sadism manifested itself when he was very young. It was just unfortunate that no one responded to these indicators and put Kemper away for good before he could harm any fellow humans. Which he ultimately did with a vengeance.

Inside their troubled heads, Gein and Kemper had lots in common. These factors included a liking for necrophilia and the inability to have normal sexual relationships, a hunger for cannibalising human bodies ... and a problem with a dominating mother. Repeated studies of sadistic killers throw up parental influences as possible factors in the 'creation' of monsters like Kemper, Gein and most of the other serial killers contained within these pages. Robert P. Brittain, whose study of the sadistic murderer has been mentioned more than once, could have been using Kemper as his archetypal case when he described the type of person for whom the police should search after the discovery of a particularly brutal crime involving mutilation. Brittain's profile of such a criminal, formulated after twenty-odd years' work in forensic pathology and psychiatry, lists characteristics of lifestyle, past experience and personality which are displayed, to a greater or lesser degree, by sadistic murderers. Kemper, like Gein, matched the profile closely, especially with regard to his mother. Brittain noted a sadistic killer's strong, ambivalent relationship to his mother, both loving her and hating her. This archetypcal 'killer' is often known as a particularly devoted son, emotionally very closely bound to his mother, bringing her gifts to a degree beyond the ordinary. He is a 'mother's boy' even when adult. There also co-exists a deep hatred of her, not superficially obvious and not always acknowledged even to himself. This kind of person sometimes kills his mother, and all male matricides should be examined with this psychopathology in mind. He often tells of childhood glimpses of his mother undressed

... In some cases, the father is known to have been very authoritarian and punitive.

In addition to this, rape is commonly thought to be 'a symbolic attack on the aggressor's own parents – particularly the mother.'[7] So what of Edmund Emil Kemper III who, after being born into an apparently normal family, the second of three children, went on to rape, murder and sometimes cannibalise his victims – fourteen in all? Brittain says of the typical sadistic murderer: 'The seeds of his abnormalities would seem to be planted at a very early age and a careful history will often show clear evidence of some manifestations of his perversions even before puberty.'

So it was with Kemper. His youngest sister recalled much evidence of Ed's 'spooky' childhood behaviour. There was a fascination with staging pretend executions, when he would make her blindfold him, then pull an imaginary lever and he would writhe around as if dying. There was the time when he took her new doll and she later found it with its head and hands cut off – something which Kemper would later do to his human victims. She also remembered teasing him about a teacher he had a crush on. 'Why don't you go and kiss her?' she joked.

'If I kiss her, I would have to kill her first,' replied the seven-year-old boy. If that was a strange remark from a small child, even more bizarre were the fantasies he nursed before he reached adolescence. In addition to an occasion when he stood outside his teacher's house one night and envisaged what it would be like to kill her and then make love to her, he also imagined killing his neighbours, having sex with corpses and killing his mother. Being a self-confessed 'weapons freak' (yet another typical characteristic of the sadistic murderer, according to Brittain), he later admitted to psychiatrist Donald T. Lunde that on numerous occasions as a youngster he had gone into his mother's bedroom carrying a weapon and had thought about killing her.

After his arrest, Kemper told officers why he hated his mother Clarnell, and of his resentment that his father was not around very much when he was young. His parents separated when he was seven and Clarnell moved her family away from California to Montana, which resulted in Ed hardly ever seeing his father. Kemper blamed his mother utterly for the non-presence of his father and also claimed that his mother was a strict disciplinarian and frequently punished and ridiculed him 'to make him a man'. Also, he said, 'She used to tell me how much I reminded her of my father, whom she dearly hated, of course.' Kemper alleged that one day when he was eight years old he returned from school to find that his belongings had been moved out of his bedroom and he was told he must sleep in the cellar thereafter, because his huge, bulky presence was, according to Clarnell Kemper, making his sisters feel uncomfortable. In later life Ed Kemper remembered being virtually imprisoned in the dark store-room where, he believed, goblins and demons lurked. 'There was only one way out – someone had to move the kitchen table and lift a trapdoor,' said Kemper. When his father heard about this incident some months later, he was angry and put a stop to it, threatening his ex-wife with legal action.

But isolated thus, and with a high intelligence and fertile imagination, Kemper's fantasies were given free rein, and they were all murderous – a combination of feelings of revenge, mutilation, power, possession and sex. And he was not yet out of short pants. His mother explained her harshness on one occasion when she looked back on her son's childhood and remarked: 'I was deeply worried during the years about the lack of a father relationship, and so I tried everything I could to compensate for that.' Perhaps Clarnell Kemper was, as her son alleged, over-punitive – and excessive parental punishment has been shown by many psychiatric researchers to result in abnormal aggression in children.[8] Alan R. Felthous concluded that parental brutality could predispose a child to aggressive behaviour, including cruelty to animals and – perhaps interesting in relation to Kemper's case – he added: 'The combination of parental brutality and the absence of a stable and emotionally available father figure may increase the likelihood of a boy showing cruelty to dogs or cats.'

Kemper certainly showed such cruelty when young, but while it is convenient to try and apportion blame to parents in these labelling exercises, it is also worth remembering that although abusive or neglectful parents are likely to have a negative effect on their children – even more probable if the parents are themselves psychologically disturbed – this does not necessarily mean that their offspring will always be criminals. Indeed, many children who suffer at their parents' hands in much the same way that Kemper claimed to have suffered – and indeed some who endure much worse cruelty – turn out to be normal, and sometimes valuable members of society. They may carry long-term effects of their trauma, but this is not always expressed in law-breaking, and in still fewer cases in murder. Likewise, some criminals come from devoted families with responsible, caring parents. The outdated behavioural psychologists' view that the newborn child is a *tabula rasa* – a blank slate – whose personality is solely dependent upon the life events and influences which are etched thereon is fairly comprehensively debunked by the above two contradictory facts.

This is not to say that a sexual sadist's early life does not offer useful insights into the likely personality of the man. In Ed Kemper's case these were numerous, the most obvious indicator of his psychopathy being the torture of animals, to which he graduated when he tired of cutting up his sister's dolls. Says Robert P. Brittain regarding sadistic killers:

'Their sadism is manifested in various ways. They are excited by cruelty whether in books or in films, in fact or in fantasy. There is sometimes a history of extreme cruelty to animals. Paradoxically they can also be very fond of animals ... the only animal which seems to be safe is one belonging to the sadist himself.'

Not, it seemed, in Kemper's case. He was thirteen when his mother noticed that the family cat had vanished. Unknown to her, it was only the latest feline victim of Ed's cruelty; he had been killing the neighbourhood cats for a long time previously, sometimes burying them alive, then putting their heads on poles and muttering incantations over his 'trophies'. Once he killed a cat in jealousy because it showed a preference for his sister over him: he sliced off the top of its head with a machete. On other occasions, he kept body parts of the cats in his wardrobe. Ed's mother found their cat in the dustbin. It had been decapitated and cut into pieces – which is, frighteningly, exactly what Ed was later to do to his murder victims ... including Clarnell Kemper herself.

Also when he was aged thirteen, Kemper was suspected of shooting a pet dog belonging to a neighbour and he was ostracised by other boys of his age. Kemper was an awkward and oversized child, much bigger than his peers, which increased his isolation. The assertive Clarnell was busy with her own life and her own marital relationships – which were legion. One of Kemper's step-fathers warmed to Ed and took the boy under his wing, teaching him fishing and shooting – the sort of masculine role-modelling of which he had been deprived. Yet his kindness was not rewarded. Eventually Ed, armed with an iron bar, tried (but failed) to pluck up the courage to attack the man, after which, he planned, he would steal his car and drive to California to see his real father.

In the nineteenth century, there was the belief that people were born criminals – studies such as those produced by Italian criminologist Cesare Lombroso even suggested that they could be identified by their physical and facial features – and the notion of 'born killers' rose again in the 1960s when the XYY hypothesis was explored. During research which related the male sex hormone testosterone to aggressive behaviour, speculation began reasoning that people with an extra Y (male) chromosome would be unusually aggressive. Some studies showed a higher incidence of violent crimes among XYY individuals and there is a higher percentage of XYY people in prisons and maximum security hospitals (however, statistics show that many of these men did not commit violent crimes). The XYY syndrome might be evidenced by an exaggerated male appearance and Kemper might be thought to fall into this category, being unusually tall, above average intelligence and exceptionally violent. Could he have been a 'born killer' with an extra 'criminal chromosome'? Was this the reason for his later aberrant behaviour? No, it was not. The XYY theory is judged to be inconclusive in general and particularly so in Kemper's case: his chromosomal pattern was entirely normal.

But his size and his manner did mark him out from the other boys. He became a loner, reading science fiction and books about the occult, playing with his guns and knives and indulging in a violent fantasy life which often spilled over into reality, when he would feel compelled to go out and chop up a cat. At thirteen, Kemper ran away from home to his father's house, hoping to be allowed to stay, but his father refused and sent him back to his mother. Clarnell Kemper was finding her son increasingly hard to handle and was at a loss as to what she should do with him. Her ex-husband solved the problem: Ed would be sent to live with his paternal grandparents, who had an isolated ranch in northern California. Clarnell expressed some anxiety about this course of action. 'You might wake up one day and find they've been killed,' she warned, but her husband dismissed her fears and began to make plans. Ed objected strongly to this 'punishment', as he saw it, but his protests were swept aside and he was packed off to live on the mountain-top ranch with his grandparents.

Soon, he transferred his murderous fantasies about his mother to his grandmother, who was an equally dominant woman. A year later, on a day when his grandfather was away, he took a .22-calibre rifle and shot his grandmother in the back of the head. He fired two more shots into her as she lay on the ground and then, his excitement mounting, in a frenzy, he stabbed her over and over again. When his grandfather returned home, Kemper shot him before he could get into the house and discover his wife's corpse. Then he locked his grandfather's body in the garage and ambled back into the house to telephone his mother and tell the shocked woman what he had done. Immediately, she told him to ring the police, which he did. Then he sat on the step and waited for them to come and get him. He was fifteen years old. Why had he done this terrible thing? The boy didn't really know. 'I just wondered how it would feel to shoot Grandma,' he said, shrugging. Psychiatrist Dr Lunde had another theory. 'In his way, he had avenged the rejection of both his mother and father,' he hypothesised in his book *Murder and Madness*.

Kemper was handed over firstly to the California Youth Authority (CYA), where psychiatrists examined him and, as well as judging that his IQ was above average at 136, also discovered evidence of his violent hostility towards his mother. If this individual is ever released, they warned, he should never, ever be placed in his mother's custody. Then, because the Youth Authority's detention facilities were inadequate to meet the seriousness of Kemper's crime, he was put into Atascadero maximum security mental hospital (now known as Department of State Hospitals – Atascadero), where he spent four of the following five years but received little in the way of treatment. He was, however, a model patient. At twenty-one he was transferred back to the CYA and came up for parole. The parole board did not contain any psychologists or psychiatrists and they chose to ignore the advice contained in the limited psychiatric reports they had regarding the six-foot, nine-inch tall youth towering in front of them. They said he was cured and ordered his release. Then they sent him home to his mother.

By now, she was living in Santa Cruz and working as an administrative assistant at the University of California. It is clear that in many ways Clarnell Kemper tried to be a caring mother and make life easy for her troublesome son: she obtained a parking sticker for Ed so that he could park his car on the campus, and as the months passed, she also put a great deal of effort into having his juvenile record sealed, so he could begin life anew without a blot on his character. But at the same time, she continued to nag and find fault with her son, sometimes, according to those who knew them, reducing him to tears with her accusations of idleness and inadequacy. He told people that the arguments were unimportant, that they were both expressive, explosive people but very close, and to prove it, he showered his mother with gifts. 'I kept trying to push her toward where she would be a nice motherly type and quit being such a damned manipulating, controlling vicious beast,' he said later. 'She was Mrs Wonderful on the campus ... when she comes home she lets everything down and she's just a pure bitch.'

As the arguments between them began to escalate, Kemper's violent fantasies were reawakened. He began preparing for a killing spree. He developed an image of himself as a gentle giant, and adopted an easy, friendly manner with women, so they would feel comfortable with him. Meanwhile, he adapted his car so that the door on the passenger side could not be opened from the inside and he took pains to learn all the back lanes in the local road system. He began collecting knives again. His favourite knife – which he was to use for killing – he called 'The General' ('The sadistic murderer has strong feelings about [weapons], may have special favourites and he can even have "pet" names for these,' notes Brittain.)

Thus prepared, Kemper began travelling around, looking for girls to pick up and finding the campus parking sticker obtained by his mother to be most useful as a means of luring students into his death-trap car. This was what earned him the nickname of 'The Co-ed Killer'.

His first murders, in May 1972, should, by rights, have failed. He picked up two hitch-hiking college girls, Anita Luchese and Mary Anne Pesce and attacked them with 'the General', but panicked when things did not go as smoothly as he had hoped. At one point he found himself locked outside the car with the two girls inside. Amazingly, Mary Anne Pesce managed to open the door to him. Kemper made Anita climb into the boot of the car while he handcuffed Mary Anne and put a plastic bag over her head. The frightened girl tried to reason with him, but he was impervious to logic: he stabbed her many times in the abdomen and back before cutting her throat. He killed Anita in the same way and then took their bodies home with him, where he decapitated and dissected the corpses and then had sex with them, taking some Polaroid pictures during the whole bloody procedure. This was an act he had fantasised about many times while at Atascadero. He disposed of the torsos in the Santa Cruz mountains, but kept the heads ... his 'hunting trophies'.

His third victim, four months later, was Aiko Koo, aged fifteen, who was hitch-hiking to a dancing class. He drove her into the mountains at gunpoint and taped up her mouth. Then, horrifically, he suffocated Aiko by blocking her nostrils with his fingers, before raping her. He was fulfilling the childhood fantasy about his teacher which he had related to his sister all those years before: 'If I kiss her, I'd have to kill her first.' Kemper threw Aiko's body into the boot of his car, drove off – and stopped for a few beers on the way home. On returning to the car, he opened the boot to look at his handiwork 'admiring my catch – like a fisherman,' he recalled later, chillingly. Then he took Aiko's body home and mutilated it as he had with his earlier victims, keeping the decapitated head in the car with him for several days.

Three more young women aged between fifteen and twenty-three fell prey to Kemper's murderous savagery during the following year. His modus operandi rarely differed. The act of killing alone often induced orgasm: sex killers frequently indulge in frenzied stabbing or beating of a victim because they need to continue the attack until they have completed ejaculation. The sadism provides a sexual release which normal intercourse fails to do. After killing his victim by shooting or stabbing her, Kemper would take the body home and, as he had done with his sister's doll all those years ago, he always removed the head and hands before having sex with the lifeless and identity-free torso, often devouring the flesh before chopping the remainder of the body up and burying the pieces in the mountains the next day. The act of decapitation caused Kemper great sexual excitement and he would wrap the heads of his victims in cellophane in order to keep them in his closet. Later he would perform sex-acts on the severed heads, on one occasion burying a head in his yard, facing his bedroom, so he could imagine it 'looking at him' and he 'could talk to it at night'. The significance of the head, Kemper later said, was that it was a trophy: 'The head is where everything is at, the brain, eyes, mouth. That's the person ... you cut off the head and the body dies.'

A psychoanalytic theory of the sadistic man is that he has a castration complex and inflicts pain to assure himself of his power and masculinity. In particular, beheading a victim is said to be part of such a castration complex and thought to have its roots in a jealous Oedipal fantasy of the son to destroy the father. Castration was common among our primitive ancestors, when men emasculated their enemies to prevent them using their sexual power, and symbolic castration – robbing a victim of power by decapitation – can be found in the mythical methods of destroying vampires. But other researchers suggest that mothers are the true Oedipal target: blood symbolises 'an unobtainable object' or 'forbidden fruit', and this forbidden fruit, Freudians would say, is the sexual conquest of the mother. Blood-letting and drinking is therefore symbolically obtaining the unobtainable mother.

Could maternal deprivation mean that a cannibal or vampire killer has a need to be nourished which was never fulfilled? Vampiristic and, by the nature of the act, cannibalistic, impulses are to be found in individuals who are retarded at an infantile Oedipal stage of development and regard the mother's body as the object of genital and oral impulses, while at the same time experiencing aggressive and controlling desires. This can be exacerbated if there is a poor or dysfunctional masculine identification during this time, perhaps because the father is absent, as in Kemper's case. Certainly, part of Kemper's stimulation came from associating his acts with his mother. On one occasion, she came home just as Ed had put a body in his wardrobe. He behaved entirely normally with her, but the next morning he committed sex acts with the body, took it into the shower and used an axe to cut it up before disposing of it in his usual way. He took particular pleasure in talking to his mother while he had a dead body in his car and sometimes visited her after a murder because of the thrill this gave him.

As the student absences began to be recorded and buried body parts were uncovered in the mountains, the Santa Cruz police realised they had a brutal and perverted serial killer on their hands. In spite of Kemper's previous record, the authorities' suspicion never fell on him – presumably, those who were unaware of Kemper's mental state regarded the murder of his grandparents as a one-off, the specificity of his victims making it a crime he was assumed to be unlikely to repeat with strangers.

But Kemper was engrossed in his own behaviour and since the police did not come to interview him about his crimes, he decided to ingratiate himself with them. He began to go to the Santa Cruz bars where he knew they gathered and he joined in their conversations, plaguing them with questions about the Co-ed Killer. Since talk revolved around each latest ghastly killing and the identity of the murderer, Kemper was able to satisfy his own desire to relive every grisly episode and at the same time enjoy a feeling of smug superiority as he rubbed shoulders and drank beers with the men who wanted him behind bars, laughing up his sleeve at them as he asked about their progress in solving the crimes. Then he went home and watched television programmes like *Police Story* for tips on how to avoid detection – something at which he excelled. On one occasion, Kemper picked up a hitchhiker and her twelve-year-old son, intending to kill both of them, but as he drove away he spotted the woman's friend writing down the number of his car's licence plate. Instead of killing his passengers, he delivered them to their destination in a gentlemanly way and returned to the city to search for an alternative victim. Another time, he drove calmly past guards at the entrance to the campus with two dying girls in his car, blankets thrown roughly over them.

Kemper's killing spree reached its gruesome, and many would say, entirely predictable finale, on 21 April 1973. It was Easter weekend when, after many days of thought and planning, Ed decided he had to fulfil what he believed was his destiny – 'It's something hard to just up and do,' he said later, as he recollected events, 'but I was pretty fixed on that issue because there were a lot of things involved.' His mother was asleep at five o'clock in the morning when her son, acting out yet another childhood fantasy, entered her bedroom with a hammer in one hand and 'the General' in the other. But this time he did not restrict himself to imagined acts. Ferociously, he brought the hammer down on his mother's head time and again, then turned her on her back and, carefully lifting her chin, slashed her throat. When she was dead he decapitated her, used her head for oral sex and removed her larynx, throwing it down the waste disposal unit. 'This seemed appropriate,' he said later, 'as much as she'd bitched and screamed and yelled at me over the years.' But when he switched on the waste disposal machine, it malfunctioned and the grisly piece of tissue flew out again. 'Even when she was dead, she was still bitching at me,' he was to complain as he recalled the incident. 'I couldn't get her to shut up.'

He propped his mother's head on a hatbox and threw darts at it before sexually attacking her headless corpse and dumping the body in a closet. Then he went out for a drive and met an acquaintance who owed him ten dollars. Kemper was in a murderous mood. His friend paid him the money he owed and this, Kemper declared later, 'saved his life.' But his craving for savagery had not abated and he needed to kill again. Returning home, Kemper telephoned his mother's best friend Sarah Hallett and invited her round for dinner. He recalled that when she arrived she said, 'Let's sit down, I'm dead.' And, said Kemper, as if the murder was a joke, 'I kind of took her at her word there.' He strangled and decapitated her, too. Significantly, he slept in his mother's bed that night and the next morning decided to leave Santa Cruz, using Sarah Hallett's car and dumping it later so he could rent another. Before he left his home, Kemper wrote a taunting note to the police, saying: '5.15 a.m. Saturday. No need for her to suffer any more at the hands of this "murderous Butcher". It was quick – asleep – the way I wanted it. Not sloppy or incomplete, gents. Just a "lack of time". I got things to do!!!'

Kemper rented a car and drove non-stop to Pueblo, Colorado, listening to radio reports in excitement as he imagined the nationwide hunt for the Co-ed Killer. He heard nothing. In Pueblo, Kemper bought newspapers, expecting splash headlines about the massive manhunt. Again, to his growing dismay, nothing. After three days he telephoned the Santa Cruz police and confessed that he was the Co-ed Killer. The police dismissed it, thinking he was just another crank. Kemper had to call three times and repeat his story before they began to take him seriously. He patiently waited in a public telephone booth for the police to arrive and arrest him. When they took him back to Santa Cruz he admitted his crimes at once and confessed to cannibalising two of his victims. He said he had taken flesh from the women's legs and had frozen it, later making a casserole with it. He also admitted having other 'keepsakes' of his victims – teeth or pieces of skin. When he was asked why he had eaten the flesh of his victims, Kemper said: 'I wanted them to be part of me – and now they are.' He also said that he had killed his mother to spare her the embarrassment of discovering that her son was a murderer, for, after a recent police visit to check his gun licence, Kemper had begun to believe that it would only be a matter of time before he was caught.

Kemper's trial on eight counts of first-degree murder took place in October 1973. He proved to be an intelligent and articulate defendant and suggested to the court that he was a Jekyll-and-Hyde character. 'I believe very deeply there are two people inside me,' he said. Psychiatrists were called to verify Kemper's mental state and one declared that Kemper would kill again if he had the opportunity. In November 1973 Kemper was found guilty but legally sane. Despite his request that he be executed, this was during a period when capital punishment was under state review and he was instead sentenced to life imprisonment. He was an early subject for interview by profilers from the newly set-up (1972) Behavioral Science Unit, including Robert Ressler, whose studies of Kemper appear in his book written with Tom Schachtman, entitled *Whoever Fights Monsters*.

Edmund Kemper was seventy-three years old in 2021. He remains incarcerated in the California Medical Facility at Vacaville. He was denied parole in 2007 and waived his right to a parole hearing in 2012, repeating a claim that he did not want to be set free because, if released, he would probably kill again. Intelligent and with a manner which is even said to make him likeable, Kemper has been a model prisoner for almost half a century, taking responsibility for timetabling administrative work among the prison population and reading aloud books on recordings for the blind – he has spent several thousand hours making such recordings. FBI profiler John E Douglas in his book *Journey Into Darkness* described Kemper as 'among the brightest inmates' he had ever interviewed and remarked that he displayed 'rare insight' for a violent criminal. Kemper clearly has an understanding of his own mental unpredictability, an instability evidenced during a magazine interview in the 1990s when he interrupted his own apparently lucid and reasonable discourse with an impulsive burst of excitement. 'Sudden thought,' he declared, unexpectedly slithering into fantasy. 'A guy could kidnap a number of good-looking women, put them on a ship for who knows where, and sell them to some sultan. You could get away with it – there are no Kojaks out there.'

Maternal failings, especially their sexual misdemeanours, are frequently to be found in the histories of sadistic killers and, indeed, are offered by them as reasons for their crimes. Overpowering and rejecting mothers, suggest psychoanalysts, can result in sexually-repressed sons who have castration-anxiety and who feel unable to express normal sexuality because of this negative, destructive mother-complex. Another aspect of the maternal conflict, according to Professor Richard Ratner, a psychiatrist at George Washington University, is that the individual feels hate towards the person whom he believes has hurt him – his mother – but at the same time is extremely dependent upon her and comes to bitterly resent that dependence, which is why it explodes in adolescence when the resentment is no longer containable. Gein's mother was smothering, intense and oppressive; Kemper's mother was over-strict and aggressively critical. These cases would seem to support such theories – but let us not lose sight of the fact that thousands of men grow up suffering similar maternal shortcomings – without becoming cannibal killers.

Cannibalism as Art?

'I would my love could kill thee; I am satiated
With seeing thee live, and fain would have thee dead.
I would earth had thy body as fruit to eat,
And no mouth but some serpent's found thee sweet.
I would find grievous ways to have thee slain,
Intense device, and superflux of pain;
Vex thee with amorous agonies, and shake
Life at thy lips, and leave it there to ache;
Strain out thy soul with pangs too soft to kill,
Intolerable interludes, and infinite ill;
Relapse and reluctation of the breath,
Dumb tones and shuddering semitones of death.
Ah that my lips were tuneless lips, but pressed
To the bruised blossom of thy scourged white breast!
Ah that my mouth for Muses' milk were fed
On the sweet blood thy sweet small wounds had bled!
That with my tongue I felt them, and could taste
The faint flakes from thy bosom to the waist!
That I could drink thy veins as wine, and eat
Thy breast like honey! that from face to feet
Thy body were abolished and consumed,
And in my flesh the very flesh entombed!

Algernon Charles Swinburne, *Anactoria*
(poem, delivered as a dramatic monologue)

While some readers may be shocked at the sexual sadism and cannibalism contained in the above poem – the work of one of Britain's acclaimed poets of the nineteenth century – it comes as no surprise to anybody who has glanced into the life of Swinburne. Like Baudelaire before him, who also placed the rotting fruits of a corrupt imagination into his literary work, he idolised the Marquis de Sade. Sade's writings, he declared, showed the aesthetic perfection which was the stamp of genius. But the truth behind his admiration was that Sade's preoccupation with the sexual satisfaction to be derived from cruelty was reflected in Swinburne's own deviant interests in pain, punishment and dying. He relished stories about death and sadism and in his writing these obsessions were frequently laid bare, as with the above-quoted poem. In another, 'Itylus', the story – based on a Greek myth – is that of a man who rapes his sister-in-law and cuts out her tongue to ensure her silence. In revenge for her sister's mutilation and suffering, his wife kills their child and serves it to him for dinner.

In another poem, *Dolores*, Swinburne writes:

> By the ravenous teeth that have smitten
> Through the kisses that blossom and bud,
> By the lips intertwisted and bitten
> Till the foam has a savour of blood.
> By the pulse as it rises and falters,
> By the hands as they slacken and strain,
> I adjure thee respond from thine altars,
> Our Lady of Pain.

And *Our Lady of Pain* was Swinburne's lifetime object of worship. In reality he may not have indulged in the vampirism and cannibalism which poems like *Anactoria* perversely celebrate with an eloquence more customarily expressive of romantic love, but he found his sexual ecstasy in sadomasochism: from being beaten or from watching others being flogged or hurt. He never had a conventional sexual relationship with a woman – in fact, when his poet friend Dante Gabriel Rossetti bribed a woman to awaken some sign of sexual arousal in Swinburne, she eventually admitted the seduction had been a failure and gave back Rossetti's money, telling him that she had been unable to persuade Swinburne that intercourse might be more pleasurable than biting. For Swinburne, writing poems like *Dolores* sublimated his lustful desires. It is in this work that he elevates a bruised and cut body into something twistedly beautiful:

> The white wealth of thy body made whiter
> By the blushes of amorous blows,
> And seamed with sharp lips and fierce fingers,
> And branded by kisses that bruise ...

But this begs a question: can such graceful writing devoted to something which stirs Swinburne's malignantly sadistic senses and is the fuel of his fantasies, while at the same time being distasteful to the majority of individuals, be seen as true art? When, in 1866, Swinburne's *Poems and Ballads* was published, a volume containing *Dolores* and other extreme offerings, there was a Victorian backlash (to use a singularly apposite word) and the writer was dubbed 'Swine-born' by *Punch* magazine.

There was similar public shock in America, but since human nature is unchanging, evidenced today by the enormous popularity in both of these countries of salacious tabloid newspapers which people outwardly profess to despise, the book was a sell-out. Disregarding this hypocrisy, again we might ask: But is it art?

This theoretical issue of how much an artist's moral or criminal behaviour should influence our regard of his work continues into the present day. Is it right in 2020 that we continue to enjoy Michael Jackson's music if we believe him secretly to have been an exploitative paedophile? Should we praise the movie genius of Woody Allen, Roman Polanski, Bill Cosby or Kevin Spacey despite their criminal or alleged amoral actions? Does the fact that Picasso was a misogynist racist or Wagner a renowned anti-semite taint our view of their art? What about if Adolf Hitler's paintings were actually independently regarded as worthy? Would we be able to openly applaud them? Almost a century ago, British artist Eric Gill's acclaimed biblical sculptured panels adorned Britain's Westminster Cathedral and their beauty was indisputable. But fifty-eight years after his death (in 1940), there was a clamour to have the sculptures erased after it was learned that Gill was a paedophile who sexually abused countless pubescent children, including his own daughters – and that he had also sexually experimented with his dog.

So can we – or should we – separate the art from the artist and still appreciate it? Admiring the work of someone we find monstrous induces cognitive dissonance (the perception of contradictory information) in us. If art is an extension of the artist, then by validating it, does that make the viewer or the reader – or even the society – complicit with the artist's monstrosity? Or is it really 'art for art's sake'? Swinburne's masterly use of language and his evocative phraseology may show literary skills which, when applied to other topics, would be very beautiful, but should such linguistic beauty eclipse the unsavoury messages contained in these poems? Is it right that we should believe someone like Swinburne to be an artistic genius, the object of human admiration, when he celebrates in words the sexual psychopathy exhibited in the deeds of cannibalistic murderers like Edmund Kemper, Albert Fish and Ed Gein?

And Issei Sagawa. If there is one cannibal killer above all who would surely applaud the beauty of Swinburne's poetry together with the notion that you can eat someone as an act of worship and love, Sagawa would fit the bill. He, too, considers himself an artist and he particularly admires tall, generously-proportioned, beautiful girls. He has enjoyed painting them, reproducing the tones of their flesh and the plumpness of their buttocks on the canvas. Now in his seventies, the tiny Japanese artist says that these days he contents himself with such depictions to fulfil his fantasies. But in Paris in 1981 he did not restrict his sensuous pleasure to the external beauty of the female form. Unlike Swinburne, who restrained the most shocking desires of his imagination within his writing, Sagawa allowed his frighteningly deviant fantasies off their leash. His longing was for soft flesh and hot blood, for complete, exploratory knowledge of those big, bountiful women – and in Paris he found satisfaction with a Dutch woman, Renee Hartevelt, with whom he claimed to have fallen in love 'at first sight' when they were both attending a lecture on Salvador Dali at the Sorbonne (University). But as in 'Anactoria', the Swinburne poem which opened this chapter, Sagawa's love and passion bore no resemblance to that of a normal human being.

Renee was twenty-five, beautiful, blonde and well-built; a serious-minded, independent woman who spoke three languages and was in France studying for her PhD in French literature at Paris's Censier Institute. She supported herself by teaching languages and encountered Sagawa when he asked her to teach him German and offered to pay her handsomely. The son of Akira Sagawa, the wealthy and influential president of prestigious Tokyo company Kurita Water Industries, Issei had been a precocious child, enjoying Impressionist paintings at the age of five and being a prodigious reader from early childhood. Like Renee,

Sagawa was an intellectual, also working on his doctorate – in comparative literature – at university in Paris. He already had his Master's degree in Shakespeare Studies. When he sat next to Renee Hartevelt in a classroom, he saw in her the living stuff of his fantasies. 'I couldn't keep my eyes off her. Out of her short T-shirt I could see her white arms,' he wrote later in his book *In the Fog*, in which he described what he called his Parisian 'affair'. In 1981 he and Renee talked about literature together. Issei wrote her love letters. They went to concerts and dances and when he held Renee to dance, Sagawa envisaged her nude body with its 'white flesh'. So far, not an uncommon normal male fantasy, one might think. But Sagawa was no average male; he was wildly deviant in relishing the dark avenues down which his imagination roamed.

'I admire very much beautiful girls, especially Occidental girls who are healthy and tall. On the other hand, I also have this aspiration, this strange desire for cannibalism,' he calmly told reporter Peter McGill in his article in the British newspaper *The Observer* more than a decade later, as if it were for all the world just a quirky preference, an antisocial habit. He recalled the childhood nightmare on which he blamed his 'strange desire'. He and his brother were being boiled inside a pot. 'It was my first nightmare of cannibalism ... not to eat someone, but to be eaten,' he said. By the age of fifteen, he was regularly fantasising about cannibalism. 'In my case it is just sexual desire. Sexual fetishism,' he explained to McGill. 'For Japanese girls I haven't any sexual desire. I am feeling as if she is my own daughter – no, sister, so it would be incestuous. For Occidentals though, I have a big adoration. The style, physically, I find very sexual ... I prefer big women, but they are also repulsive.'

Sagawa had studied for his first degree in English literature at Wako University in Tokyo. While there, he attacked a German woman, who, as Renee would later do in Paris, taught him German. 'In my head there was always a fantasy of cannibalism, and when I met this German lady in the street, I wondered if I could eat her,' he told McGill. With 'a mischievous smile' he related how he had climbed through the window of the woman's Tokyo ground-floor apartment on a summer's afternoon. 'She was sleeping and almost naked. I wanted to attack her with an umbrella, but I was a little scared, and when I got close to her, she woke and screamed. She was stronger than me. I fell down, and tried to escape. I couldn't tell people it was because of cannibalism. I was too ashamed.' After the attack, he saw a psychiatrist who declared that Sagawa was 'extremely dangerous', but the incident was hushed up and in 1977 Sagawa, aged twenty-eight and supported by the wealth of his father, went to live in Paris. He immediately bought a rifle – as self-protection, he would later tell the police. There were, he explained, many murderers in Paris.

In 2016 Sagawa recollected to *South China Morning Post* journalist Julian Ryall that during the years prior to his murder of Renee, he had frequently invited prostitutes to his French apartment, 'but not for sex.' He said: 'I wanted to eat them. Every time they had their backs to me, I had the gun but I could not pull the trigger. It was not for a moral or religious reason; I was scared that by pulling the trigger I would be giving in to my desires. But it was more than a desire – it was more of an obligation. It was something that I would have to do in the end. That's the thing about an obsession; it means that whatever your brain or body tells you to do, you have to do it. You become a slave to your obsession.'

Renee apparently liked Sagawa. She wrote to her parents telling of her friendship with 'a brilliant Japanese student' and invited the slightly-built, strange-looking oriental man to her room to discuss literature and to have tea with her.

He did not appear threatening in any way: less than five feet tall, weighing only six stone and with a limp, he was soft and rabbit-like. His lisping voice was gently plaintive and feminine; his hands and feet were tiny and childlike. Renee would tease him about his French, laughing that it was so execrable that she would have to teach him French as well as German, and when, in turn, he invited her to visit him in his apartment to continue their discussion of literature, she willingly went. He served tea and his own special whisky brew. The two were kneeling on the floor, facing each other Japanese-style when Sagawa told Renee he loved her and asked her to go to bed with him. She dismissed his declaration of love and told him she would not sleep with him, for she saw him as a friend – that was all. Sagawa appeared to take her refusal placidly, nodding as if indicating his assent. He stood up to pluck a book of poetry from a shelf and asked Renee to read a poem aloud to him. While she was preoccupied with this, he fetched his rifle and shot her in the back of the neck.

'I just had images of the prostitutes with their backs to me,' Sagawa told Ryall in 2016. 'The wheels of delusion in my mind started to spin and it was like the scenario I had been through so many times in my head. It's still a mystery to me how so much of my life has not gone according to plan, but that day did. I feel bad for saying it, but it went so well.' Sagawa told what happened next in *In the Fog*, the book he wrote when he was incarcerated in France and in whose pages he enthuses about eating human flesh. But before Sagawa dined on Renee's corpse, he indulged in what to him was foreplay: after undressing he had sex with the body. On discovering that neither his teeth nor his kitchen knives were suitable for butchering a corpse, he left the apartment to go and buy a sharp curved knife, with which he cut off the tip of Renee's nose and part of a breast, which he devoured raw. 'I touched her hip and wondered where I should eat first. After a little consideration, I ate right in the centre of the abundant, bouncing part of the right hip ... when I stabbed it went right in ... When I started cutting, I could see some corn-like yellow stuff. I thought it was probably a white woman's own peculiar thick and soft fat. Beyond that I could see a red colour, it looked like beef, red meat ... a little came out and I put it into my mouth ... it had no smell or taste, and melted in my mouth like raw tuna ... finally I was eating a beautiful white woman, and thought nothing was so delicious!' Using an electric carving knife, Sagawa cut up Renee's body carefully, removing strips of flesh to store in his refrigerator, and keeping the other parts he wanted to eat later. Some pieces he ate raw, others he fried with salt, pepper and mustard. Those parts in which he had no interest he cut into pieces small enough to be easily discarded. In between his butchering, Sagawa took photographs of his handiwork. He also took time off to go and watch a film with friends. After a supper of raw flesh, Sagawa went to bed to get a good night's sleep in preparation for the busy day ahead.

The next morning he went out and bought a luggage trolley and two large suitcases, together with a carpet-cleaning machine. He placed the remains of Renee Hartevelt in black plastic bin-liners and then put them into the suitcases, called a taxicab and tried to find a suitable place in the city to dispose of the suitcases. He failed. He made three attempts to get rid of them, but there were always too many people nearby and he was forced to abandon his mission. It was the following day when he finally dragged his wheeled trolley to a lake in the picturesque Bois de Boulogne, where he intended to dump the cases in the water. It was hardly surprising that he was spotted by passers-by. Sagawa was such an unnaturally small person that the suitcases weighed more than he did and dwarfed him. Diners at a restaurant watched with interest as the tiny Japanese man puffed and panted his way across the grass with his heavy load. He was about to push the cases into the water when he saw a couple watching him. Sagawa panicked and ran away, abandoning the bags. Drawn by curiosity, the couple approached them. The cases were heavily bloodstained, but what horrified the couple more was the hand which protruded from one of them.

The Paris police were greatly puzzled when they found the butchered female remains together with Renee's clothes and shoes in the suitcases. While most murderers would dismember a body in order to prevent identification, the purpose here seemed solely to make the body fit into the cases: the young woman's head and hands were almost intact – apart from the missing nose-tip – and together with her belongings it was a simple and speedy matter to discover who she was. And they were to find their suspect when a cab driver remembered collecting Sagawa from his apartment. Within forty-eight hours the police had closed in on Sagawa, who greeted the officers pleasantly as he welcomed them into his apartment and confessed freely to the murder, claiming he had a history of mental illness. When the officers opened the refrigerator door to discover Renee Hartevelt's breast, one of her lips and both buttocks on the shelves – and when Sagawa said he had eaten the other missing parts of her body 'sliced thin and raw' – they were inclined to agree that they were dealing with a madman.

While waiting for his trial to begin, Sagawa was confident that his influential father would do something to help him and, indeed, the senior Sagawa provided a lawyer for his son's defence. Issei Sagawa expressed no regret for his victim, but he did say he had learned a lesson from his experience of committing murder. He was quoted as saying: 'I know now what to do when killing a girl, how not to be arrested.' It was 1983 before a judge decided that Sagawa was mentally incompetent to stand trial, that criminal charges would be dropped because Sagawa was in a 'state of dementia' at the time of the murder and that he should be placed in a secure mental hospital – the Hospital Paul Guiraud, an asylum in a Paris suburb – indefinitely. Hospital psychiatrists said that he was an untreatable psychotic. And there the story should have ended. But that is to disregard the curious appeal that this man held for the Japanese people. Sagawa had described Renee Hartevelt's dead flesh as tasting 'like raw tuna in a sushi restaurant', and those Westerners whose stomachs already lurch at the Japanese predilection for eating raw fish can only feel even more disgust at what happened next to 'insane' Issei Sagawa: he became a star.

No sooner had Sagawa arrived at the Hospital Paul Guiraud than a Japanese film company was looking at his story in just the way Sagawa had regarded Renee: in terms of consumer appeal. This could be a hit, they told Japanese playwright Juro Kara, who immediately began exchanging letters with Sagawa, which in 1983 were published in the form of a fictional novel called *Sagawa-kun kara no Tegami* (*Letters from Sagawa*). In it, with a distasteful – and entirely inappropriate – picturesqueness, Kara described French women as having huge breasts 'swinging to and fro like monsters, with blue veins running through them like Martian rivers'. The book was a sell-out and won a literary prize for its 'interesting intellectual approach'. Sagawa's story inspired the 1981 Stranglers' song 'La Folie', the Rolling Stones' track 'Too Much Blood' on their 1983 album *Undercover* and the 2004 Human Factors Lab song 'Dinner with Renee'. *Adoration*, a 1986 short film by Olivier Smolders was based on Sagawa's story and the same year the European TV channel Viasat Explorer released a forty-seven-minute documentary film about Sagawa called *Cannibal Superstar*.

Meanwhile, Sagawa was writing *Kiri no Naka* (*In the Fog*), a series of five books about his experiences, which contain lavish and intricate descriptions about the murder and cannibalisation of Renee, written in a way which reveals the erotic fetishism which dominated Sagawa's psyche. The blurb on the cover includes a quotation from Sagawa describing Renee as 'the most delicious meat I ever had' and the book was an instant success in Japan, where the newspaper *Tokyo Shimbun* declared it to be 'beautifully done and outstanding among recent Japanese literature, which has become boring'. Sagawa also began making plans for directing a film of his experience, with himself in the starring role.

One would think that these writings and plans were proof enough that Sagawa was a hopeless and dangerous sexually deviant fantasist who should remain incarcerated until the breath left his body. As Dr Bernard Defer, one of Sagawa's psychiatrists in France, remarked in 1991:

'Sexual desire, especially perverse desire, is something lasting, something permanent. It forms part of the personality. He can still have the desire to eat a woman. It is preferable that he still be in an institution.'

But Issei Sagawa is not still in an institution. Following approaches from his father shortly after his hospitalisation, within a year Sagawa was removed from the French hospital and taken back to Tokyo – Sagawa's macabre celebrity probably contributed to the French authorities' decision to have him extradited. The killer was placed in the Matsuzawa Hospital 'by the agreement of his parents', rather than being officially committed, and fifteen months later, in 1985, Akira Sagawa decided that his son should leave the hospital. Unable to object, purportedly because they lacked certain important papers from the French court, the Japanese authorities freed Issei Sagawa, whereupon he became a celebrity with a story combining sex and violence with fetishism that commanded untiring fascination. He was feted by the popular press and on television, a real-life Hannibal Lecter to whet the strange appetites of the Japanese masses. One interviewer fawningly told Sagawa: 'Human beings like you are very rare. You act as a prism. You are Sagawa, who ate a human being.' Sagawa was featured on the gourmet page of a magazine, eating barbecued food at a restaurant.

Over the almost four decades since Sagawa was lauded for his 'art', there have been other violent murderers whose creativity has achieved popular notoriety after their imprisonment: Charles Manson and Richard Ramirez are two, serial killer Henry Lee Lucas – who claimed to have killed hundreds of people – is another. Probably the best known 'murderabilia' artist is John Wayne Gacy, who tortured and killed more than thirty boys and youths in Chicago throughout the 1970s. A sinister aspect of Gacy's modus operandi was the use of his alternative working persona of 'Pogo the Clown', frequently hired for children's parties, where he found his victims. Thus known as the 'Killer Clown', during his fourteen years on death row he occupied himself by painting, his favourite subject being himself in his clown costume. It is estimated that more than two thousand of Gacy's 'Clown' paintings are in circulation today, more than twenty-seven years after his 1994 execution and they are in much demand, having been sold at auctions or online for as much as $175,000. There are dealers in the West who specifically sell art created by death row inmates and other people who are heavily critical of this practice. Andy Kahan, a defender of victims' rights in the United States, wryly remarks: 'When you end up on death row now, two things happen ... you get reborn and you turn into DaVinci.'

But in the pre-internet Japan of the 1980s, Sagawa, who painted, wrote books and was prepared to talk endlessly to anyone prepared to listen about his self-expression of 'love by cannibalism', was regarded as a novelty. Japanese media has always shown a peculiar appetite for the bizarre, especially if there is a macabre element of suffering or pain to enhance the entertainment value.

Yukio Mishima (1925–1970), arguably the most important and successful Japanese writer of all time, was a homosexual sadist with a fascination for death, whose writing was full of violent homoerotic imagery, sadomasochism, rape and vengeance. He was said to be stimulated by the sight of blood and allegedly only joined the army in order to be able to observe blood, agony and death at first-hand. His dreams, according to his biographer Henry Scott Stokes were of 'bloodshed – massacring youths, preferably Circassian [white] on large marble tables and eating parts of their bodies.' Obsessed with strong young male bodies, the young Mishima was unattractive, short in stature, weak and thin – curiously echoed in the appearance of Issei Sagawa – and later in his life he became obsessed with bodybuilding to improve his physique. Yukio Mishima was his pen-name; he was originally named Kimitake Hiraoka and was a descendant of the Samurai. His fascination with their ritualistic suicide tradition, harakiri, was unsurprising, since one of his favourite erotic images – seen graphically time and again in his work – was of a knife being thrust into an abdomen, which was then ripped asunder.

In the 1960s Mishima became a right-wing political activist. He and his Imperialist sympathisers would swear allegiance by dripping blood from a cut finger into a cup, which would then be passed around for drinking. His public behaviour became more and more extreme. He appeared in a trashy film and posed for a series of narcissistic photographs, one of which depicted him as Saint Sebastian during his execution, his flesh pierced by many arrows. Death, he declared, was 'the only truly vivid and erotic idea' and in November 1970 the stuff of his erotic imagination entered reality. He and his small army stormed the headquarters of the Eastern Army in Tokyo and took the commander hostage. After notifying the media of his actions, he emerged from the building to speak out against democracy, but receiving only jeers he went back inside, knelt down, drove a dagger into his own abdomen and ripped it sideways to disembowel himself – a ritual suicide practised by members of the Samurai class, called 'seppuku'. He was forty-five.

Sagawa grew up during a time when Mishima's genius was being lauded and Mishima's deviant eroticisation of death and violence can be compared with Sagawa's attempt to bestow artistic values upon his act of murder and his unstable sexual proclivities. Sagawa still likes to speculate upon whether the murder of Renee was one of exquisite and pure love, of crime redeemed by art. In the world of normal sexuality, the debate over where erotica ends and pornography begins may be argued by defining the erotic in the beauty or expressiveness of words or images, where coarseness or exploitation is absent. But this argument concerns images of normal sexuality. What of the abnormal – and what of 'flawed genius'? There are those who say that with true genius also comes instability – that creativity cannot co-exist with normality – which is why many of the world's greatest artists and writers have displayed mental, emotional or sexual trauma in their lives. So what if talented artists – like Mishima or Swinburne – utilise their admirably positive literary or expressive devices in their creation of 'erotica', while acknowledging that what is erotic for them is a perversion which they find arousing, but which disgusts the normal human being? Deviant desires like sadism, murder, necrophilia, cannibalism? If lyrically expressed, can such subjects still be admirable art?

Issei Sagawa regards himself as an artist, the walls of his apartment hung with his own oil paintings – mostly of Western women, with particular attention paid to their fleshy pink buttocks. Today he remains unsupervised, despite the fact that decades ago Dr Tsuguo Kaneko, the superintendent of the Japanese hospital where Sagawa had been kept prior to being released, reportedly declared him to be a dangerous psychopath who should be prosecuted: 'I think he is sane and guilty. Maybe he is a danger to foreign females. He must be in prison.' Instead, Sagawa, as the established media figure he became, was prepared to do and say just about anything for attention: in 1989 he was announcing his intention to open a vegetarian restaurant in Tokyo; by 1992 he was planning his autobiographical film with Juro Kara and wondering who to choose to play the part of the victim. The books he wrote about his cannibalistic fantasies were all best-sellers and he contributed regularly to pornographic magazines, repeating his cannibalistic exploits in gory detail. In film reviews for another magazine he opined that *The Silence of the Lambs* movie lacked psychological depth but he approved of *Trance*, a German film 'about the very beautiful girl who kills her boyfriend when he wants to leave her, and ate him up'. This, he confided during later magazine interviews was one of his sensual aims: a 'long-cherished desire is to be eaten by a beautiful Western woman' and to eat a woman's flesh ... but without murdering her and only with her consent. Such irrationality was evidence of the unbalanced mind of Sagawa as he basked in the Japanese limelight thanks to his heinous deeds.

In 1992 there was outrage, particularly from the Netherlands embassy in Tokyo, when Sagawa was issued with a passport so he could appear on a German chat show and talk about how he killed and ate Renee Hartevelt. Sagawa's celebrity status was inflated by the support he received from a nucleus of intellectuals in Japan who regarded him as an anti-establishment outsider deserving of admiration for the fulfilment of his fantasy and for his 'artistic insanity'. High-flown debate raged in respected artistic circles concerning the 'artistry' of Sagawa: whether he showed the purest form of love by devouring his girlfriend or whether it was simply a bizarre fetish. The intelligentsia declared Sagawa's 'crime' had to be committed, otherwise his 'art' would have suffered. In a detached manner, they spoke philosophically about Sagawa's enjoyment of Renee Hartevelt's body, as if this had been an imaginary learning experience rather than a real horrific sex murder. 'Eating human flesh is the same thing as assimilating yourself to the body you are eating,' coolly explained psychologist Shu Kishida. 'In the Western world there are many historical cases in tribes, that you eat the flesh of the man you respect. In Sagawa's case it is an extreme form of the inherent admiration of every Japanese for the white race. His admiration … took the extreme form of killing and eating that white woman's flesh.'

Yasuhisa Yazaki, the editor of a magazine which carried a flattering article about the cannibal, described him as 'a human being who has undergone a very special experience', declaring: 'In this world some human beings want to eat the flesh of other people. We have to admit their existence and accept it in the future.' Other publications carried pictures of his paintings while Sagawa told his rapt audiences he was artistically stimulated by 'tall and robust' Western women, announcing: 'I'm essentially a romantic.' Some women were persuaded to pose nude for him to paint. One of them, a young Dutch model, Ingrid, whom he contacted when he saw her photograph in a magazine, returned to Holland without ever knowing his real name or anything of his past.

In 1992, at the height of Sagawa's fame, British reporter Joanna Pitman of *The Times*, actually went and took tea with him – not unaccompanied, of course – and was alarmed when he handed out cups of the special tea-and-whisky brew he had given to Renee before killing her. She described:

'He welcomed us to his cramped and dingy home with fawning hospitality, displaying an ominous and hair-raising delight at the sight of a foreign female visitor. "I still adore the sight and the shape of young Western women, particularly beautiful ones," he said, his wolfish eyes staring out from behind dark glasses. "I was a premature and unhealthy baby, I am ugly and small, but I indulge in fantasies about strong healthy bodies."'

Most alarmingly, Sagawa continued to talk to Pitman with enthusiasm about cannibalism being an 'expression of love' and his 'obsession' he had known since his childhood. 'It is a pleasure lying deep in the human spirit,' he said. His insistence that artistic fantasy had become a substitute for his very real desires prompted Joanna Pitman to observe his 'disturbingly carnal' paintings and remark: 'One of the most distressing aspects of this solitary man is the fact that he believes he is normal.' Sagawa told her: 'My time in the mental ward was like hell. Everyone else in there was crazy, but the doctors saw that I was not like them, that I was cured. I am normal. I eat an evening meal with my parents every day and spend my spare time painting and writing.' He was equally insistent about his normality in another published article during that period. Beneath the headline *I Ate Her Because of Fetishism* he declared: 'My fantasy of cannibalism is not crazy. Everyone has fantasies. The special thing about me is that I acted upon mine.'

But as the decades passed, the Japanese media lost interest in the shock value of Sagawa's declarations. He discovered that without sensational celebrity, doors were no longer opened to him. Still displaying a complete absence of moral concern, publishers who had viewed him as a money-spinner thirty-odd years ago rejected Sagawa's writing once he had tumbled from the headlines. Hundreds of his job applications were unceremoniously turned down. His parents died in 2005 and Sagawa ended up penniless and living alone in public housing in a region south of Tokyo under an assumed name, surviving only on welfare support and fees for interviews. In 2013 he suffered permanent damage from a cerebral haemorrhage. This, along with his chronic diabetes, meant that since his release from hospital he has been cared for full-time by his younger brother Jun – the same brother who featured in his childhood cannibalism dreams. Recently – and some may say ironically – the *Shukan Shincho* news magazine reported that Sagawa was unable to eat normally after having undergone a gastrostomy. He is now fed through a tube directly into his stomach.

His fame was briefly revived in 2018 with the release of a French-made documentary film about him, called *Caniba*, described as reflecting 'the discomfiting significance of cannibalistic desire in human existence through the prism of one Japanese man'. Made by Verena Paravel and Lucien Castaing-Taylor, the movie, shot entirely in facial close-up as Sagawa reflected upon his life and crimes, won a prize at the Venice Film Festival – despite many people who attended the screening allegedly walking out. 'And one can only imagine how many walkouts *Caniba* will inspire,' said Michael Nordine, a reviewer from *IndieWire*, who watched the preview in October 2018. Sagawa now says he is 'no longer a cannibal', although in the movie his brother says of him that despite his poor health, he still gets the urge to eat a woman. In an interview ten years ago Sagawa had spoken of this continuing longing being especially strong 'around June when women start wearing less and showing more skin'. Latterly he has spoken often of his fantasy to 'savour the process of being killed' by a woman, suggesting that this pleasure would also carry with it a sense of redemption for him.

Sagawa's media attention outside Japan has, in large part, been owing to his being a rarity: a criminal who committed the most heinous of murderous crimes but who escaped conviction and was freed to live at liberty for almost forty years, thanks to the Japanese system as it was then. Makoto Watanabe, an associate professor of media and communications at Hokkaido Bunkyo University spoke to the *South China Morning Post*'s Julian Ryall in 2019 of his horror that the attention of the Japanese media turned Sagawa into a celebrity in the 1980s. He said he was 'at a loss' to understand how they could have deemed it appropriate to hire a man who freely admitted to killing and consuming a woman. Today they would behave differently, he said, suggesting the episode was an unsettling reflection of Japanese society at the time. 'Sagawa was never forced to take responsibility for his actions, but because he was never found guilty, then in the eyes of many Japanese he was not responsible,' Watanabe said.

Meanwhile, Sagawa continues to bleat about his suicidal thoughts and his mistreatment by society and the media. Back in 2009 Sagawa complained in a *Vice* magazine interview that the freedom he had enjoyed had been worse than the death penalty or even life imprisonment. Ever the blinkered narcissist, his continuing self-absorption leaves no room for remorse or pity for anyone other than himself. 'You can't imagine how difficult it is to live under surveillance from society … The victim's family always say things like "I'll never forgive so-and-so, even if they're put to death" … Even with a life sentence, they give you clothes, food and shelter in jail, plus they let you work. But if you're out in society, you have to somehow make a living and find a place to stay. What harsher punishment can there be? It's brutal.'

'Do what thou wilt shall be the whole of the law'

(Aleister Crowley, citing the Satanic commandment)

'He has an awful lot of love for me ... He always wanted to do things for me. He's a boy who likes things I like. He loves flowers, roses. He doesn't hesitate to show his love for me.'

In the above, a doting grandma is describing her grandson, who has just been arrested for an abominable series of crimes. The man's stepmother is talking to a British journalist and says: 'If you could meet him he would wring your heart out. He is such a sad person, he brings out all your maternal instincts.'

'Sit down and talk with him,' says his lawyer, 'and you'll say he's as nice a young man as you could meet.' The man's neighbour recalls: 'We used to hear sawing coming from his apartment at all hours ... I said [to my husband] one night at about two in the morning, "What in the world is he building at this hour?"' And: 'He seemed like a regular guy,' says the frightened individual who narrowly avoided becoming the 'regular guy's' eighteenth victim – and supper.

Tracy Edwards, aged thirty-two, had fled the man's apartment in panic after being drugged, handcuffed and threatened with a knife. He gibbered this to two passing police officers – who, bored, sighed deeply and offered to check out the handcuffed man's story, all the time assuming it would be just a routine rapping of the 'regular guy's' knuckles. Their first glimpse of Jeffrey Dahmer certainly would not have indicated that he was anything other than a normal, somewhat serious young man. The good-looking thirty-one-year-old who opened his front door to them on that night in July 1991 was skinny and blond with a gentle, unhurried manner and a calm voice. Perhaps this makes it easier to understand why three other police officers, two months earlier, had returned to Dahmer a fourteen-year-old boy who had somehow escaped his captor and, bruised, bleeding, naked and in a near-catatonic state of drugged confusion, had wandered out on to the street where the policemen found him after being called by a neighbour. Dahmer had then turned up and, in pacifying tones, explained that the boy was a friend who was staying with him and had drunk too much. Those officers had been convinced that this was the case, and had allowed Dahmer to take Konerak Sinthasomphone back into his apartment, where the uncomprehending boy had watched the door close on his last hope of survival.

But in July these two police officers, Robert Rauth and Rolf Mueller, knew nothing of that incident as they asked Jeffrey Dahmer if they could look around his apartment, having heard Tracy Edwards, who stood at their shoulders, still cuffed, say that from being a friendly, normal guy one minute, this placid-seeming resident had suddenly become crazy and tried to kill him. Dahmer quietly acquiesced and offered to go and fetch the key to the handcuffs from his bedroom. Edwards loudly warned the officers that Dahmer's knife was in the bedroom, so Mueller went to search instead. What he found jolted and revolted him. In a drawer were gruesome Polaroid pictures of bodies at different stages of mutilation and dismemberment, photographs of skulls and skeletons ... and a picture of a severed human head. The horrific importance of this discovery was not lost on Mueller, and Dahmer was immediately arrested. Mueller showed Edwards the awful picture of the severed head. 'This could have been you,' he told him grimly with barely-controlled revulsion.

Edwards, in a state of high excitement by now, told Mueller that the moment when Dahmer had freaked out was when his guest had gone to open the refrigerator earlier in the evening. 'Maybe there's a head in there!' he cried. Mueller smiled nervously at this outlandish idea – fuelled, he assumed, by Edwards's hysteria. 'Yeah, maybe,' he laughed, pulling open the door.

But there was a head in there. In fact, there were three heads in there.

Mueller screamed.

★ ★ ★ ★

The question everyone wanted answering was: what turned Jeffrey Dahmer into a monster who cannibalised the bodies of the young men he murdered? And the answer is unsatisfactory: nobody knows. Those who like to claim that early environment – perhaps an unhappy childhood, severity of punishment or being starved of affection – is to blame for a man's later heinous crimes, would scratch their heads over Dahmer and his failure to fit any bill of deprivation.

Born in 1960, Jeffrey was the elder son of Lionel and Joyce Dahmer, who led a comfortable middle-class life in Bath, Ohio. Lionel Dahmer told a reporter that Jeffrey was an ordinary little boy. He recalled how his son would become excited when his grandparents came to visit, just like any normal kid. He denied a story, which was circulating at the time of Dahmer's arrest, that his son had been sexually abused by a neighbour when he was eight years old – as, indeed, did the killer himself. And although another journalist turned up a school report suggesting that the six-year-old Jeffrey seemed to feel neglected after the birth of his brother David, this is hardly unusual. There seems little in the way of childhood trauma to explain adequately why this sweet small boy grew up to be a sick cannibalistic serial killer who would shock the world. One psychiatrist put forward an idea that it might have been because Jeffrey had had a hernia operation at the age of four: a suggestion born, one feels, of desperation rather than real in-depth analysis.

Jeffrey's home life was not without love and affection; he was adored by his grandmother in particular. True, there were problems between his parents and soon after brother David's birth they moved into separate bedrooms – friends even claimed that Lionel Dahmer had a string of bells outside his room to warn him of his wife's imminent arrival – but the couple stayed together for the sake of their sons until Jeffrey was eighteen and David twelve. Jeffrey Dahmer would later tell a probation officer that if there was anything he would have liked to change about his childhood, 'it would be the way my parents behaved towards each other,' but again, countless children from broken homes endure far worse. And while David developed normally, Jeffrey's peculiar interests and fantasies began to evolve early. The child was only eight when his interest in dead bodies began to manifest itself. Dahmer's lawyer was to tell the court at his eventual trial that he was fascinated by the insides of bodies, the bright colours. At trial it was also revealed that Dahmer preferred to have sex with the viscera of the young men whom he had killed.

Lionel Dahmer, a chemist, may have thought his son would follow in his footsteps when he bought little Jeffrey a chemistry set. The most enlivening use to which most children put their chemistry sets is in creating flashes and bangs; Jeffrey's experiments were more sinister. His early interests lay with insects, which he preserved in jars, but later he moved on to amphibians and mammals, impaling cats and frogs on sticks. He would collect the corpses of road-kill animals and skin them, using the substances in his chemistry set experimentally. Dried-out animal skins and their decapitated heads impaled on spikes were scattered around the woods at the back of the Dahmer home and he was fascinated with the innards of the creatures, cutting them up to see how they worked. Dahmer later told the police that when he was young he and a friend would drive around looking for dogs which were walking along the road, and run them over. He recalled hitting a beagle puppy and relished the look of terror on its face as it hit the windscreen of the car.

At the age of fourteen, he said, he had his first homosexual experience and confessed that even then he regularly fantasised about using a corpse for sex. Necrophilia became an obsession and, like other sadistic killers, he had a fertile imagination. As his lawyer Gerald Boyle was to remark after Dahmer's imprisonment, 'When you're fourteen and you want to make love to a dead body, you've got a hell of a problem.' Schoolmates cast back their minds and described the teenage Dahmer as an isolated individual with a peculiar sense of humour. One girl remembered: 'I felt uncomfortable around him because he was so weird and so emotionless,' and another recalled that Jeffrey had an established drink problem by the time he was sixteen, which led to him drinking neat Scotch during class. Gerald Boyle said that by this age Dahmer was 'a desperately lonely person with no friends,' and further claimed that, 'If Jeffrey Dahmer had gotten help when he was sixteen he'd be a free man today.'

Dahmer's home life was obviously imperfect at this time, but it was not until he was eighteen – an independent adult, according to the law – that his parents finalised their divorce, which involved a wrangle over custody of Jeffrey's younger brother, then aged twelve. Lionel and Joyce accused each other of neglect and cruelty and Lionel alleged that Joyce should not be awarded custody of David because of 'extreme mental illness'. However, Joyce did win custody and a month later, in August 1978, she left Jeffrey in the family home and took off with her younger son to settle firstly in Chippewa Falls, Wisconsin, and later in Fresno, California. Lionel, robbed of his regular meetings with his younger son, applied to the court again for custody – and this time it was granted. Meanwhile, throughout these family battles, during that summer of 1978 Jeffrey was left very much to his own devices. The month before his parents' divorce hearing, Jeffrey Dahmer murdered the first of his seventeen victims. 'One night,' Gerald Boyle would later tell a packed Milwaukee court, 'he is driving around and he sees a hitchhiker, and the hitchhiker doesn't have a shirt on, and Jeffrey Dahmer wants his body.' Boyle was to pause before repeating significantly: 'His body.'

Dahmer picked up eighteen-year-old Steven Hicks, who was hitchhiking from a rock concert, took him home, got drunk, had sex with Steven and then killed him, hiding the corpse in the crawl-space beneath the house. 'The guy wanted to leave and I didn't want him to leave,' he said later. Then, as he had done with the road-kill animals ten years previously, Dahmer dismembered Steven Hicks's body with a kitchen knife, placed the pieces in plastic bags and carried them around in his car with him. Much later he scattered Steven Hicks's remains around the wood at the back of his home. The murder was not to come to light until thirteen years later, when Dahmer made a confession to Milwaukee police, although he could remember the hitchhiker only as 'Steve'. When shown a photograph of

Hicks, he said: 'Yeah, that's him,' displaying no emotion at all.

Back in 1978, Dahmer's family had no clue as to the teenager's unspeakable fantasies or his awful secret. Jeffrey went off to Ohio State University to study business but dropped out after one term, his drink problem having become increasingly hard to handle. In December that year Shari Jordan married Lionel Dahmer. Jeffrey was eighteen and she remembers him as 'practically an alcoholic'. Like his father, she was to express bewilderment at Jeffrey Dahmer's dreadful crimes: 'None of us know why, out of two children with a similar upbringing, one should become a killer.'

Dahmer enrolled in the army where he was to spend the next two years. The following July he was posted to Baumholder, West Germany, as a combat medic. Unlike many soldiers he did not join in the 'buddy culture' and remained a loner on the periphery of his fellow-soldiers' social interactions. Occasionally he drank heavily and hurled racist abuse at black soldiers and in the course of duty it seemed he was squeamish. He was afraid of needles and could not bear to take anyone's blood – which makes it even more curious to consider that, only a year after his discharge for alcohol abuse, he got a job at the Milwaukee Blood Plasma Center doing exactly that.

But his first work on leaving the army was in a Florida sandwich bar where he worked for a time before moving back to the home of his father and stepmother. Lionel Dahmer, unable to cope with his son's heavy and frequent drinking at the local bars, decided to send him to his grandmother's house to live, on the grounds that Catherine Dahmer and Jeffrey had always been very close. It was true that there was a loving bond between the two of them. But a stable home environment over the next five years did not alter Dahmer's lifestyle. At the end of this period he was working at a chocolate factory during the daytime and in the evenings he cruised around the gay bars. He was arrested a couple of times for exposing himself and masturbating in public, and on one occasion he was accused of drugging people at a gay bath house, but this was the 1980s and, predictably enough, no man wished to declare himself to be present at such places, so no one pressed charges. There was nothing and no one to stop Dahmer. Towards the end of 1987 and, still living with his grandma, he began his killing spree in earnest.

Steven Toumi, one of the few white males who became a Dahmer victim, shared a hotel room for a night with Dahmer after meeting him at a gay bar in Milwaukee. Dahmer claimed in his later confession that he woke up the next morning to find Toumi dead and bleeding from the mouth. Experts, puzzled as to why he should give graphic accounts of other murders but insist he remembered nothing of this one, are inclined to believe that for some reason he has blocked out all memory of the events that night. However, he clearly recalled his actions the following morning: he bought a large suitcase, put the corpse inside and took it back to Catherine Dahmer's house where, after having sex with the body in his basement room, he mutilated and then dismembered it, putting the pieces into the dustbin.

Two months later he repeated his actions with fourteen-year-old James Doxtator, whom he had picked up outside the same club. This time, Dahmer avoided the cost of a hotel room by bribing the boy with cash in return for his posing naked for him, and took him straight home. After having sex with James, Dahmer gave him a drink with some sleeping pills in it – a technique which was to become a routine part of his killing method. When the drugs had the required effect, Dahmer strangled James and dismembered the boy's body, throwing it out with the rubbish as he had done with Toumi. After another two-month period of abstinence the scenario was repeated: the next victim was Richard Guerrero, aged twenty-five.

Dahmer did not keep any 'mementos' of these three victims, unlike later in his killing career when he began preserving their heads, genitals, bones or other organs. At his trial, Dahmer's attorney, Gerald Boyle, said that Dahmer viewed the act of mutilation as 'just making a human being disappear' – as if he was driven to dispose of his victims in this way by sheer expedience. That was certainly not the case towards the end of his murderous spree – and judging by what we know of Dahmer's warped childhood interests, it was probably not his prime motivation at the time of these murders. His behaviour with corpses was, however, going to become more and more extreme to meet his necrophiliac desires. Eventually he demanded greater stimulation to gain the same sexual satisfaction, and would achieve it in a number of ways, including the practice of cannibalism.

Jeffrey's drunken behaviour was becoming as intolerable for his grandmother as it had been for his father. In summer 1988 she asked him to move out and he found an apartment in Milwaukee. Almost immediately, he intercepted a thirteen-year-old boy on his way home from school and offered him fifty dollars to go home with him and pose half-naked for photographs. The boy obliged and Dahmer made homosexual advances to him, kissing him and touching his penis. He also gave the boy some drugged coffee, but perhaps he misjudged the quantity of drug required to knock out the teenager because, although dopey, the youth did not fall asleep. Instead he went home where, after behaving in a disoriented way, he eventually passed out and his family took him to hospital. Tests revealed that he had been drugged and Dahmer was soon under arrest. His family rallied round. Catherine Dahmer took her grandson into her home again and Lionel Dahmer put up bail and hired a top lawyer, Gerald Boyle, to defend him. At first Dahmer denied the events, explaining away the drugging as an accident – because, he claimed, when he took his sleeping tablets, he always drank them from the cup which he had given to the child. Obviously, he said, there must have been some residue left in there. But when the case was heard the following year, he pleaded guilty to second-degree sexual assault and to enticing a child for immoral purposes.

While he was on bail, Dahmer was seeing a psychologist from the probation department. These consultations had, declared one report, been most useful, noting optimistically that Dahmer was more amiable and relaxed and more willing to talk about himself. The probation department did not know that Dahmer had been busy during those months on bail when it was supposedly monitoring him. A matter of weeks before he was due to be sentenced, he picked up twenty-year-old Anthony Sears at a gay bar, took him home to his grandmother's house for sex and killed and disposed of him in his customary way. But this time he kept a souvenir: Anthony's head, which was to be discovered when police raided Dahmer's apartment two years later. After boiling the head to remove the skin, he painted the skull grey, so it would appear to be like a medical model, such as doctors or medical students might use. Later he would admit that he enjoyed masturbating in front of this and other skulls.

In court for sentence on the enticement charge, the Assistant District Attorney Gale Shelton pleaded that Dahmer should be imprisoned for many years – on the grounds that although he was superficially co-operative he had 'deep-seated anger and deep-seated psychological problems.' Two psychologists agreed with her, between them offering opinions that Dahmer was manipulative, had problems with his sexuality and was a schizoid personality who needed intensive treatment. His defending attorney, Gerald Boyle, unaware that the man in the dock had already killed five people, the last one only weeks previously, pleaded for lenience, citing Dahmer's sense of responsibility in holding down a job and his belief that Dahmer was 'semi-sick' – that he had not reached the stage where he was a chronic offender. 'I believe that he was caught before it got to the point where it would have gotten worse – a blessing in disguise,' Boyle said, adding that as far as he was aware, there had been 'no recurrence of this type of conduct.' In an ironic sense, this was true; Dahmer had made sure that things were different with his most recent victim Anthony Sears, giving him such a hefty dose of drugs that he was too sedated to get up and leave Dahmer's room to blow the whistle on him.

But Dahmer was the very model of contrition in court, blaming alcohol for his misdemeanours, saying he had never before done anything as awful as this assault on the boy and that it had shocked him out of his bad behaviour pattern. He pleaded that the court allow him to continue to do his job. 'Please don't destroy my life,' he begged piteously, knowing all the time that he had destroyed several other lives more completely than this court could ever hope to damage his.

But the judge was convinced of Dahmer's wish to reform. He sent Dahmer to a correction centre for a year with day release so he could continue his job, plus he imposed suspended prison sentences on both the charges together with a five-year probation order and an order to get counselling and treatment for his drink problem. Three years later, Gerald Boyle was to say that this sentence was appropriate at the time, no one having had any idea of Dahmer's dark secrets, adding: 'He fooled a lot of people.' When Dahmer was released from the correction centre ten months later, he moved into the apartment which was to become the most infamous place in Milwaukee. Dahmer turned it into a human abbatoir.

In just over a year, Dahmer murdered twelve people in that apartment, typically luring them there for sex, photographic sessions or to watch homosexual videos with the promise of payment. The murders were part of his weekend entertainment and followed a similar pattern. Before Dahmer left to cruise the gay bars and select a victim, he would shift the furniture to make more room to carry out the murder when he returned later. He was preoccupied with the horror film *The Exorcist III* and would often play the video of it to his potential victims. He would sedate them, strangle or stab them, have anal and oral sex with the corpses and then dismember them, always doing this in the nude to avoid messing up his clothes. Before dismemberment he would frequently wait until the bodies were stiff with rigor mortis, then he would stand them up, cut them open and take Polaroid pictures, which he put in an album. He would remove the genitals to preserve in formaldehyde and he would decapitate his victims, usually boiling the heads to keep as trophies and sometimes painting them grey. He saved the penis of one victim and painted it a 'natural' flesh-colour. Dahmer told police he disposed of six victims' torsos by soaking them in acid until they became 'slushy' and then flushed them down a toilet.

Dahmer ate the flesh of three victims and performed sex acts on two of the severed heads. He admitted experimenting with various culinary seasonings in order to make the flesh taste better and kept human-meat 'patties' in the freezer. During his later confession to the police, he was reluctant to give details about which victims he ate, but admitted cutting flesh from one man's thigh and eating it, to saving a heart in his freezer 'to eat later' and to frying and eating the biceps of twenty-four-year-old Ernest Miller 'because they were big' and he 'wanted to try it'. Miller, a dancer, evidently held many attractions for Dahmer – he also flayed this man's body, removed the flesh from the bones and saved the skull and skeleton, which he hung in his apartment. A photograph was found of the skeleton hanging in the shower. As time went on, even this horrific behaviour became inadequate to satiate Dahmer's lust and he began to perform experiments on his sedated victims. Testimony at his sanity trial described how Dahmer drilled the skulls of some unconscious victims and poured acid into the drill-holes in a crude attempt to lobotomise the men and create zombie-like sex partners for himself. Needless to say, the gruesome experiments failed. Sometimes, in a further twist of cruelty, Dahmer would anonymously telephone the families of his murder victims and tell them their sons were dead and that he had killed them.

The majority of Dahmer's victims were non-white, which makes their murders at the hands of Dahmer unusual in terms of serial murder statistics. FBI profiles of serial killers show that they usually only attack people within their own ethnic group – and serial killers are almost always white. Also uncommon was that Dahmer had no car and killed most of his victims at his home. After his arrest, many people came forward to declare that Dahmer was a racist who frequently made anti-black remarks.

At Dahmer's trial, however, Dr Frederick Fosdal, a forensic psychiatrist hired by the state, said that in his interview of Dahmer he found no evidence that the killings were racially motivated, although he established that Dahmer was homosexual. All Dahmer's known victims were gay – a fact which Dahmer was keen to point out at the time of his confession, as if he thought it might exculpate his murders. Why should he point this out when he was himself gay? There are clues to be found to this puzzle. All the time that Dahmer was committing these dreadful crimes, he was turning up – fairly regularly, at least – for his monthly appointments with his probation officer, Donna Chester, who noted his depression and his problem with his sexual identity. He admitted being gay but said he felt guilty about it. This attitude is borne out by a twenty-one-year-old single mother who, in 1992, under the banner headlines of: *The Only Woman Who Loved Hannibal the Cannibal* told a British newspaper, *Today*, about Dahmer's hatred for homosexuals and his preoccupation with God and religion.

She met Dahmer in 1988 when he was living with his grandmother before his arrest on the indecency charge – about which the young woman knew nothing until Dahmer's atrocities were made public – and they became friends. She even helped him to choose the apartment in which he later butchered his victims. The woman would sit in Dahmer's room for hours and he would sometimes recite the Lord's Prayer or preach passages from the Bible to her. Sometimes, she revealed, he would ask her what she thought about homosexuals and he made plain his own opinion. 'He couldn't stand them,' she said. 'He said sex between men and men or women and women was wrong ... that they were committing a sin.'

Dahmer's antipathy towards homosexuals is interesting in that it provides a possible shred of insight into his behaviour. This knowledge tells us that he must necessarily have been filled with self-disgust at his own homosexual desires and, possibly wishing to deny the homosexual acts in which he indulged, he projected this disgust onto his partners. By eradicating them, in some twisted way he may have believed he was attacking himself and destroying the evidence of his 'shameful' actions. However, while this internal conflict might offer a theory about why a person with a severe personality disorder would feel compelled to kill, it fails to explain why they would indulge in the sordid cannibalistic and necrophiliac activities in which Dahmer revelled.

*　*　*　*

In May 1991, two months before the full horror of what had gone on in Jeffrey Dahmer's apartment was discovered, the police had a telephone call from Sandra Smith, one of his neighbours who, with her mother, Glenda Cleveland, was alarmed to see a naked boy, his legs covered with blood, running down the street, having fled from Dahmer's apartment. By the time officers Joe Gabrish, Richard Porubcan and John Balcerzak arrived, so had Dahmer, on his way back from an off-licence. Dahmer had already had oral sex with fourteen-year-old Konerak Sinthasomphone while the drugged boy was inert and unconscious and he had left his flat only briefly to buy some beer, relishing the thought that his next blood-sacrifice was drugged into oblivion and would be there for his pleasure when he returned. Instead his plan was going wrong, for he was alarmed to see this boy standing stark naked in the company of three police officers. But Dahmer was gratified to observe that the drugged coffee had taken effect: the boy was dazed and incoherent. Having summoned up a surge of strength and courage to run, he now slumped into glassy-eyed silence. In the glib, manipulative way which Dahmer had practised before and was to display again, he quietly told the police that their charge was a nineteen-year-old friend who was staying with him and had taken too much drink. The three officers were clearly fooled by Dahmer but decided to check out his apartment anyway. There they found Konerak's clothes neatly stacked on a chair with no apparent sign of any struggle. Konerak sat on the sofa and said nothing, no longer trying to escape, and the officers put the incident down to a lovers' tiff.

Had they investigated a little further, they would have discovered the decomposing body of Tony Hughes spread out on Dahmer's bed, where it had been since Dahmer had killed him three days previously. Sure, the police officers noticed the appalling, blocked-drains-type smell in Dahmer's apartment – as did everyone else who visited it – but they had no reason to suspect that this was because the pleasant, polite, sandy-haired chap before them had several rotting corpses in a fifty-gallon container in his bedroom. As Balcerzak said later: 'Dahmer was a straightforward, calm, convincing person who came forward voluntarily with information with no hint of stress and no hint that he didn't want us to continue with our investigation.' Nevertheless, they were glad to leave the stench of the room and the squalor of the Milwaukee building and be on their way. In flippant mood they radioed into HQ. 'The intoxicated Asian naked male was returned to sober boyfriend,' Balcerzak reported amid much laughter, adding, 'my partner's going to get deloused at the station!' as a graphic comment on the unsanitary conditions of the Milwaukee apartment.

As soon as the police had gone, Dahmer is said to have drilled into Konerak's head and poured acid into his brain in one of his attempts to create a zombie sex slave. Then he strangled Konerak, sexually violated his corpse and dismembered it, taking photographs and keeping the boy's skull. When Dahmer was eventually arrested and tried for murder, the details of this bungled incident emerged and the three officers found themselves in deep trouble. As Janie Hagen, the sister of victim Richard Guerrero said: 'Jeffrey Dahmer will get what he deserves – life in prison. The three police officers are next.' Joe Gabrish and John

Balcerzak were fired almost instantly; Richard Porubcan was suspended. In retrospect it is easy to blame these officers for failing to carry out their duty to the hapless Konerak and no one doubts that they should have been more suspicious of Dahmer. But Dahmer, as a psychiatrist was later to declare, was 'a formidable liar'. Already, at the indecency trial where he had deceived everyone from his attorney to the judge, he had shown that if you're smart enough, you can fool all of the people all of the time.

Tracy Edwards, the man who lived to tell the tale of his encounter with Milwaukee's most infamous murderer – and whose successful escape put a stop to Dahmer's slaying of young men – claimed that there was no mention of homosexuality when he went back to Dahmer's apartment with him on 22 July 1991 'merely for a drink' (although Dahmer said that Edwards was there for a 'photo session'). However, he told the court at Dahmer's trial, he suspected that his rum and Coke had been drugged when he began feeling dizzy. In the bedroom, where the walls were plastered with pornographic pictures of gay sex acts, Dahmer handcuffed Edwards and pulled out a knife. The horrified young man said he saw a large bloodstain on the bedspread and later said that there was a human hand sticking out from under the bed – although he does not appear to have mentioned this to the police at the time they rescued him. Dahmer, claimed Edwards, told him he intended to eat him. 'You'll never leave here,' he said and pulled a skull out of a filing cabinet, saying: 'This is how I get people to stay with me – you will stay with me too.' Then he listened to the terrified Edwards's heart beating and announced, 'Soon it will be mine. I'm going to cut your heart out.' (It must be noted that doubt has been cast on Edwards's retrospective claims about these theatrical threats; such killers as Dahmer do not usually announce their intentions so colourfully in advance, say some psychiatrists.) Seizing an opportune moment – when, according to Edwards, Dahmer was rocking manically back and forth and chanting 'It's time, it's time' – Edwards said he punched and kicked him and fled the apartment, to flag down officers Rauth and Mueller, who exposed the bloody slaughterhouse which was Jeffrey Dahmer's home. The remains of eleven victims were found there. Most were identified by dental records.

Meanwhile, officers investigating Dahmer's history discovered other unsolved murders in places where, coincidentally, Dahmer had lived. While Dahmer was in the army and stationed in Baumholder, Germany, there were five unsolved 'mutilation' murders in the area. Later, the Baumholder connection was abandoned as theoretically unlikely because there were females among the victims. When Dahmer left the army he lived for a time in Miami. Four months after his arrival, a six-year-old boy called Adam Walsh was abducted in Hollywood, Florida, and two weeks later his head was found in a canal 120 miles away. No other remains were found. Dahmer refused to admit any involvement in this murder and police appear to have ruled out any connection.

Dahmer confessed to killing seventeen young males, sixteen in Wisconsin and one in Ohio, but when he came to trial on 13 January 1992 he was only charged with fifteen. One of the Wisconsin murder cases was abandoned because of lack of evidence and Dahmer's first victim, Steven Hicks, was killed in Dahmer's home town of Bath, Ohio, where he was due to stand trial separately. Dahmer pleaded guilty but insane to the fifteen murders. When the jury was selected, Dahmer's attorney, Gerald Boyle, cautioned that the trial would include 'human carnage, killing, mutilation, cannibalism – everything you can possibly imagine.' Two female jurors who said they couldn't endure it were excused. After the trial the jury were offered counselling to help them cope with the gruesome details they had heard. Dahmer sat silently during most of the jury selection, looking at the floor or at the judge, although he occasionally looked at potential jurors with sideways glances. If found insane, he would be sent to a mental hospital and could petition for release every six months. If judged to be sane, he would receive a mandatory life prison sentence for each murder. Wisconsin has no death penalty.

One of the officers who had taken down Dahmer's confession described to the court how calm and composed the killer was as he talked for hours about how he had mutilated his victims, smoking cigarettes and drinking coffee as he went over the details. Detective Murphy said that Dahmer told the police he 'would have preferred that the victims stayed alive. However, he felt that it was better to have them dead than to have them leave.' He added: '[Dahmer] became more relaxed as conversations went on. At the beginning there was no eye contact. Toward the end he would look at us and occasionally smile.' Officer Murphy said Dahmer was like someone who had been caught doing 'something wrong and was a little embarrassed about it.' He said Dahmer told him of taking the bicep of one of his victims and frying it, using a meat tenderiser and then eating it. 'He said it tasted like beef.'

Gerald Boyle argued that Dahmer's craving for sex with dead bodies and his fear of loneliness escalated into a killing spree that he could not control. Dahmer's acts were not those of a normal man, he said, but a man who was caught up in the 'personification of Satan'. Dahmer's early dabblings in necrophilia had involved an attempt to dig up a body from a cemetery but he had failed because the ground was frozen, said Boyle. He said that although Dahmer had tasted blood while working at the plasma clinic in Milwaukee in 1983, he did not like it and had never tried it again.

However, later in his killing spree he did perform acts of cannibalism. There were two occasions confirmed, but up to ten reported by Dahmer, it was said. Boyle expanded on the idea that Dahmer was 'keeping' his victims with him to prevent them abandoning him – a grisly attempt to fulfil a need for human contact. 'He ate body parts so these poor people he killed would become alive in him,' said Boyle, claiming that when Dahmer's victims wanted to leave, this was what drove him to kill them to keep them with him, out of loneliness and out of his desire to have their bodies and enjoy them sexually in numerous ways. Dahmer could not perform sexual acts with men when they were awake, so he would drug them and then kill them. He said that after sex Dahmer missed feeling the heartbeats of his partners – and that was when he began experimenting with lobotomies to turn his victims into 'zombies or sex slaves ... people who would be there for him.' As stated earlier, after Dahmer had drilled holes in the skulls of his unconscious victims, he injected muriatic acid into their brains. Some died instantly, but one victim, Jeremiah Weinberger, walked around for two days after being 'lobotomised'.

One clinical psychologist, Dr Judith Becker, revealed that Dahmer had planned to build a magical shrine which would enable him to receive 'special powers'. Dahmer had drawn a picture of this shrine, which featured a black table and chair, incense burners and the skulls and skeletons of his victims. He had already bought the base of the table and planned to illuminate it with blue lights directed on to a backdrop curtain featuring a goat. Dahmer had also bought a statue of a mythical monster, the griffin, which – like the goat – is sometimes used in Satanic ceremonies. Dahmer told the psychologist that the griffin captured the way he felt, in that it represented evil. Yet to the courtroom crowds, Dahmer's calm and unthreatening manner made it difficult to see him as the Devil incarnate. Throughout the terrible evidence which was presented, the untidy, somewhat insubstantial young man kept his eyes downcast and remained passive. His manner changed only once, to display a grisly sense of humour. The day that the case went to the jury, he brought into court a copy of a supermarket tabloid with his picture on the cover. The splash headline read: *Milwaukee Cannibal Kills His Cellmate* and the story said that Dahmer also ate the cellmate. Dahmer flashed the paper around in disdainful amusement. 'Isn't it amazing what they come up with?' asked the man who may not have eaten his cellmate but had killed and partially eaten seventeen other people, failing to perceive the irony of his words.

Dahmer's father and stepmother had attended the trial, listening intently and sometimes hugging relatives of Dahmer's victims. 'They knew that we were hurting too,' Lionel Dahmer told reporters and Shari added: 'It's tragic. And what do we say to those families out there who don't even have the child to bury in many cases?' 'I don't think I'll ever come to terms with it,' Mr Dahmer said. 'Nothing will ever be the same again.'

At the end of the trial, Dahmer issued an elaborate apology to the families of his victims and begged to be forgiven for his 'holocaust' of evil. 'I hope God can forgive me,' he said. Lionel Dahmer, a religious man who could never have imagined that when he bought his small son his first chemistry set all those years ago it would one day lead to this horror, listened in sorrow, saying later that Jeffrey would willingly have chosen death as punishment. But the court was not to grant Dahmer's wish. He was declared sane and sentenced to fifteen consecutive life sentences, which would have kept him in prison for the rest of his life, ineligible for parole for 936 years. Three months later, Dahmer pleaded guilty in Ohio to the murder of his first victim, Steven Hicks, and was sentenced to a sixteenth term of life imprisonment. He was sent to serve his sentence at Columbia Correctional Institution at Portage, about eighty miles north west of Milwaukee, to be held in solitary confinement for the first year in a glass cage, reminiscent of the cage which housed 'Hannibal the Cannibal' in the movie *The Silence of the Lambs*. The high-tech equipment and design made Columbia one of the most secure and safe prisons in the country.

Secure, that is, if the dangerous inmates were inclined to attempt escape. But holding them in such a prison in no way reduced their dangerousness, especially in relation to each other. In July 1994, a year after Dahmer had been moved at his own request to a less secure unit within the prison where he was assigned to a work detail cleaning the toilet block, a fellow inmate, Osvoldo Durruthy, attacked him by trying to slash his throat with a razor blade embedded in a toothbrush. The wound was superficial and Dahmer recovered. But a few months later, on 28 November 1994, he and another inmate, Jesse Anderson, were discovered with serious head wounds in the prison gymnasium after an attack by a third inmate, Christopher Scarver. Scarver, who was four years into a life sentence for murder, admitted beating Dahmer with a twenty-inch metal bar and also repeatedly smashing his head against a wall. Dahmer, then thirty-four, was declared dead an hour after being admitted to hospital and Anderson died two days later. Scarver insisted that the attack had not been premeditated. He was later given two more life sentences for the murders.

'Now is everybody happy?' demanded Dahmer's mother Joyce in angry response to the stories in the media about Dahmer's death. 'Now that he's been bludgeoned to death, is that good enough for everyone?' The answer, in general, appeared to be in the affirmative; most of the families of

Dahmer's victims were pleased to hear of the killer's death. After cremation, Dahmer's ashes were divided between his parents.

★ ★ ★ ★

POSTSCRIPT

Twenty years after he was instrumental in the arrest of Jeffrey Dahmer, escapee Tracy Edwards himself was jailed for eighteen months for his role, with two others, in the drowning death of a homeless man in the Milwaukee River. Now in his sixties, homeless Edwards has struggled with alcohol and drugs problems for many years. At his trial in January 2012, Edwards's attorney said that the Dahmer incident had had 'a profound effect' on his life and he had never received counselling or other help to aid his recovery from the trauma.

'The stubborn beast-flesh grows day by day back again'

(from *The Island of Doctor Moreau*, novel by H. G. Wells)

'Doctor: A very pestilent disease, my lord,
They call lycanthropia.
… they imagine
Themselves to be transformed into wolves;
Steal forth to churchyards in the dead of night,
And dig dead bodies up, as two nights since
One met the Duke, 'bout midnight in a lane
Behind St Mark's church, with the leg of a man
Upon his shoulder; and he howl'd fearfully:
Said he was a wolf: only the difference
Was, a wolf's skin was hairy on the outside,
His on the inside … '

John Webster, *The Duchess of Malfi*, Act Five, Scene 2

Andrei Romanovich always stayed close to his mother. He knew what could happen to small children who wandered too far from home. Terrible stories were told of wolves in the wild land, just waiting in the undergrowth, their yellow eyes glittering, waiting, waiting. Waiting for a boy like himself who had strayed away from the safety of his village, who had chased foolishly after a thrown stone or to investigate a sudden fluttering in a bush. Waiting for a loyal blanket of dusk to conceal their stealthy advance on a village to find that lone, straggling boy idly humming as he scrawls in the dust with a stick. They pounce. Showing no mercy, they gobble him up. Andrei Romanovich knew. His mother had warned her sweet-faced boy.

And he had heard tales of other monsters: dragons with fierce teeth that ached to tear into the tender flesh of little children; witches who would wheedle children into their houses and, hurling them into cages, would keep and fatten the boys, then would chop them into little pieces and eat them all up. Andrei Romanovich shivered with a thrill of exciting horror at such stories. Other boys might scoff at tales of werewolves and witches, other boys might laugh at him and call him names for clinging to his mother's skirts, just as they jeered at his inept responses at school when he failed to give correct answers, even though the words he needed were there, on the blackboard. The other children could not know how bad Andrei's eyesight was, how the chalk writing became a blur as he gazed as hard as he could, to no avail. They could not know what he knew about the true savagery of the world. That was why, timid and shy, he never strayed far from his mother. For he knew that along with the dragons and witches, there were real human monsters out there who could commit worse acts than the wolves he sometimes heard howling at night. His mother had told him.

He knew what had happened to his brother Stepan, only a few years before he himself had been born in 1936. The Soviet famine of 1932–33, also known as the Holodomor, and caused by Stalin's regime, had caused widespread famine. Between three and seven million Soviet citizens in the southern republics died of starvation as Stalin tried to force private farmers into collectives (the collective farm system). The population of Andrei's village, Yablochnoye in the Ukraine, was decimated along with the rest of the

Soviet Union. But he had knowledge of those who had sunk to the level of desperation which, it was said, some had. Little Stepan had wandered too far from home, his mother had told Andrei time and again, her eyes filling up with tears every time she repeated the tale. And Stepan never returned. The child was captured, killed and eaten, by hungry people, she explained, weeping as she told Andrei and his sister Tatyana the full horror of what had happened to Stepan. It was an awful warning. Andrei was appalled. The story haunted his mind.

As he grew older, his passive reserve caused him to be isolated from the other boys at school. He lived in terror of them discovering his other secret: that although he was a big boy now, he still had a small child's problem in bed at night. He could not understand why so often he woke up having wet himself – but he knew he could not bear the ridicule if his schoolmates found out. Andrei retreated into the world of his imagination. Into his mind, again and again, would come terrifying images of what had happened to his older brother, the brother who, had he lived, would have been united with him against the jibes of the other children. Already they scolded him with taunts of 'Traitor!', hissing the word as he passed. He was ashamed. His father was to blame. A Soviet soldier, he had been captured by the Nazis during the war and placed in a prisoner-of-war camp. On his return to the Soviet Union, he was arrested again as an enemy of the people for allowing himself to be captured, placed in a work camp far from home and was regarded as an outcast because of it. His family suffered their neighbours' spite because of this ... and the boy bore it badly.

As Andrei Romanovich approached adolescence, the haunting images developed more richly. The terror, the screams, the blood. The feast. Instead of revolting him, the fearsome fantasies came to evoke in him a response of another sort. The boy was turning into a man – his bodily responses to his fantasies told him that. Yet his only attempted seduction of a girl had ended in humiliating failure, and the stirring in his lower belly only occurred when he was held in the thrall of his extraordinary dreams. The sex-talk which caused lewd merriment in the other boys, the crude pictures they would pass round, all these things left him cold and disgusted. The source of Andrei Romanovich Chikatilo's stimulation was rather more disturbing ...

* * * *

As she checked herself over in the mirror, Fayina wondered whether she would care for Tatyana's brother. If Tatyana was to be believed, Andrei Romanovich sounded like quite a catch: twenty-seven years old, shy, gentle and well educated. Tall, too, which was always an attraction as far as she was concerned, being on the large side herself. It was 1963. In Britain, the Beatles were inducing hysteria in teenage fans; in America, John F. Kennedy was planning his fateful Dallas trip; and in Novoshakhtinsk, Fayina, the twenty-four-year-old daughter of a pit-worker, hummed as she prepared for the meeting with Tatyana and Andrei which was to change her life. As she had expected, she liked Tatyana's brother. He was good-looking in a soft sort of way, and although his shoulders sloped in a manner which was perhaps unmasculine – for it gave his neck the appearance of being elongated – Andrei was otherwise powerfully built and treated Fayina with such reverence and respect that he captivated her. As their relationship progressed, she realised that Andrei was shy and insecure, so shy that he never even kissed her, but this added to his appeal. For although she was not head-over-heels in love, Fayina liked so many things about him: he did not drink or smoke, he was quietly spoken, subdued in his dress – he was no flashy fly-by-night. Ordinary, that was what he was. Some might call him boring, with his drab clothes and quiet reserve. He might never be very rich or very famous, but she didn't care: she liked his ordinariness. They were married that same year.

On the first night of their marriage, Fayina knew there was something wrong. Andrei's shyness was embarrassing. His attempts at love-making were painfully inept and she seemed unable to arouse his passion. They gave up. For a week, Fayina tried to persuade Andrei to try again and finally, using all her skills of seduction and patient dexterity, the marriage was consummated. As the couple's life together continued, it became clear that sex was an ordeal for Andrei, that he was almost repelled by intimacy with the female body. On the rare occasions they had sex, he performed perfunctorily, without emotion, passion or variation, and only managed to complete the act with a great deal of manual help from his wife. But the infrequent sex was enough to produce two children – Ludmilla in 1965 and Yuri in 1969 – and Fayina consoled herself with the thought that the relationship was satisfactory in other ways. Andrei was determined to better himself and studied at home, eventually gaining degrees in Russian literature, engineering and Marxist-Leninism. He was a faithful, almost fanatical, Party member (the Communist Party of the Soviet Union, or CPSU, the monopolistic ruling party of the USSR) and wrote articles for newspapers on Soviet patriotism and morality. Eventually he got a job as a teacher. Sex wasn't everything, thought Fayina. Andrei was a good father and never became angry with the children. She was proud of her hard-working, non-flamboyant, clever husband, who was teaching the Soviet children, future Soviet citizens, at his school.

What he was teaching them apart from the standard curriculum, was another matter. Not many years passed before Andrei Chikatilo was caught molesting little girls at his school. He discovered he liked their fear after grabbing one girl, who screamed and pushed him away. Such resistance gave him pleasure. Was there a subconscious link there between his act of grasping a child and the story of the seizure of little Stepan struggling with his captors forty years earlier? Who knows? But when his sexual peccadilloes were uncovered, he eventually lost his job.

However, there was no official inquiry and no charges were brought, so Fayina remained in ignorance as to the cause of his sacking. He took another job, an inferior one at a mining school, and moved into a school-owned house in Shakhty. Fayina also got a job at the school. And unknown to his wife, Chikatilo bought another house in Shakhty as well: a run-down, three-roomed shack in the shabbiest part of town. Here, he was to bring a succession of prostitutes in an effort to overcome his impotence. To him, with his prudish sensibility, they were forbidden fruit. Unlike his good, pure Fayina to whom he looked up to so earnestly, these women were low creatures: loose and promiscuous, to be despised. They were prepared to perform sexual acts which he would never have dreamed of suggesting to Fayina. He also brought small girls to the filthy, broken-down hut where he would sexually assault them. But, in a community where secretiveness was second nature, he never attacked them seriously enough to attract the attention of police. This 'house of depravity' was to be the place where, almost by accident, he first discovered the true nature of his own terrible desires.

It was 1978 and little Lena Zakotnova was nine, the same age as Chikatilo's son, Yuri. Chikatilo spotted her at the tram stop in Shakhty. In her red coat and brown fur hat, she was on her way home from an after-school skating trip when Chikatilo began chatting easily to her. He talked of school, her friends, her interests; he knew how to talk to children for he had been communicating with them for years in his work. Lena was dancing from foot to foot and confided in this pleasant, grandfatherly man, that she badly needed the toilet. 'I only live round the corner,' said the man, smiling. 'You can go there.' It was as easy as that for Andrei Chikatilo. As soon as he had Lena in the squalid little house, he threw her to the ground and tore at her clothes, silencing her screams with an arm on her throat. Unable to stand the look of reproachful terror in her eyes, he blindfolded her with her own scarf and tried to rape the child, but he could not sustain an erection. Seized by a sudden impulse, he took out his knife, which he carried for self-protection, and thrust it into the child's lower abdomen, the unflinching steel substituting for his limp penis. As if transformed into a wild, carnivorous beast, he revelled in the blood and gore. He thrust the knife in again. And again. And, miraculously to him, there was no mistaking the sexual relief that this terrible act drew from him.

Chikatilo marvelled as he realised, after all, how simple his needs were. And how simple, too, it was going to be to pluck victims from the streets; weak and helpless people like this small girl, whose life-blood was still pumping stickily out of her tiny body. Such people would give him the sexual satisfaction that had eluded him all these years – and it had taken him until now, at forty-two, to know what was necessary to arouse and satiate him: blood and the infliction of pain. Emerging from his monstrous reverie, Chikatilo looked absently at the body of the child and knew that he must dispose of it speedily. Tucking Lena beneath his arm, as if she were a doll, he left the house quickly and hastened to the banks of the nearby Grushovka River, tossing the little body in, with Lena's school satchel thrown after her. Then, feeling a warm glow which could have been stoked by the fires of Hades, he hurried home to Fayina.

Lena's body was not swept far from Shakhty, as Chikatilo had hoped it would be, but remained close to the house where he had murdered the child. The police inquiry should, by rights, have put Chikatilo under grave suspicion. They had evidence that he had frequently taken children and women back to the house; a neighbour had reported that, unusually, that night the light had been left on overnight although the house was empty; there was blood on the road outside; most importantly of all, they had an eye-witness, a woman, who had seen Lena leave the tram stop with Chikatilo just before her disappearance. She gave a police artist an excellent description of the tall, bespectacled man with sloping shoulders. They also learnt about the child-molestation complaints which had been lodged against Chikatilo in the past and discovered that a man answering his description had been seen hanging around the girls' toilets at local schools. But the sketch alone was enough to identify Chikatilo and he was pulled in for questioning. He hung his head in shame and admitted his 'sexual weakness' where interfering with little girls was concerned, but insisted that it was in the past; his interest in sexual matters had declined. Fayina, who went with him, would have seconded that – and she swore that her husband had spent the entire evening at home. The police let Chikatilo go, but kept his file open. Then they had what they believed to be a big break in their hunt for the murderer.

Only yards from the place where Lena's body was found lived a man called Alexander Kravchenko, who had served a prison sentence for the murder of a teenage girl eight years previously and was just making a new life for himself with his wife and family. But with astonishing self-destructive misjudgement, a month after Lena's death, Kravchenko was in trouble with the law again. He indulged in some petty theft, was caught red-handed with the stolen goods and was hauled into the police station. Having discovered that Kravchenko had the same semen type as that found on Lena's body, the police used all the means at their disposal – some of them dubious, to say the least – to break his alibi for the night of her death. Eventually they succeeded and Kravchenko confessed to Chikatilo's crime. Later he denied his confession, but his denials were disregarded. No one bothered asking the eyewitness who had been the last to see Lena alive if she could identify Kravchenko as the man who had accompanied the child. And no policeman visited Chikatilo again. Five years later, Kravchenko, protesting his innocence, was executed for Lena's murder.

* * * *

After his first murder, it was almost three years before the beast within Chikatilo rose up to feast again. By this time he had changed jobs once more: now he was a supply clerk for an industrial firm, which, conveniently for Chikatilo, involved travelling further afield to collect and deliver goods, often with an overnight stay. When he was not required to stay on somewhere, he invented a reason – 'business', he would tell his fellow delivery-man. On 3 September 1981 he found himself in Rostov where, as in any large city, there was a large population of itinerants, vagrants, homeless runaways and wretched, unhappy young women who would do almost anything for the offer of a meal. One such was Larisa Tkachenko, aged seventeen, whose red jacket caught Chikatilo's attention as she stood at a bus stop. Red: which was the colour of his fantasies. They chatted, and Larisa indicated that she was prepared to have sex with Chikatilo in exchange for a little supper. Together they set off for the overgrown badlands on the other side of the River Don, a place popular with young lovers. But of this ill-matched pair, only one was to walk back over the bridge.

As soon as they were out of sight of passers-by, Chikatilo became a monster. Despite experiencing the thrill of seizing Larisa roughly to feed his domination fantasy and violently ripping off her red jacket and her other clothes, his potency still failed him. This time he knew exactly what he needed: suffering, screams and, most of all, blood. Strangling Larisa to near-unconsciousness, he tore into her with his teeth, biting her neck like a wolf deranged by the smell of blood, bathing his face in it. He bit off part of her breast and swallowed it, then mutilated her genitals, discovering anew that this taste for sadism guaranteed him orgasm.

Perhaps he justified his actions by telling himself that Larisa was a depraved, loose woman who deserved her fate. With the extraordinary primness which had commanded him to be celibate until marriage, and then to respect his wife as a Madonna figure, this contradictory logic is a probability, particularly since he was to describe his victims after his arrest as 'degenerate elements' whose 'right to life' was questionable. Before he left the scene of carnage, he cleaned the blood off his face and hands with Larisa's clothing, with her red coat. He planned to change his clothes as soon as possible – in the bag he always carried with him there was another outfit for just such an occasion – but as he prepared to leave, he found himself offended by Larisa's naked body, exposed for all to see. To preserve her decency, he covered her body with pages from *Pravda* and the *Young Communist*, which, being a loyal Party member, he just happened to have with him.

Nine months passed before Chikatilo was again seized by his vicious alter ego. This time the victim was a thirteen-year-old girl from a good family. Lyuba Biryuk was waiting at a bus stop close to her home village of Zaplavskaya on a warm summer's day in 1982 when Chikatilo saw her, chatted to her, then obtained her agreement to abandon the wait for the bus and permit him to walk with her towards her home. The path took them close to the woods and Lyuba's fate was sealed. Chikatilo's shy, insecure persona was swamped from then on by the monster within him.

Over the next six months, he committed as many murders as possible in the far-flung districts where his job took him. Now he was more opportunistic and less choosy over whom he took: these six victims were males and females, aged between nine and sixteen; all they had in common was their powerlessness, which made them easy prey. Chikatilo was essentially a cowardly man, and would never have tried to tackle someone who might fight back or escape. Using the knife he carried with him, he stabbed his victims in a frenzy, his 'trademark' being knife injuries around the eyes. Sometimes he gouged eyes out. Such a thing was rare in investigated murders, causing the police to speculate that the killer believed the old superstition that a person's eyes are imprinted with the last thing they see before they die, in this case Chikatilo himself. Perhaps the killer was trying to obliterate the accusing, agonised stare of the person dying so cruelly at his hands. Or perhaps he was merely prolonging the suffering, enjoying the screams, causing maximum pain – the pain which gave him such acute pleasure – in the most devastatingly brutal way imaginable.

Certainly Chikatilo's other actions with the bodies bore this theory out and eventually his sensation-seeking necessitated more and more bizarre horrors. He would bite off victims' tongues and breasts and eat them, cut off noses and lips, slice off boys' genitals – or remove the testes, leaving the empty scrotal sac – and excise girls' internal reproductive organs, then devour them on the spot, sometimes cooking them over a rough fire he built nearby in the forest. So vicious was his butchery that a number of policemen broke down and requested to be removed from the case. Some investigators even theorised that the murders had been committed by Satanists or a gang collecting testicles for transplants.

Most chilling of all, was that sometimes forensic evidence suggested that the savagery had taken place while the victim still lived, that it was seeing the pain of torture, more than the circumstance of death, which gave Chikatilo his ghastly pleasure. This, too, set him apart from the majority of sex murderers for, as Dr J. Paul de River said in his 1950 book, *Crime and the Sexual Psychopath*: 'The lust murderer usually, after killing his victim, tortures, cuts, maims or slashes the victim in the regions on or about the genitalia, rectum, breast in the female, and about the neck, throat and buttocks, as usually these parts contain sexual significance to him and serve as sexual stimulus.' In his actions, Chikatilo had much in common with Albert Fish and with a historical monster like Gilles de Rais who, in the fifteenth century, killed, raped and sodomised more than 150 children after inflicting the most barbarous tortures upon them, purely for the sadistic pleasure their agonies offered him.

The police in Rostov and its surrounding areas were beginning to recognise the killings as the work of one person, but this fact took time to dawn upon them because the various murders were committed in different districts, with each district's police force dealing with individual cases and not pooling their knowledge. During the 1980s, the notion of a serial killer was relatively unknown in the

Soviet Union and they were without the sophisticated techniques of the West, such as the Criminal Investigative Analysis Programme, the computer profiling technique which had been developed by the FBI at their Behavioral Sciences Unit in Quantico, Virginia, over the previous decade. Using information gathered from hundreds of interviews with serious offenders, some on death row, the Unit still operates in the United States today in compiling psychological profiles of criminals. When a crime is committed, evidence gathered from the scene is translated into behavioural characteristics, enabling an analyst to build up an 'offender profile'. Although this is used in many varieties of crime situations, it has proved an invaluable tool for American crime-fighters in apprehending serial killers, for even if a serial killer crosses State lines, his murders are fed into the same computer and common indicators are then discovered.

A sadistic killer's modus operandi – the implementation of his oft-rehearsed fantasies – tells psychologists into which of several categories he might fall. Broadly, the two main ones are the 'Organised Nonsocial' killer and the 'Disorganised Asocial' killer. The Organised Nonsocial murderer presents a cunning façade of warmth and friendliness to society while secretly committing his carefully-planned and methodical crimes, which he knows will shock that same society; indeed, this is part of his aim. He is also likely to cruise around, looking for a victim and a safe opportunity to commit his crime undetected. The Disorganised Asocial individual, on the other hand, is a loner, a friendless outsider who feels rejected, but who murders in a more uncontrolled and less methodical way and is then more likely to abandon the body and make no attempt to hide it. In contrast, the Organised Nonsocial type may, in an attempt to control matters further, even go so far as to remove the body and then later put it somewhere else to be found, whereupon he may follow its discovery and the subsequent murder inquiry with excitement.

What would the FBI's Behavioral Sciences Unit have made of Andrei Chikatilo? The driven frenzy of the attacks maybe would have placed him into the 'disorganised' mould, as would Chikatilo's alienated personality, yet he was calculating in the extreme. His fifty-three murders bore testimony to that. Without doubt, then, Chikatilo was an Organised killer. If he had been a Disorganised type, how would he have controlled his violent urges until he had lured his victim to a suitable killing field ... at least fifty-three times? Additionally, his method was to spend hours trying to pick up a suitable victim – indeed, when he was pulled in on one occasion, plain-clothes detectives in Rostov had watched him for nine hours while he attempted to persuade one woman after another to go with him. His patient approach to female down-and-outs was friendly and chatty with an invitation to have sex. Children who fell prey to him were usually waiting at bus stops when he opened a conversation, telling them after he had won their confidence: 'I'm going there. We'll never catch a bus from here; I know a short cut.' And each child – one little boy was only eight years old – would place his or her small hand into that of this monstrous beast who led them into the forest ... in much the same way, Chikatilo would later suggest, that someone had abducted his infant brother Stepan in the 1930s. And the fates of his victims were not dissimilar. 'He made contact with people very easily,' a policeman was to reflect many years later. 'He had an amazing talent for it. He could join a bus queue and say to the person in front: "Hey, where did you buy those beautiful mushrooms?" and before you knew it he would have the whole crowd chatting.' At his trial, when Chikatilo himself was asked why he thought children went with him so willingly, he had his own suggestion: 'I must have had a kind of magnetism.'

Chikatilo had what appeared to be a normal public life. His workmates did not like him, regarding him as robot-like, unable to make independent decisions and controlled by his wife, but Fayina, suspecting nothing of his double life, was contented. He was a 'perfect husband' she was to declare later. Chikatilo was to reveal to psychologists that Fayina had upset him by having an abortion without his knowledge – as if he had high regard for the sanctity of life – but the couple were not in disharmony. However, it was during 1984 that Chikatilo's unsatisfactory sex life with his wife ended completely; she even urged him to see a psychiatrist about his loss of libido, but he had found a more rewarding substitute and pursued it with a vengeance. Chikatilo's need for cruelty and cannibalism was driving him with more frequency and to the use of increasingly sadistic methods to indulge it.

During two months of summer 1984, he killed ten people – more than one a week. But at the end of 1984, with more than thirty murders on their hands, the police were no nearer to catching him. They were, it is true, beset by difficulties in profiling their killer. The victims were very different in age, gender and social class, even though a number were drifters, prostitutes, mentally handicapped youngsters and kids from broken homes who ended up on the streets and sleeping in railway stations. Such lowly status meant that many were not reported missing and even that first step in a murder inquiry – the identification of the body – was often a problem. But the police also rejected their most powerful weapon of detection: publicity. A mixture of the customary Soviet secrecy and the desire not to cause panic made the police suppress the news that Rostov had on its streets a sadistic murderer who picked up people at random and slaughtered them in the most unspeakable of ways – and that by 1984 he had done this thirty-odd times already. The media, still controlled by the authorities, dutifully obeyed the police and kept the terrible news quiet.

The vagrant nature of many of his victims was, then, to Chikatilo's advantage and just like Britain's 'Yorkshire Ripper' Peter Sutcliffe – a killer of, mainly, prostitutes – Chikatilo even tried to pretend to himself that he was performing a street-cleaning service. He was disgusted by the squalor and the promiscuity of the women, the alcoholism, the shabbiness and dirtiness of these fallen people. They were little more than objects to him – 'rootless elements', he called them – there solely to provide him with gratification. He reasoned that they deserved what they got. After his arrest Chikatilo openly tried to justify his treatment of these people. 'They followed me like dogs,' he said. 'Vagrants ... they beg, demand and seize things ... They crawl into your very soul, demanding money, food, vodka and offering themselves for sex ... I saw scenes of these vagrants' sex lives and I remembered my humiliation, that I could not prove myself as a real man.' But like Jeffrey Dahmer who, despising his own homosexuality, justified his murders on the grounds that his victims were gay, Chikatilo had much in common with the 'vermin' he eradicated: like them, he was a misfit, an outsider of a society which he felt had rejected him, rather than the other way round.

The police were also to be condemned for their shocking sloppiness (as, in fact, they would be by the Public Prosecutor's office and the judge at Chikatilo's eventual trial). At every turn they revealed themselves to be ludicrously inept. At murder-scenes, forensic clues were lost because of the bulldozing clumsiness of the officers; other items of evidence were simply mislaid. In their anxiety to clear up the case, the police pinned blame wherever it might stick. Two mentally disabled young men, pulled in for another offence, confessed to ten of the murders, and the police were jubilant. Then, while these two men were held in custody, more murders occurred, whereupon two more educationally subnormal youths were arrested. They also confessed. With each new discovery of a body a succession of mentally handicapped males were arrested and induced to confess. The police called them 'the halfwits' and protested long and hard in defence of their actions, but while they were content to sit back and believe in the guilt of their handicapped youths, they were not putting maximum effort into catching Russia's worst serial killer of all time. Eventually, after the intervention of the Public Prosecutor's Office, the young disabled men were freed and the murders were acknowledged to be the work of one man. Because Chikatilo buried the bodies in woods beside railway tracks, it earned him the nickname 'The Forest Strip Killer'.

* * * *

In September 1984, Chikatilo was arrested by the Rostov police. Officers Zanasovski and Akhmatkhanov were on plain-clothes patrol near the city's central bus station one evening and observed Chikatilo behaving oddly, getting on buses and trying to pick up women – staring at them, smiling and chatting, or pressing up against them – then getting off to catch one bus after another in opposite directions. 'He was ill at ease and was always twisting his head from one side to the other ... I had the impression that he was trying to make sure that he was not being followed,' Detective Akhmatkhanov reported. With hindsight, we can assume that Chikatilo, carnivorous beast that he was, was out hunting. What Inspector Aleksandr Zanasovski recalled was that this man was the same one he had questioned a couple of weeks earlier when he was behaving in exactly the same way at the nearby railway station. Chikatilo had let him know he was an educated man, telling the inspector that being a teacher, he liked and was interested in young people. Zanasovski checked with one of the women he had approached and it seemed he had done nothing more than chat in a friendly way. Chikatilo was sent on his way, and now Zanasovski was watching him; once more he was showing the same dogged persistence.

And what persistence. The officers watched for more than nine hours throughout the night as Chikatilo relentlessly pursued one woman after another. His patience almost paid off when a young girl performed an indecent act with him, but then he returned to his hunt for prey. However, the sex act was enough of an excuse for the policemen to arrest Chikatilo for licentious behaviour. When they opened his briefcase and discovered it contained a kitchen knife with an eight-inch blade, together with some lengths of rope and a jar of petroleum jelly – and then they found out he came from Shakhty, where many murders had been committed – Zanasovski and Akhmatkhanov believed they had caught the serial killer of whom the public, at last, had been told.

Chikatilo was questioned for two days during the time he was held for the public conduct offence and confessed, again, to his 'sexual weakness' for young girls and his lack of relations with his wife. This, he told officers, was no longer important to him because he was approaching fifty. But the biggest blow to the police was that a blood test showed that Chikatilo's Type A blood did not match the semen type found on and in the victims' bodies, which was AB. Just as nobody thought about bringing in the handful of witnesses who had been the last to see some of the murder victims alive, nobody considered testing Chikatilo's semen, for at the time it was an accepted scientific 'fact' that blood and semen type always matched. Since then, science has proved that in rare instances this is untrue. Chikatilo was an exception to normal humans in so many ways and unfortunately he was exceptional in this, too, and it was a tremendous stroke of luck for him. The only incriminating thing the police had on their captive was the reported theft of a roll of linoleum and a car battery from a company he had worked for in Shakhty – a crime which was to cost him his membership of the Communist Party, causing him enormous shame and increasing his sense of society's injustice. In due course he came up in court over the theft and was sentenced to a year's corrective labour. But because he had already been held in custody for some time, he was freed. He refrained from murdering for many months, but before 1985 was out, two more people had fallen victim to his killing compulsion.

The Soviet Union's Department for Crimes of Special Importance became involved in the manhunt in 1985, when its deputy head, Chief Inspector Issa Kostoyev, arrived in Rostov to head up the investigation. More than half a million people had been interviewed by the time Chikatilo was caught. The investigation was so widespread that it solved 1,062 unrelated crimes, including ninety-five murders. Every school was contacted, its children urged not to go with strange men and asked if anyone had ever approached them. Psychologists were called upon to take a leaf out of the FBI's book and try to draw up a psychological profile of their serial killer. One of these was Aleksandr Bukhanovsky, who was also to interview Chikatilo at length when he was finally arrested in December 1990. The profile was remarkably accurate: Bukhanovsky painted a portrait of a middle-aged, self-pitying misfit, heterosexual but impotent. With only the victims' remains and the circumstances of their deaths to work on, Dr Bukhanovsky suggested that the killer would be apparently normal with a regular job. In addition he believed that the subject would be unable to stop killing.

He was right again. 1987: three murders; 1988: three murders; 1989: five murders. As the police began to get more desperate, Chikatilo began using even greater cunning by committing his murders further afield. Another change of job, into the supplies section of a company in Novocherkassk, gave him even more freedom to travel on business trips and he exploited this, killing in places as far apart as Moscow, the Urals and Leningrad (now St Petersburg) – proof of the premeditated nature of his attacks. Predictably, the methods he used changed too: there was less frenzy and more precision in the way he used his knife. The cutting or biting off of male genitals and the excision of a female uterus was followed by his chewing the organs. Uteruses, he said later, 'were so beautiful and elastic.' Like a surgeon, he performed his abominable 'operations' upon the helpless, terrified youngsters he had stolen from the streets and from those who loved them. His victims, more often than not, were little boys now, not girls. Like all sadistic killers who fail to be stopped, he began to search for variation. Since his satisfaction came from inflicting pain, rather than from a recognised conventional sexual interest in a person of a particular gender, the identity of the individual became immaterial.

As was also inevitable, the bloodlust began to come upon Chikatilo so frequently that it dominated his life, his thoughts constantly occupied by plans for the next sacrifice to his power. 1990 saw him killing a total of eight more people. But as his boldness increased, so too did the alertness of the population. Eye-witness reports began slowly to come in, offering descriptions of a tall, middle-aged man with glasses seen in the vicinity of, or in conversation with, those who were later found murdered.

Or he was seen trying to induce small boys to go with him, telling them, 'I know your mother, I'll take you to her.' Encouraged, the police stepped up their manpower even more. Six hundred officers in plain clothes rode the trains and buses up and down routes which were judged to be favourites of the killer. The police were to be found staking out the Forest Strip area, hiding in ditches or posing as mushroom-pickers in the woods. And eventually it paid off.

At four o'clock in the afternoon of 7 November 1990, a sergeant based at the railway station in Donleskhoz watched a tall, middle-aged man with glasses, wearing a grey suit and carrying a shoulder-bag, emerge from the woods and wash his hands and his shoes at a nearby water hydrant. He had a bandaged finger and a red stain on his cheek, which looked like blood. Leaves and twigs were stuck to his clothes. The policeman asked for his documents and discovered the man was Andrei Chikatilo – a name which meant nothing to him, even though it was soon to cause a chill to run up and down the spines of all who were to read or hear of his dreadful acts.

Chikatilo, glib and unflustered, was not detained, but when the report of this sighting found its way on to Kostoyev's desk, as it eventually did a full six days later – yet another example of police sloppiness – the name rang a bell with him. He pulled out the file on Andrei Chikatilo from his 1984 arrest when he was freed because of the difference between his blood type and the semen found at crime scenes, and was reminded of recent Japanese research which stated that, rarely, a conflict between blood and semen type was possible in an individual. The police returned to the woods near the station in Donleskhoz where the sergeant had intercepted Chikatilo. There, after a long search, they found the body of Sveta Korostik, aged twenty-two, killed by Chikatilo just before he had so casually chatted to the officer at the Donleskhoz station. She had suffered many knife wounds, her tongue and nipples had been cut off and were missing and the mutilation was clearly the work of the Forest Strip Murderer. Sveta was to be Chikatilo's last victim.

When investigations were made with Chikatilo's employers, they discovered that his long-distance business trips coincided with places where murders had been committed. But, in an effort to catch Chikatilo red-handed, he was tailed and, as in 1984, detectives watched his determined efforts to pick up youngsters on the trains, particularly those weakling stragglers of the herd, the children who had become separated from the mainstream of passengers. Reluctant to risk Chikatilo murdering again, after a few days they arrested him. For a week, Chikatilo denied the crimes. But this time his blood and semen were both tested and the difference between them was revealed. Twenty-one lives would have been saved if only this had been done in 1984.

Kostoyev began to subtly suggest to Chikatilo that the crimes could only have been committed by an insane man. Gradually Chikatilo realised that only insanity could save him from the executioner, and, encouraged by the psychiatrist Aleksandr Bukhanovsky, who was brought in to coax words from him, he began to talk. In one statement he described his lifelong depression and humiliation because he had been the butt of people's jokes and because he was impotent. Self-pityingly, he remarked on the unfairness of managements who 'took advantage' of his 'weak character' to make him leave 'without reason' (neglecting to mention his molestation of small girls and the charge of theft which had been proven against him). He described his victims as 'déclassé elements' and 'scum', implying that it was their own fault that they had been killed, and even categorising them with a private code: EM for easy morals, D for drifter, A for adolescent. He claimed to be unable to control his actions during his perverted sexual acts. 'How much of this is my responsibility?' he asked. 'What I did was not for sexual pleasure. Rather it brought me some peace of mind … What I did, I did after watching videos of perverted sex acts, cruelties, horrors.'

Kostoyev charged Chikatilo with thirty-six murders dating from 1982 to 1990 and also with raping or sodomising his victims. Chikatilo indignantly denied the latter charges; his impotence would have made that impossible, he said. He was also insulted at any suggestion of theft from his victims. Then he amazed his interrogators by confessing to nineteen more killings, including his first, Lena Zakotnova in Shakhty, whose picture he picked out from a selection of photographs of little girls and for which another man had been found guilty and executed. Understandably, the police were horrified to learn that Chikatilo had been the culprit, their reluctance to believe his claim evaporating as he gave details about the killing which only the murderer would have known. His memory for each of his victims and the events surrounding each killing was remarkable, and he took the police to many places where he had buried bodies of people that the police had not even known were missing, or whose murders had been attributed to other, unknown killers. An important part of any Russian criminal investigation is the 'experiment', during which the accused demonstrates in front of a camera exactly how he committed the crime. Using a tailor's dummy, Chikatilo showed how he had murdered each person, including that first time with little Lena. Showing no remorse, he chatted and made jokes as he performed his grisly death-act. The remains of two of the victims Chikatilo remembered killing could not be found, despite his certainty about their location. The police gave these up.

Fayina Chikatilo felt sick. When she had first been told her husband had been arrested, she thought it was because he had been making a nuisance of himself with the authorities, protesting in numerous letters about some garages being built close to his son's house. She could not believe Andrei was really capable of the terrible things they were saying he had done. After all, hadn't he always been a devoted father who loved his own children? How could he perpetrate such abominably evil acts upon other small children? As for these crimes being sexually motivated, she found this hard to understand, because of his lack of interest in sex with her.

When she accepted the truth, she also began to fit pieces of the jigsaw puzzle into place: the business trips and the nights away; the blood he sometimes had on his clothes, which he claimed was from cuts he had suffered when unloading goods. Unreasonably, Fayina felt a huge burden of guilt: that she was to blame for trusting him and not inquiring too deeply into his activities. If she had, she said, she would have done something to stop him, but 'I could never imagine him being able to murder one person, let alone fifty-three ... he could never hurt anyone.' Overcoming her repulsion, she visited her husband once, to get his authorisation for her to have access to the couple's savings. Hanging his head like a naughty child, Chikatilo could not meet his wife's gaze, but used his pet name for her. 'If only I had listened to you, Fenechka ... If only I had followed your advice and got treatment,' he whined. Fayina was too appalled to have any more to do with Chikatilo, and the two children, Ludmilla and Yuri found it equally hard to come to terms with the fact that they had been fathered by such a monster. The family were later forced to change their name and move away after receiving death-threats. 'I crossed him out of my life as if he had never existed,' Fayina later told writer Peter Conradi.

Chikatilo believed he could claim that temporary insanity had fired his actions, and suggested that he could be treated. Scientists would be interested in him because he was unique, owing to the number of his victims, which made his case 'exceptional', he said. After his confessions, Chikatilo was sent for psychiatric evaluation to the Serbsky Institute in Moscow, where he spent three months being tested by many doctors. In the old Soviet Union, this was the place where the authorities infamously used Soviet psychology as a form of political control rather than to investigate the complexities of the psyche. Here, 'enemies of the state' were likely to be certified and interned in asylums, but with the break-up of the Soviet Union, the Serbsky Institute gained a new, healthier profile influenced by Western methods. Under the guidance of psychiatrists like Boris Shostakovich and Andrei Tkachenko, who specialise in the study of the criminally insane, the Serbsky psychiatrists noted that Chikatilo discussed the murders 'calmly and coldly', and that he was not deranged enough to fail to realise he was committing wrong. On the contrary, said the reports, he was a sadist who was cautious in the extreme when carrying out his premeditated acts. It was noted that he was even discouraged from murdering when the weather was cold – during the winter months his murder rate dropped away. This 'uncontrolled compulsion', it seemed, only took hold when it was convenient and comfortable for Chikatilo. He was declared legally sane.

The trial of Andrei Romanovich Chikatilo began on 14 April 1992 in Rostov-on-Don Regional Court. It was to last six months – unsurprising, given that the documentary evidence collected by investigators over the previous six months filled 200 volumes, covering as it did twelve years of murders committed in an area stretching from southern Russia and Ukraine to the Central Asian republic of Uzbekistan. Although Chikatilo had claimed fifty-five murders, only fifty-three were regarded as conclusive by the police, including Chikatilo's first murder in Shakhty, that of Lena Zakotnova, for which Alexander Kravchenko had been executed.

It took three days for Judge Leonid Akubzhanov to read out the evidence to a court packed with relatives, the media and other spectators magnetized by the ghoulishness of the crimes committed by the world's foremost serial killer; three days of interruptions as people repeatedly erupted into outbursts of anger, tears and abuse. As Chikatilo, dressed in grey trousers and an old shirt decorated with the rings symbol of the 1980 Moscow Olympics, stood or sat staring sullenly from behind the bars of a metal cage designed, not to keep him in, but to keep others out, the prosecutors detailed the grisly crimes he committed against women, boys aged between eight and sixteen, and girls aged between nine and seventeen. Relatives of victims – and even hardened soldiers keeping guard – fainted as they heard how Chikatilo boiled and ate the sawn-off testicles or nipples of his victims, or carved slits in some corpses to use for his own brand of necrophiliac sex, often not bothering to kill his trussed teenage victims before the butchery started. 'He was constantly on the look-out for victims,' Judge Akubzhanov said. 'On holidays, on business trips, visiting relatives. He was always ready to kill.'

Chikatilo countered this by remarking coolly at one point: 'I did not need to look for them. Every step I took, they were there.' He tried to convince the judge that he was a victim of Soviet totalitarianism. He had led a wretched life, having to travel constantly for work, stay in 'dirty railway stations and miserable hotels' and put up with the rudeness of his bosses, he said. Then he changed tack and claimed abnormality. 'I am a mistake of nature, a mad beast,' he declared – and it was true that Chikatilo appeared far from grandfatherly now. No longer with the appearance of a respectable teacher of literature, his head had been shaved, giving him a malevolent appearance, and this was compounded when, after spending the early days either silent or making articulate pleas for a new trial on the grounds that everyone, including the judge, had allegedly already found him guilty, he suddenly decided to play crazy.

Portraying the beast which the world had expected when the search was on for the 'Rostov Ripper', Chikatilo began lolling his head, rolling his eyes, gnashing his teeth and drooling, loudly singing the Communist anthem 'Internationale', producing pornographic magazines, rattling the bars of his cage and even, on a couple of occasions, dropping his trousers or tearing off his clothes to wave his penis at the court, screaming: 'Look at this useless thing. What do you think I could do with that?' Obviously a desperate Chikatilo knew that being found insane was his sole chance of survival. 'I am not a homosexual!' he ranted one day. Another day he yelled: 'I have milk in my breasts; I am going to give birth!' Then he suddenly retracted his confession to the murder of Lena Zakotnova. Next, he claimed to remember other murders he had committed, saying at one point that he had killed seventy people. Later, he recanted on six murders to which he had already confessed. One time-wasting strategy was to declare that he wanted the trial conducted in his native Ukrainian language, and to demand an interpreter. Another was to claim hallucinations and announce that the KGB was firing invisible rays at him: standard schizophrenic symptoms suddenly harnessed by a killer playing a madman to Oscar-winning standards. Repeatedly, he was hauled from the court back to his cell and beaten by guards.

Throughout it all, the crowds keened, wailed and shouted. An elderly woman denounced Chikatilo as 'a damned soul and an evil sadist'. The aunt of one murdered boy shouted at one point: 'This trial is rubbing salt into the wounds of the relatives of the victims.' Voicing a popular view, she demanded: 'Liquidate the criminal. Too much money is being spent on supporting his life.' Many others concurred. Chikatilo had confessed, they said. What was the point of having a trial? 'What's the use of announcing the verdict? It would have been a better idea to shoot him here at once,' said a student from a nearby college. Several times distraught relatives of victims tried to attack Chikatilo through his bars. Eventually they were penned upstairs in the gallery. One day the brother of a victim hurled a small metal ball at Chikatilo. It flew through the metal bars and missed his head by centimetres. When the guards went to arrest the man, other spectators gathered protectively around him. The guards did not pursue the arrest.

The grief of parents who had lost sons and daughters was pitiable. Nina Beletskaya, whose twelve-year-old son Ivan disappeared and was murdered in Zaporozhe, Ukraine in 1987 after going to pick apricots in the forest near their home, broke down while giving evidence. 'The day I buried my son, I gave him my word that I would try to live long enough to see his killer with my own eyes,' she said. 'I wanted to see this man who could rip open my son's stomach and then stuff mud in his mouth so that he would not cry out. I wanted to know what he looked like, to know which mother could bear such an animal. And now I see him.' She told reporters: 'Look, he's still smiling. He's taken part of my life ... He's an animal. He doesn't deserve a human trial.' Lida Khovata, whose ten-year-old son Alyosha was murdered in August 1989, said: 'It's so painful I can't even describe it. I have no wish other than to kill him. I just want this to end.'

Dr Aleksandr Bukhanovsky's scientific fascination with the killer extended to regular visits to Chikatilo during the trial. He would take him his breakfast every day and the cannibal enjoyed discussing himself with the doctor, asking that Bukhanovsky be with him at his execution. The psychiatrist – alone in his professional opinion that Chikatilo was insane and should be sent to a mental hospital – was intrigued by both the killer's intelligence and the conflicts within his psyche. 'He was a great theatre-goer. He could sit in a performance of something by Chekhov and be moved to tears, but then go out and murder someone,' Bukhanovsky said. 'His internal world is a thousand times richer than the surface expression of that world.' It was to Bukhanovsky that Chikatilo gave details of what he claimed was his dreadful childhood. 'When he started telling me about his life it was already the story of his illness,' said Dr Bukhanovsky. Chikatilo told the doctor about his brother Stepan, the subject of his mother's fearful tales. 'He was told the child was kidnapped, stolen and eaten. He found out about it when he was four. He reacted with such terror to the idea that it was possible to kidnap and eat a child that he remembered it all his life. On the one hand he found it terrible and frightening, on the other he had an unhealthy interest in it and his fantasies were all constantly concerned with it,' said the psychiatrist.

On 15 October 1992 Judge Akubzhanov found Chikatilo guilty on all but one of the fifty-three murder charges – a confession to the killing of a fifteen-year-old girl offered inadequate evidence – and amid shouts of fury and applause the judge sentenced him to death by shooting with a single bullet fired in the back of the head. As he spoke, the killer shouted 'Swindlers', shrieked and snarled, threw himself around the metal cage and hurled his bench to one side. Guards tried to grab the spitting and biting man as the angry crowd bayed for his blood. 'You gave him nothing! Give him to us, give this murderer to us!' cried one woman. Others screamed: 'Give him to us so we can tear him to pieces, as he did to our children!' Chikatilo's lawyer, Marat Khabibulin, rejected the court's finding that his client was sane and announced that he would appeal to the Supreme Court of the Russian Federation in Moscow against the verdict, claiming the court had not properly evaluated Chikatilo's mental health. While awaiting the appeal hearing, Chikatilo was held in a special cell on death row at the Novocherkassk prison, isolated from ordinary prisoners for his own safety; the father of one of his victims was also an employee at the prison. The appeal was rejected by the Russian Supreme Court in 1993. A further appeal for clemency from the then Russian president Boris Yeltsin was also turned down in January 1994 and a month later Chikatilo was taken to a soundproofed room at the prison and executed with a gunshot behind his right ear – a death considerably more merciful than those he had inflicted upon his victims.

Since Chikatilo's dreadful crimes, the stories of his murders have become valuable cautionary tales for Russian parents who want to warn their children against going with strangers. Just like the child Andrei Romanovich Chikatilo before them, Russian children are told by their mothers that there are real-life human monsters around, eager to snatch them away, kill them and gobble them up. Andrei Romanovich turned out to be that archetypal bogeyman, that wolf in the forest he himself had once feared.

But there is one significant difference between the genuine scare-stories told to today's children, and the one that was told to the four-year-old Chikatilo by his mother. For he certainly was told the story: his sister confirmed this. But the authorities checked up on Chikatilo's childhood and they could find no records or documents confirming the birth of a Stepan Chikatilo in Yablochnoye. None of the villagers remembered this boy, still less recall the terrifying fate which was said to have befallen him. It seems that the awful tale that his mother told him was probably fictional.

On the other hand, Chikatilo, in all his impossible monstrosity, really did exist.

Unnatural Selection

'*You maggots make me sick. I am beyond your experience*'

Richard Ramirez, the 'Night Stalker', killer of fifteen in California

'*I think you can provide some insight and advance this study.*'
'*And what possible reason could I have to do that?*'
'*Curiosity.*'
'*About what?*'
'*About why you're here. About what happened to you.*'
'*Nothing happened to me, Officer Starling. I happened. You can't reduce me to a set of influences. You've given up good and evil for behaviourism, Officer Starling. You've got everyone in moral dignity pants – nothing is ever anybody's fault. Look at me, Officer Starling. Can you stand to say I'm evil? Am I evil, Officer Starling? A census taker tried to quantify me once. I ate his liver with some fava beans and a big Amarone.*'

Thomas Harris, *The Silence of the Lambs*

Jeffrey Dahmer's crimes in Milwaukee came to light in the summer following the release of 1991's Oscar-winning film, *The Silence of the Lambs*. Small wonder, then, that the discovery of a man whose flat was littered with the body parts from eleven corpses, including a human heart in the freezer ('I was saving it to eat later,' explained Dahmer) and a set of male genitals in a pot, provoked a rash of *The Real Hannibal the Cannibal* headlines. But only months later the abhorrence felt towards Dahmer's crimes was to take a new direction: the Russian cannibal killer Andrei Chikatilo, arrested in December 1991, perpetrated such numerous and repulsively cruel acts that eclipsed even Dahmer's. Once again Thomas Harris's most famous creation was called upon to help out the headline-writers: *Russia's Hannibal the Cannibal* shrieked the newspaper stories. Yet Dahmer and Chikatilo could not have been more unlike Anthony Hopkins's portrayal of Harris's sinister psychopath, a man who emitted a tangible, almost magical, aura of sheer power. It was a compelling Oscar-winning performance which, rather worryingly, turned Hannibal Lecter into an anti-hero and cult figure. So worrying, in fact, that Anthony Hopkins – later to become Sir Anthony – expressed doubts about reprising the role in a proposed sequel to the film (but he did set aside his concerns to make *Hannibal* in 2001 and *Red Dragon* in 2002).

Hannibal Lecter was make-believe, but real-life monstrosities are rather different. Away from the fictions and film scripts, it is rare to find an easily-identifiable beast with a seductive tone, piercing eyes and a powerful aura of sexual magnetism which evokes inexplicable fear or desire in anyone who encounters him. It is not potency, but inadequacy, which drives the actual sadistic killer. They more often appear to be quiet, withdrawn people, isolated and lonely maybe, but regarded as unmemorable by many who meet them. They have mothers, fathers, relatives, people who care about them – or at least, people who once cared. One has to remind oneself that these killers have not just appeared like screen aliens in our midst as fully-fledged, evil adults. Once, they were newborn babies cooed over by their mothers, they were laughing toddlers learning to talk, they were small boys in short pants reciting their five-times table and playing boats with bits of sticks in muddy puddles. What on earth happens inside the brains of these children to set them upon a blood-drenched path of such horror? As a woman said outside the Rostov court where Chikatilo was tried: 'They kept on explaining how and whom he killed but nobody explained why. That's the most interesting thing.'

So can we answer this question? Can we find common factors among these killers, something which makes them prey like carnivorous animals on those weaker than themselves? Were they made that way, or born that way? Are they just genetically evil? The rash of contemporary cases of cannibal or vampire killers might also pose another question: did this sort of grotesque murder actually escalate during the twentieth and twenty-first centuries – and if so, then again, why? Or have such crimes always happened with similar regularity? As was noted in the introductory chapter, there have certainly been instances in past centuries to indicate that sadistic killers existed then – pre-internet – as they do now.[9] Claiming that random bloody acts were the work of mythical beasts such as werewolves would seem to support the hypothesis that attempts were made during times of cultural ignorance to account for abhorrent crimes, but documentation is muddied by the persecution, superstition and hysteria which accompanied medieval law enforcement. Additionally, the incidence of these ancient crimes cannot be comprehensively assessed owing to the limitations of communication and reportage. The most bloody would not necessarily involve cannibalism or blood-drinking, although this is one likely aspect of a crime which is the work of those we call sadistic killers. By the end of the twentieth century, sadistic sex killings made up eighteen per cent of all murders – and cannibalism featured among these cases.

The infliction of fear, suffering and mutilation are essential ingredients for sexual gratification in the sadistic killer – or lust-murderer, as he is sometimes called. They discover that the sight or feel of blood stimulates them. Often they move on to tasting blood or biting ... and swallowing. In these killers, the advance to cannibalism might seem almost imperceptible; this aspect of deviant sexual behaviour is contained within essentially the same abnormal framework. And by virtue of the compulsive nature of their drive, sadistic killers develop into serial killers if they are not caught.[10] Similarly, in striving to 'perfect' a crime and reap its sensual rewards – satisfactions which are destined never to live up to the sexual fantasies a killer has entertained for years – they enter an 'improvement continuum' and become more and more experimental in their brutality. In fact, despite the thrall cast by Hannibal Lecter upon the cinema-going public, it is his lack of an urgent sexual dimension which clearly marks him as a highly unrealistic character. The remarkably-controlled Lecter, whose heart-rate never increases when he kills, mutilates and devours at random with apparently no sexual motive – this in no way conforms to the fictional cannibal's real-life counterparts.

During the preceding chapters there was a recurring pattern: Andrei Chikatilo's mutilations became ever more frenzied and bloody, his infliction of torture on his victims gathered momentum and for the Russian killer to achieve satisfaction necessitated greater suffering and pain on the part of his victims, together with cannibalising their bodies. Jeffrey Dahmer's modus operandi became similarly more channelled. In his childhood his necrophiliac satisfaction came from dead animals. When he moved on to killing humans, at first he did not keep any 'mementos' of his victims and if one had not known of Dahmer's childhood history the dismemberment might almost seem to have been born of expedience. While his deviant cravings initially appeared to be adequately met by his actions of drugging, strangling, having sex with male corpses, mutilation and dismemberment, as his methods became more streamlined he demanded greater and greater stimulation – and achieved it in a number of ways, including cannibalism. It has been suggested that Dahmer was different from many serial killers in that his power and domination thrill did not come from observing his victims scream, suffer and beg for their lives; instead, his gratification began post-mortem. He could even be considered merciful because at first he drugged those he killed. But we should note that over time Dahmer graduated to wilder and more bizarre obsessions – preserving skulls and organs and eventually drilling the heads of his drugged victims in the belief he could transform them into 'zombies'. If he had not been caught, if his victim-count had reached the staggering heights of Chikatilo's, would he have ultimately needed to inflict ever-greater suffering on his victims to achieve that same elusive satisfaction which his fantasies promised?

That is, of course, a speculative theory. But this grisly model is followed by others who rape and mutilate, when such extreme violation forms the stuff of their long-held fantasies. Just as Dahmer and Chikatilo eventually sated their appetites with cannibalism, who knows how many other sadistic killers – certainly those whose perversions include necrophilia – would ultimately have progressed to cannibalism as a supreme act of power when primitive instinct ruled their actions? I am thinking here of killers like Neville Heath and William Heirens, who, in 1946, were both arrested in Britain. Heath was apprehended after two sadistic murders of women, during which he inflicted terrible mutilations, including the biting-off and mangling of breasts. Heirens was a fetishist who stole women's underwear from washing-lines and who was sexually stimulated by breaking and entering houses to burgle them. He also committed two mutilation murders – including that of a six-year-old girl whom he kidnapped from her bedroom as she lay asleep and whose body he dismembered. It is chilling to conjecture about the primordial taboos which these two heinous murderers may have further breached had they remained free to continue killing. It was noted that the sadistic fantasies which Heirens had enjoyed for many years 'far exceeded' those he had carried out.

In the criminal history of the Western world, the number of serial killers increased over the centuries, especially in the United States, until the figure reached a peak in the 1990s. At the beginning of the twentieth century there was an average of one homicide a year for every 100,000 people, a figure which was most elevated in the 1930s, receded post-war, but then rose inexorably during the 1960s to make it ten in 100,000 by 1980 – a tenfold rise since 1900. Sixty years ago, in almost all homicides the killer had some relationship with his victim. But by the 1980s, twenty-five per cent of murders were 'stranger murders' – accounted for, said sociologists, by increased mobility and a society which had become impersonal and culturally filled with sexual and violent images. The last decade of the twentieth century saw the USA homicide rate having trebled since the 1960s, and despite the significant decline during the twenty-first century, nevertheless within the homicide statistics, according to John Douglas, a former Chief of the FBI's Elite Serial Crime Unit and author of the book *Mindhunter*, 'a very conservative estimate is that there are between thirty-five and fifty active serial killers in the United States' at any given time.

America accounts for about two-thirds of the world's serial killers. The UK's Radford University, partnered with Florida Gulf Coast University in the United States, has an ongoing database of serial killers which is updated annually, the last update being in 2021. Its statistics show that between 1900 and 1910, out of a total of twenty-nine serial killers globally, eighteen were to be found in the USA. By the 1960s, this had increased to 217 worldwide, out of which 156 were in the USA. The 1980s' world total was 767 with 604 in the States but in the 1990s, after an all-time peak halfway through the decade, there was a notable change: a definite decline began in the United States (498) while there was a rise elsewhere in the world (215) – a world total of 713. This decline continued until by 2010–2014 the estimate was sixty-five serial killers in America and ninety-five serial killers listed worldwide. Other studies of serial killers suggest that this figure, to be realistic, should be more than doubled and, speaking in 2012, the FBI's John Douglas admitted that his previously-mentioned 'conservative estimate' figure was difficult to ascertain because an undetected killer may murder two or three people and then have a 'cooling-off' period, sometimes for years, before killing again. Those figures, also, are now thought to be an underestimate. Rene Chun's investigative report in the October 2019 issue of *The Atlantic* remarks that: 'while the number of serial killings has supposedly fallen, so too has the rate of murder cases solved ... In other words, about forty per cent of the time, murderers get away with murder.'

Serial killers are thought to be responsible for a significant number of these unsolved murders. The writer quotes Thomas Hargrove, the founder of the Murder Accountability Project, which compiles data on homicide, as believing that at least two per cent of murders are committed by serial killers, translating to more than two thousand unidentified serial killers. Michael Arntfield, who has written many books about serial murder, also believes that the FBI's figures are an underestimate and believes that the number of active serial killers at present is somewhere between three and four thousand. The ease with which a serial murderer in America may operate in separate counties many hundreds of miles apart led the FBI in 2005 to set up the 'Highway Serial Killings Initiative', a database to investigate murders potentially committed by truckers. By 2019 this had a matrix of more than 750 victims found near major roads and highways with the identification of 450 potential suspects, many of them long-haul lorry drivers who, as regards opportunity, are well-positioned to pick up their prey in one state – perhaps hitchhikers, or someone stranded at a service station – and then dump the body by a highway several states away. The FBI analysts expect that numbers of victims will increase during future years.

While other economically-developed nations, including the United Kingdom and Western Europe, do not match the USA proportionately (mainly because of more restrictive firearms laws), the rates of murder, serial killings and violent crime broadly reflect the USA pattern over the last hundred years, including the apparent recent decline. The Radford database over this period suggests that the UK is second to the USA in terms of recorded serial killers: 116 over the last century, compared to more than 2,300 in the States. But in recent years the overall murder figures in London have shown fluctuating increases of up to fifty per cent: from ninety-four cases in 2014, the number rose to 149 in 2019. By March 2021 this annual overall London homicide rate was down to 119 – which is still significantly higher than the 2014 overall murder rate that was lower than at any time since the 1960s and violent crime in the entire UK was at its lowest since 1981. It should also be noted that within these statistics, the annual number of rapes (24,043) and other sexual offences (48,934) were the highest recorded by the police since 2002–03. As well as improvements in recording crime, this is thought to reflect a greater willingness of victims to come forward to report such crimes.

What is more alarming is the increasingly callous and sadistic nature of the offender over the last thirty years or so. Increasingly, there have been cases of sadistic 'killing for kicks' – 'recreational murder' or 'wilding' as it is sometimes known. Horrifyingly, such sexual sadism is inflicted by people in groups. That the barbaric are able to seek out and find others of a similarly vicious persuasion instead of being alienated by virtue of their depraved inclinations must make us question the nature of our progressive society and, disturbingly, such individuals are aided by the freedoms and communication offered by the internet and the mobile 'smartphone', with which they are able to film and then share their actions with others. Back in 1992 the 'wilding' case that shocked the UK concerned the abduction and abhorrent murder of sixteen-year-old Suzanne Capper in Manchester, England, by a group of six people who held her captive for a week, during which time she was blindfolded and tied to a bed, then tortured with increasing brutality. This included having her head shaved, being cut and beaten, having her teeth snapped off with pliers and her flesh scrubbed raw with a wire brush. Finally she was driven to a remote place, doused with petrol, set alight, and left for dead. Suzanne was found after, unbelievably, she managed to stagger to a main road. In hospital, her burns were such that she was unrecognisable. She was put into an induced coma and died four days later, but not before she had been able to tell police the names of her persecutors: a group of four men ... and two women.

Recent academic studies of sexual violence against women estimate that in the United States more than one in three women (35.6%) have experienced rape, physical violence and/or stalking at some point in their lives, but Radford University's serial killer study suggests that in the US as many as 44.5 per cent of the victims of serial killers are male. However, their perpetrator statistics in terms of gender are rather different: only nine per cent of the last century's serial killers have been female. Although the idea is apocryphal that 'a woman's weapon' is stereotypically poison, female motives for murder are not, broadly speaking, identical to those of men and it is exceptionally rare for female killers to indulge in sexual or sadistic acts, as occurred in the Suzanne Capper murder. Possibly this is owing to females' lower levels of testosterone, the male hormone which is the driver of both sex and aggression, or perhaps it is because the sense of inadequacy, low self-esteem, powerlessness and frustration which manifests as aggressive behaviour in males is more likely to be internalised in women, resulting in such self-harms as mutilation and suicide.

During the twenty-eight years since the Capper case, several US female serial killers have also occupied the front pages of newspapers, possibly the most infamous being Aileen Wuornos, a Florida prostitute who, without obvious motive other than rage, randomly shot dead eight of her clients and was executed in 2002. Wuornos was later made notorious by the 2003 movie, *Monster*, although it should be mentioned that these killings do not fall into the 'lust-murder', that is, sexual sadism category. But in the UK, the black cloak of infamy which for thirty years had belonged to the 'Moors Murderer' child-killer Myra Hindley passed during the 1990s to Rosemary West who, with her husband Fred, sexually tortured and killed at least ten young girls including her own daughter at their

Gloucester home. Fred West committed suicide in his cell while awaiting trial; his wife was sent to prison for life in 1995 and in 2022 remains there, only the second woman after Hindley to be given a whole-life tariff in England and Wales. In February 2014 there was added a third: Joanne Dennehy of Peterborough won the additional dubious distinction of being the first woman to be sentenced to the whole-life tariff by a judge rather than by the Home Secretary under new powers introduced that year: she was jailed for killing three men by stabbing them through their hearts – two of the three were random strangers. During a ten-day killing frenzy, she had also stabbed a further two men who survived her attacks.

Trial judge Mr Justice Spencer said medical reports made it clear that Dennehy, then aged thirty-one, was a sadomasochist who enjoyed sex with extreme violence. He described her as 'a cruel, calculating and manipulative serial killer' who had killed 'to satisfy her sadistic lust for blood' and was remorseless. The mother-of-two had, prior to these crimes, untruthfully boasted to associates that she had killed many other men including her own father. The court heard that after each of the three murders to which she pleaded guilty, she had been keen to draw attention to her crimes, on one occasion showing the corpse to a fourteen-year-old neighbour. Another witness testified that Dennehy was delighted when she saw a picture of herself on the TV news. Dennehy laughed as she was led away to the cells, and offered no reason for her crimes, other than that – as she told the two survivors during the act of stabbing them – she was murdering for fun. Also remarkable in the UK is that unlike Hindley and West, she acted alone rather than in conjunction with a male partner. Dennehy told a psychiatrist: 'I killed to see how I would feel, to see if I was as cold as I thought I was. Then it got more-ish.'

So increasingly, cruel murderers are not exclusively male. Or, in fact, adult. The crime which – occurring as it did immediately after the Suzanne Capper 'wilding' case – stopped Britain in its tracks was the sadistic 'killing for kicks' of a two-year-old child who had been abducted from a shopping centre in Liverpool in February 1993. When discovered, the little boy's body had had such appalling injuries inflicted upon it that policemen wept in horrified disbelief – but the security cameras in the shopping centre had captured his abductors on video-film, and the suspects were later arrested. They were two ten-year-old boys who, according to allegation, had previously limited their tortures to neighbourhood animals. That same month, in the wake of the two terrible murders, British Prime Minister John Major backed new legislative measures on punishment, declaring: 'Society needs to condemn a little more and understand a little less.'

SOCIAL BACKGROUND FACTORS
Can society really be blamed for this deplorable state of affairs? What makes people commit crimes like torture, mutilation, cannibalism or vampirism? Have we created a non-pejorative climate in which the sadistic murderer can flourish? There has been a tendency over the past six decades for a criminal's antisocial deeds to be attributed to everyone and everything except the criminal himself. Parents are blamed. Peer-pressure is blamed. Racism, poverty and unemployment, substandard housing and tower blocks are blamed. Schools used to be blamed for imposing too much discipline. Then years later, schools were blamed for not imposing enough discipline. Churches are seen as having failed in their duty. The media, together with the movie and computer gaming industries – and of course, the internet – is accused of glamorising crime and violence and of graphically portraying escalating

levels of explicit brutality and cruelty in order to boost ratings and sales. Even the advertising industry is held to be blameworthy for offering desirable images of goods to potential criminals, exemplifying a lifestyle which they cannot attain. When the poor commit crimes they are seen as victims of a society which has deprived them of hope: seeing privilege and wealth everywhere robs them of self-esteem. But when middle-class youths similarly break the law, there are some who suggest that they too are casualties of society, rebelling against parental values of materialism and the pressures to succeed. As Stanton E. Samenow points out in his book *Inside the Criminal Mind*, economic hard times have historically been associated with an increase in crime ... but then, so have good times.

Sociological explanations for crime, plausible as they may seem, are simplistic. If they were plausible, we would have far more criminals than we do. Criminals come from all kinds of families and neighbourhoods. Most poor people are law-abiding, and most kids from broken homes are not delinquents. Children may bear the scars of neglect and deprivation for life, but most do not become criminals. The environment does have an effect, but people perceive and react to similar conditions of life in very different ways.

Psychological studies of adopted children who are later diagnosed as psychopaths or who have become criminals suggest that heredity may play a predisposing part in each of the types. Some of the studies have found a higher-than-average proportion of both of these dysfunctionalities in adopted children whose biological relatives were criminals or who were diagnosed with antisocial personalities. Samenow puts his own opinion bluntly in his book: focusing on forces outside the criminal is futile, he says, because it is criminals who cause crime, not family or social factors. Sure, he says, remedy intolerable social conditions because this is a worthwhile task, but do not expect criminals to change because of such efforts.

But Mr Samenow's view is an unfashionable one, in its way just as extreme as the ideas of those psychologists and sociologists who cast around for social causes of crime while ignoring the nature of the criminal, but it is supported in part by the social planning trend begun during the era of high-crime in the 1960s. This was based on the worthy assumption that improving conditions in inner-city areas would reduce the crime and murder rate in the locality. After all (the reasoning went), the stress caused to laboratory rats by imposing upon them poor conditions and overcrowding makes them, too, behave in unaccustomed antisocial, violent, cannibalistic and murderous ways. However, despite many cities operating urban renewal schemes – creating better homes, better schools, better health-care – for the following thirty years the crime rate increased, and did not decrease. As for the belief that poor living conditions are more likely to particularly predispose people to becoming serial or sadistic killers, while these criminals are always more than eager to lay the blame anywhere but upon themselves, it is interesting to note that among those whom we may consider to be the most socially disadvantaged in our Western urban midst – ethnic minorities – it is statistically very unusual to find a serial killer. Considering that in America black males have elevated offending-rates relative to other ethnic groups, particularly for homicide, and although they make up a disproportionate (and possibly skewed) one-third of the prison population, serial killing is not generally their province. Indeed, the profile of an archetypal serial killer, according to VICAP (the Violent Criminal Apprehension Programme) at the FBI's National Centre for the Analysis of Violent Crime in Quantico, famously begins with the description: 'single white male, aged twenties or thirties ...'

So, bearing in mind the apparent impotence of a policy of improvement in living and care standards during the latter third of the twentieth century, what changed towards the dawning of the millennium to precipitate the resulting dramatic reversal in violent crime figures over the next twenty years, contrary to the expectations of many worried criminologists earlier in the 1990s? According to, among others, James Alan Fox, a criminologist at Northeastern University in Boston, there are several reasons for this in the USA, including a huge increase in the incarceration of criminals, together with more severe sentencing – which keeps more of them off the streets for longer periods. By 2000, at any one point there were four times as many people held in prison than there had been thirty years previously – more than two million, in fact – and half of this quadrupled growth had taken place during the 1990s, giving the United States the highest incarceration rate in the world.

Over the same period there was a significant increase in the number of police officers. The Violent Crime Control and Law Enforcement Act signed by President Clinton in 1994, allowed for more than thirty billion dollars to be spent on prisons and crime prevention over the next six years, resulting in a fourteen per cent average increase in officers across all states. In New York City the expansion of the size of the force was considerably higher – forty-five per cent. It was a crackdown on crime led by Mayor Rudy Giuliani and Police Commissioner William Bratton which resulted in a seventy-three per cent decline in the homicide rate by 2001. In addition to these law enforcement strategies, there have been continuing advances in computer communication and innovative technology such as DNA-sampling to give detectives powerful new tools which enable them to co-ordinate multiple agencies when tracking down criminals. Additionally, media coverage and communication means there is now more awareness of risk among the public: behavioural changes may, for example, include an increased wariness about hitchhiking and enhanced parental recognition of the possible threats to lone children on the streets or in parks.

There is one other influential factor of interest: that the US crime-drop of the late 1990s could have been related to the legalisation of abortion in the 1970s with the landmark Roe v. Wade Supreme Court decision of 1973, stating that women had the right to choose to abort an unwanted baby. In 2001 a study by two academics, John J. Donahue of Stanford Law School and Steven D. Levitt, an economist from Chicago University, linked the dramatic reduction in the number of unwanted births in the 1970s to the decrease in crime in *The Impact of Legalised Abortion on Crime*, a paper calling upon research showing unwanted children to be 'at higher risk of less favourable life outcomes', including economic hardship and being raised in dangerous neighbourhoods, which could expose them to criminal behaviour and increase the likelihood of their offending as adults. They looked at five states which had allowed abortion in 1970 – earlier than the rest of the nation – and observed that there was a corresponding sharp decline in crime in the 1990s, when those aborted foetuses would have been of 'criminal age', compared to the other states. Donahue and Levitt continued monitoring the crime statistics and in 2019 announced that the data over the previous eighteen years had borne out their original research hypotheses into abortion legalisation and crime. Further research showed that 'high-abortion states' experienced greater decreases in crime and arrest-rates than 'medium-abortion' and 'low abortion' states (which fared the worst in crime trends). The researchers predicted that 'legalised abortion will account for persistent declines of one per cent a year in crime over the next two decades'. (It is thus unfortunate that in 2021 several of the USA's right-wing southern states, including Texas and Mississippi adopted an extremist anti-abortion approach, demanding that the Roe v. Wade law be scrapped and banning abortions past six weeks of pregnancy.)

SADISTIC MURDERERS

In this study I am concentrating on the sadistic murderers among serial killers, for it is within this sector that cannibal killers are to be identified. It is true that they are not a novel phenomenon,[11] but whereas in nineteenth-century England the appearance of such men was rare enough to cause the sort of panic which has given Jack the Ripper – whose identity was never discovered – historical infamy, in contemporary times it seems they are more plentiful. Accordingly psychiatrists, while not always understanding the motivation for sadistic murders, can assess the culprits who have been apprehended and endeavour to point to predisposing and diagnostic factors which, it is hoped, will help us to pinpoint the individuals who are likely to develop in this deviant way.

A classic study of the sadistic murderer was written by Robert P. Brittain in 1970, in which he lists many characteristics, some or all of which are commonly found among these men; the individuals in this book amply bear out Dr Brittain's theories. Among these characteristics are:

- Usually introspective and withdrawn, he has few associates and no close friends and enjoys solitary pursuits like reading or going to the cinema alone, often to see horror films.
- He feels inadequate and inferior except in regard to his crimes, which make him feel god-like, and is likely to offend when he has suffered a loss of self-esteem, such

as loss of job, or being ridiculed by someone, especially in a sexual context.

- He can be a hypochondriac and display squeamishness.
- He has an elaborate fantasy life, imagining sadistic scenes which he acts out in his killings. He is fascinated by atrocities and excited by cruelty, such as that committed by the Nazis, and collects books or pictures of such images.
- He has an inordinate interest in weapons, often having a large collection which he may lovingly handle, and he may even endow some with pet names.
- He is usually under thirty-five, unmarried and of high intelligence.
- He is usually sexually dysfunctional, having had little or no experience of normal sexual intercourse, and may hate all females.
- Many take jobs which satisfy their sadistic inclinations, such as butchery or slaughter-house work – in much the same way that necrophiles are known to obtain jobs as mortuary attendants and grave-diggers.
- He has a strong, ambivalent relationship with his mother, both loving and hating her. He is often seen as a 'mother's boy' when adult. Sometimes he commits matricide.
- Sometimes the father is excessively punitive and authoritarian.
- There is a great interest in pornography, particularly sadistic pornography.
- A history of cruelty to animals is particularly significant when it relates to cats, dogs, birds and farm animals. Stabbing or hanging is common, although worse cruelties can be inflicted.
- The method of killing his human victims is almost always strangling, which gives him a greater sense of

power over his victims, playing with them 'like a cat with a mouse.'

- Although these are sexually motivated crimes, sexual intercourse or orgasm does not always occur. Sometimes the murderer masturbates and sometimes a penis-substitute – such as a piece of wood or a knife – is used to violate the victim.
- When captured and institutionalised in hospitals or prisons, he is very well behaved, which can result in his being released or sent to a less secure unit.

Trying to assess the motivation of such men is no new thing. As Dr Brittain's list (above) shows, there are certainly common childhood factors which could be regarded as influential and indeed, there are common behaviour patterns displayed in childhood by sadists which many investigators regard as extremely predictive. The three most notable of these are:

A preoccupation with fire-setting – sometimes seen in children as young as five or six.

Cruelty to animals such as dogs, birds and cats (animals which scream, bleed and show fear), rather than the common, if horrid, practice of pulling the wings off flies.

Lastly – and perhaps most surprisingly since it is does not appear to be overtly hostile or destructive – is enuresis: defined as regular bed-wetting, which continues beyond the age of twelve.

With regard to this possibly puzzling third indicator, in *The Psycho-Analysis of Children* (1932) Melanie Klein, whose particular interest was psychotic conditions in children, draws upon Freudian theories concerning destructive and cannibalistic fantasies and sadistic behaviours of children which are rooted in oral-sadistic fantasies of the infant towards its mother, the object who holds the power to give or withhold satisfaction. When its hunger needs are not met, the infant reacts with rage and anxiety and interestingly, Klein observes that the sadistic tendency most closely allied to oral-sadism is what she calls 'urethral-sadism', an aggressive subconscious impulse by the child against the mother's body. Klein connects it with an extreme fantasy of 'flooding and destroying by means of enormous quantities of urine in terms of soaking, drowning, burning and poisoning', as 'a sadistic reaction to their having been deprived of fluid by their mother and ... ultimately directed against her breast'. She goes on to reiterate what I have stated above, the known connection between playing with fire and bed-wetting as 'merely the more visible and less repressed signs of the sadistic impulses which are attached to the function of urinating'.

Other factors are said to be indicative of potential violence in adult life, such as observing that the child indulges in prolonged day-dreaming (in fact, the suggestion is that he may be engaged in sadistic fantasies), and persistent lying and aggression. But of the three main behaviours – cruelty to sentient animals, fire-setting and bed-wetting in older children – many psychologists firmly believe that if a child displays two-thirds of that predictive triad, eventual aggression towards people is indicated. And of the three, deliberate, repetitive infliction of severe injuries upon animals is arguably the most specific sign. Studies have shown that children who are cruel to animals also show other aggressive behaviours such as temper tantrums, bullying and fighting. It is easy to see that a child who is not only unable to empathise with the suffering of an intelligent animal but is also eager to witness or inflict that suffering is not displaying normal behaviour. And neither, one might suggest, are grown men who display the same traits by revelling in cock-fighting, dog-fighting, hare-coursing or badger-baiting.

However, there are also other influences at work here. Many studies have also shown that severe parental punishments can foster aggression in children, predisposing them to animal cruelty. Some parents actively encourage their children – especially boys – to violate cultural norms and behave in aggressive ways, both with animals and other children, and since parents are primary role-models for their children, in such instances it would be more surprising if a child developed into a sensitive human being than if he became a bully and a thug. The absence of a 'stable and emotionally available father figure' will also increase the likelihood of a boy showing cruelty to dogs or cats, researcher Dr Alan R. Felthous claims, and points out that in a study of thirty-one 'motiveless' murderers, eighteen had a history of parental deprivation together with 'remorseless physical brutality' by a parent. Convincing statistics – until one pauses to consider that the remaining thirteen murderers presumably had not.

What does seem to be clear is that serial killers in general almost invariably suffer childhoods of emotional deprivation, are often from broken homes with a weak or absent father figure and a dominant mother. Discipline and demonstration of affection is inconsistent. Sometimes, crime is a way of life in families. Emotional abuse is very common, but there is also a relationship between killers who mutilate their victims and sexual abuse in childhood. According to one 1986 study[12] sexually-abused murderers are more likely to mutilate their victims (and to have begun their sadistic career by torturing animals) than those who were not sexually abused. Because the sadistic killer does not come from an environment of love and understanding, he grows up feeling rejected, alienated, worthless, frustrated by social failure, impotent and powerless. The relationship with the mother is usually dysfunctional – perhaps unsurprising since a child usually relies primarily upon its mother to fulfil its love and nurturing needs.

Robert Ressler, the FBI detective whose excellent book *Whoever Fights Monsters* delves into the lives of many serial killers, noted that as children they all grew up without any limits set upon their behaviour, without being taught right from wrong and without any comprehension that they must interact with and accommodate other people in the world around them. Consequently they are stunted at an egocentric stage of infantile development – that stage when babies understand that they are the centre of the universe and that others exist merely to fulfil their selfish demands. Normal development involves learning that this is not the case and educating children in these things – socialising them – is the task of the loving mother during the first half-dozen years of an infant's life, says Ressler. But the mothers of the murderers in his study, in addition to falling down on this duty of socialisation, also deprived their offspring of attention and affection. They never properly, actively loved their children but instead ignored them, pushed them out of the way. The child's relationships with other members of the family, such as siblings, were also absent. A perfect example here would be Ed Kemper, who told Ressler of returning home from primary school one day to find that he was being banished to the basement because he was so abnormally large, powerful and clumsy that he was making his sisters uncomfortable.

But is blaming sadistic murder on unhappy childhoods actually mistaking correlations for causes? There have always been bad homes, and in many of them other siblings of the offender have been equally badly treated, yet they have not become serial killers. Stanton E. Samenow, with his customary cynicism regarding the extent to which environment can shape an individual, remarks that criminals often claim that they were rejected by everyone of importance in their lives, but rarely say why. Suggesting that these embryo criminals are sneaky, defiant, untruthful, argumentative and manipulative of their parents, he submits that it is the criminal who rejects his parents rather than vice versa. Criminals may tell horrific tales of their deprived childhoods to portray themselves as victims, gain sympathy and avoid blame, but Samenow urges a deeper look into the family landscape: 'We ought not to limit our inquiries to what parents have done to children but strive to determine what children have done to their parents,' he advises. And perhaps, in this context, it might be worth reminding ourselves that Kemper was freely fantasising and slaughtering local pets by the time he was sent to sleep in that basement room, that long before puberty he had decapitated and cut the hands from his sister's doll and that as a child of seven he had said about a teacher he had a crush on: 'If I kiss her, I would have to kill her first.'

When people ask whether such men as Kemper, Gein, Fish and the rest are born or made, perhaps the truth lies somewhere between the two: that something in their neurological make-up has given them a predisposition towards such deviant behaviour and that real or imagined emotional deprivations in childhood enable this susceptibility to surface, just as someone whose genetic constitution predisposes them to heart trouble is more likely to bring this on if they eat fatty foods or take no exercise. The question that this invites, though, is whether that means killers like those in this book would have been diverted from their blood-drenched lusts if they had been loved and valued as children. Robert Ressler believes that the millions of people from deprived backgrounds which are as bad as or worse than those suffered by the killers catalogued here without growing up to kill, are 'saved' by forming other attachments – 'rescued by strong hands', as he says – in pre-adolescence.

In his book *Hunting Humans*, Elliott Leyton proposes something similar, suggesting that the vast majority of people who may have the same tainted origins can be averted from their murderous destiny by being 'touched' by some individual or institution which serves to make their lives bearable and offers them fulfilment. Leyton acknowledges, however, that this theory is impossible to prove in any scientific fashion, for we only have the end results to guide us. Florida psychologist Ann McMillan is doubtful and offers as an example Gerald Stano, executed in 1998 for murdering women (he confessed to forty-one murders, although, controversially, this number was later queried). For the first six months of Stano's life he suffered extreme neglect but was then adopted and raised by a loving couple. He still turned out to be a monster. 'Sometimes it's not going to matter who raises them,' says McMillan. 'If the parents were Mary and Joseph, it would still turn out the same.'

We have no evidence that, to cite a couple of examples, Richard Chase was the abused victim of an unhappy childhood or that Jeffrey Dahmer's childhood was emotionally barren – we know, for instance, that he had a doting grandmother. His time in the army offered another opportunity for achievement and integration, but he achieved neither. Much the same applies to Andrei Chikatilo. His childhood might have been economically harsh, but as far as it is possible to ascertain his mother was caring and although he was teased at school, this seems to have been no more unpleasant for him than it is for thousands of youngsters. In addition, he had a secure job, an attentive wife and a family who loved him. In fact, Chikatilo's psychiatrist Aleksandr Bukhanovsky appears to suggest that the principle reason Chikatilo became the cannibal killer of fifty-odd people was because he had been told a frightening story about cannibalism in his childhood

– which is exactly what Albert Fish gave as the 'reason' behind his deviant crimes.

Leyton also suggests that the serial killer is a product of his age and can be judged according to social theory principles. His ideas can be compared to Colin Wilson's somewhat startling assertion in his book *The Serial Killers* that there were no sex-killers before the late nineteenth century, mainly because life was hard for the working classes, and when they committed murder the motive was most likely to be robbery, not sex. Economic deprivation makes sex a secondary issue, Wilson states.

Leyton suggests that murder is a form of class assertion, since serial killers are primarily from the working classes or the lower middle classes, but feel alienated from and rejected by that class or the class that they wish to join. To illustrate his political point, he intellectualises that Gilles de Rais, who raped, tortured and killed 150 children in fifteenth-century France, could have been expressing an aristocratic fear of the power of the peasants, who were advancing themselves at this time and threatening his autocracy. Therefore, by murdering the children of peasants, de Rais was imposing the tyranny of his class. From here, Leyton goes on to say that murders like those committed by Kemper, the 'Co-ed Killer' he offers as an example, are not primarily sexual but social, citing Kemper's claim that he targeted young upper-class women because, he says: 'I was swashbuckling, I was destroying only society's finest young girls.' He adds to this Kemper's evidently weak sex-drive as supportive of his hypothesis.

Apart from the notion that self-esteem and self-aggrandisement play a part, I would question the speculative placing of a socio-cultural motive above the sex-drive. 'Death, not sex was the ecstasy,' says Elliott Leyton, interpreting the sexual aspect as merely a secondary benefit because it came after death. Other researchers have also suggested that the relief a killer feels is only coincidentally sexual. But this is applying healthy sexual norms to extreme deviance, where the sexual drive is operating at a much more primitive and atypical level. It ignores the sadistic fantasies which preoccupy such men and are used as a masturbatory aid. Death and blood are irrevocably tied up with sex because sexual stimulation is achieved only by incorporating them into the fantasy or the reality. These things replace normal sexual stimulation – but that does not make the murder non-sexual. The fact that lust-killers invariably kill within the sphere of their own sexual preferences would seem to support this. The stalking of a victim parallels foreplay and the killing represents the orgasm, offering either physical or mental release. The American sex-killer David Berkowitz once explained that after his first murder: 'I felt happy ... that built-up tension dissipated temporarily. While I didn't have a physical, sexual orgasm, I certainly had a mental one.' Dr Martin Orne, a psychiatrist from the University of Pennsylvania, believes sexual gratification is the primary motive and suggests that this might be why the victims of serial killers are usually superficially alike: the killers may simply pick victims that fit their sexual fantasies.

Sex and aggression become inextricably linked early in life for these men and they are unable to differentiate between them by the time they are adults – but how this happens is not precisely known. Can it really be as simple a matter as classical conditioning, as some suggest? It has been speculated that the physiological arousal from inflicting and experiencing pain is not unlike sexual excitement, therefore in the early stages of sexualisation it might be harder for some individuals to discriminate between them, especially if the pain-inducing act also includes sexual elements. Gein attributed his perverted behaviour to having seen pigs being butchered when he was in his teens – and this awakened his sex-drive. Albert Fish spoke of the cruelty he suffered and witnessed in his childhood; the infant Peter Kürten saw his brutal father rape his wife and thirteen-year-old daughter and then, at nine, he would enjoy watching the local rat-catcher torture and sexually violate animals, reinforcing the association of sex and cruelty in the child's mind. Jeffrey Dahmer found himself powerfully sexually attracted to viscera about the time he began dissecting animals at school and would masturbate while thinking about this, sexualising something which for most people, is non-sexual. Some psychiatrists[13] argue that the nature of the first sexual experience followed by orgasm at a critical stage of a person's development may be crucial for any establishment of sexual deviation, which is then maintained by fantasies of that behaviour. Of course, that 'critical stage' is individually variable.

That is not to say that this sort of childhood incident actually brings about such extreme deviation so much as that it draws upon an existing bias. For Fish, it must be remembered, recalled his childhood beatings with a pleasure which we assume his companions did not. Most people would find the sight of pigs being butchered anything but sexually stimulating – but not Gein. Dahmer's classmates also dissected animals in the biology lab – yet they did not find animal entrails alluring and were not, as Dahmer told police that he was, sexually aroused by the heat which came from a body during disembowelling. Is it possible that people really learn to enjoy such things, or are humans born with cruelty as a component of their nature? And if so, does that apply to some humans or all humans? Are some people more likely than others to adapt readily to killing?

If we imagine a scale of psychopathy (also called sociopathy) – that is, a continuum along which each of us may be placed according to the degree of the sociopathic traits we display, like narcissism, lack of reliability and responsibility, poverty of deep emotions, lack of shame and untruthfulness – we might hypothesise that, depending upon how far along this scale an individual is, life-events may elicit certain aggressive behaviours more effortlessly. Professor Anthony Storr, who has made a study of aggression and destructiveness, points out that some aggression is necessary in humans for advancement and survival. Total passivity (as demonstrated by the fictional Eloi in Wells's story *The Time Machine*) would ultimately result in our annihilation. But Professor Storr points out that compared to other animals, humans show a 'marked hereditary predisposition toward aggressive behaviour' and are exceptionally destructive. Between 1820 and 1945 a total of 59 million people died as a result of 'war, murder or other lethal activities' according to one researcher.[14]

History has indeed shown us that stewing not far beneath the veneer of civilisation are Man's brutally aggressive instincts – and it is primarily (although not exclusively) adult males under consideration here. Fuelled by the complexity of primitive emotional mechanisms, including suggestibility, such instincts can be aroused with relative ease when harnessed by religious dogma or a state's conditioning strategies. It is 2020, yet in some countries – those where religious dogma actually is the state's conditioning strategy – adulterous women might no longer be slaughtered and eaten by their accusers, but they may still be stoned to death, just as those who have suffered rape face similar death penalties. To appreciate the human capacity for deliberately causing suffering and agony with an excuse that one is just following orders, it has become customary to cite Adolf Hitler's Germany of the 1930s and 1940s, when the Nazi-led atrocities against Jews who were their fellow countrymen were driven by methods of population brainwashing identical to those which enabled the persecution and slaughter of 'witches' during the Middle Ages.

A disbelieving world's post-war pledge that such iniquity would never be repeated proved hollow when, two decades later in 1969, the ferocity of American soldiers towards unarmed Vietnamese villagers in a massacre at My Lai caused shockwaves. In the 1990s, events in Bosnia saw the planet reeling again, particularly at the acts of genocide committed by the Serbs and the Croats upon Muslims who had been, quite literally, their neighbours. They cited as 'justification' the instruction from President Franjo Tudjman of Croatia that:

'Genocide is a natural phenomenon, in harmony with the societal and mythologically divine nature. Genocide is not only permitted, it is recommended, even commanded by the word of the Almighty, whenever it is useful for the survival or the restoration of the kingdom of the chosen nation, or for the preservation and spreading of its one and only correct faith.[15]

When these are ideals which are embraced publicly and urged upon people whose learned compliance with authority – especially religious authority – is total, the bindings which keep primitive impulses in check can unravel with alarming speed to return some of us to a centuries-old culture where hatred can be a propaganda tool used by the powerful to manoeuvre the weak-minded into committing outrageous acts. The significant emergence in the twenty-first century of the suicide attacker prepared to lose his life when committing a murderous act of terror exemplifies clearly the degree of control that such manipulation can exert. This applies in particular to the rigid extremist dogma used by Islamic radicals, which promises far-fetched 'rewards' in Paradise to those who sacrifice themselves. The shocking realisation that there is nothing which the conditioned individual is not willing to do for a fanatical religious cause, fully hit home with the Western world when al-Qaeda attacked Washington and also New York's Twin Towers on 11 September 2001, using four hi-jacked passenger airliners. Including the nineteen al-Qaeda Islamic terrorist hijackers, 2,996 people died in the incidents. Despite the prompt condemnation of the attack by Muslim organisations in the USA, there were several instances of harassment and hate-crime attacks upon Muslims and their religious buildings during the days following the attack. The late-2001 retaliatory intervention by the USA and its allies to overthrow the Taliban regime in Afghanistan because of its harbouring of al-Qaeda members resulted in a significant US military presence in Afghanistan up to 2014 until their final departure in 2021, leaving the Taliban, a brutal and regressive regime, back in control of the country.

Meanwhile in the twenty years following the New York attack and the American reprisals in the Middle East, a new terrorist group of Islamic extremist terrorists rose up to declare war, not only on the West and other non-Muslim nations, but on Muslims who fail to share their particularly slender and ruthless interpretation of their religion. The so-called Islamic State (ISIS) spread cancerously through Iraq, Syria and other Middle East countries, its militias using barbaric methods of ethnic cleansing to drive hundreds of thousands of their opponents – men, women and children – from their homelands, torturing, executing or enslaving those who were captured. In 2014 al-Qaeda itself distanced itself from ISIS, citing the terrorists' 'notorious intransigence' as the reason. An international group of Muslim imams and Islamic scholars renounced ISIS as having 'misinterpreted Islam into a religion of harshness, brutality, torture and murder' which was 'an offence to Islam, to Muslims and to the entire world'.

But for many subsequent years, ISIS expanded to occupy an area in the Middle East the size of the British Isles and bragged of its global ambitions, resulting in the return to the region of Western and other military forces led by the USA to drive it out – which as the second decade of the twenty-first century neared its end appeared to have largely succeeded. One tactic which set ISIS apart from tyrannical regimes of recent centuries was its parading of its own hideous monstrosity to the world via the internet. Unlike other historic despotic systems which have tried to conceal the inhumanity of their atrocities, ISIS boasted about its own prehistoric barbarity, posting sickening scenes of primordial butchery on YouTube, so as to terrorise the enlightened world. Gruesome videos of the beheadings or live incineration of innocent captives and abductees – most of them humanitarian aid workers kidnapped in areas of conflict such as Syria – were shattering and created a sense of disbelief at these twenty-first century evolutionary anachronisms.[16]

Considering the genocides which the last century has seen, is it possible that every one of a regime's unspeakably cruel perpetrators can bear the label of psychopath, sadist, deranged psychotic – call them what you will? The Nazi concentration camp guards for instance. Surely they were not all of them sexual sadists? The Croat soldiers who in April 1993 set fire to Muslim women and children, who allegedly made weeping mothers hold their babies while they shot the infants dead – these were apparently 'normal' men. The human rights abuses of ISIS did not repel everybody. On the contrary, its policy of religious violence and terror attracted an alarming number of young Muslim males who were born, educated and raised in a cultural climate of freedom in Western countries but who, perhaps because of a low IQ-level, or because they felt – as teenagers frequently do – disaffected or disenfranchised in their home society, fell under the influence of radical clerics and agitators and travelled to Syria to fight, kill and frequently die alongside the ISIS terrorists. In February 2015, even the heir to the British throne, Prince Charles, was compelled to publicly proclaim in a radio interview his bewilderment, sorrow and concern about this 'alarming' radicalisation of young British people and the need to 'build bridges' between different faiths (although it has to be said that ISIS, despite a declared aim of creating an Islamic 'caliphate', showed by their actions that religious faith had little to do with such barbarity of political purpose).

It is a fact that killing becomes easier after the first time; research among the armed forces confirms this. Psychologist Paul Cameron, who conducted such research in 1976, also found that people who had killed before – as soldiers, for example – were more likely than those who have never killed at all to say they would murder for money, suggesting that inhibitions about murder are overcome relatively easily. The 'military theory' was the focus again in 2002 when a study of serial killers made by Castle and Hensley explored the correlation between serial killing and past military training. Castle and Hensley theorised that serial killing can be 'learned' during military training, which involves the desensitisation of soldiers for situations when, they learn, it is acceptable to kill, and they are rewarded with praise when they do so. In both military confrontation and serial killing, the desensitised offender or soldier may come to view his victims or, in the case of soldiers, their enemies, as not human.[17]

This suggests that very large numbers of 'normal' people can be induced to see others as disposable non-human objects with no worth, there to fulfil their own selfish desire – or as in the above cases, the warped religious or political directive of a regime. They may do this by abdicating personal responsibility and citing their obedience to authority, but, all the same, they have eschewed any constraints of conscience and have detached themselves from the suffering of the helpless person they are inflicting pain upon – exactly like the murderers under observation in this book. 'We cannot assume that the forces which account for aggression between nation-states are the same as those which drive individuals,' says Anthony Storr – but are not the same distancing devices at work? Can we not relate the ability of psychotic killers to reduce humans to the status of disposable objects, to what supposedly un-psychotic 'normal' people do in a war setting when they kill or degrade, their actions justified to themselves by a belief that even torture is sanctioned by whatever they take as their authority?

This transformation in the sadistic killer's imagination of living human into inanimate doll is an oft-repeated pattern, enabling him to feel powerful. Krafft-Ebing (1886) suggested that 'mastering and possessing an absolutely defenceless human object ... is part of sadism' – as it is, indeed, a primary ingredient of rape. Denigrating, dominating, hurting and humiliating a victim offers a sadist ultimate control and the need for control is an overwhelming motivating force. The more extreme the controlling devices the more powerful the controller is in his own mind and the more helpless the victim, the more like an object he or she becomes. Chikatilo blindfolded his victims and cut out their tongues to prevent them seeing and speaking; Dahmer became obsessed with turning his homosexual conquests into zombies by drilling into their heads; Kürten regarded all his victims simply as throwaway objects for his enjoyment and never expressed remorse about their fates; Chase admitted killing baby David Ferreira and decapitating him to 'get at the blood', but said that at the time he thought the baby was 'something else'; Kemper described: 'making a doll out of a human being ... and carrying out my fantasies with ... a living human doll.' And the ultimate control is devouring a victim.

Search History

'O wonder!
How many godly creatures are there here!
How beauteous mankind is! O brave new world,
That has such people in't!'

William Shakespeare, *The Tempest*, Act Five, Scene 1

One of the primary faculties which distinguishes humans from lower species is the possession of an imagination of astonishing richness. As my frontispiece quotation from Goya declares, imagination is a wondrous thing, the 'origin of our marvels', responsible for all human intellectual achievement whether technological or scientific, the greatest works of art and literature or the ability to empathise by imagining ourselves in another's shoes. But this most precious quality is ripe for sabotage. The power of imagination is exploited to incite and fuel a group's hatred and aggression towards an opposing faction or country, religion or race. Numerous psychological studies have shown that when group obedience to authority is obtained, the individual conscience is subdued and personal responsibility is abdicated, assigned to leaders. Thus, as outlined in the previous chapter, human beings are induced to dehumanise their perceived enemies and inflict cruelties upon them, a process which bears comparison to that of the psychopathic sadistic lust-killer. Imagination inspires him and, already devoid of conscience and the inhibitory devices which constrain the normally-socialised man, he lives out his fantasies, amply demonstrating in microcosm the human potential for cruelty and destructiveness which our history has displayed in macrocosm.

Since male aggression and sexuality are hormonally linked, it has been suggested that boys who grow up to be sex killers are often regarded in childhood as having been very highly sexed, but they are not alone in enjoying deviant fantasies. Research has shown that a proportion of 'normal' men engage in controlling and sadistic fantasies.[18] Yet only a tiny fraction of these fail to contain the fantasies within their own imaginations, permitting a spillage which leads to the horrific realities contained in this book and elsewhere. Why this happens, and why only some men entertain such controlling fantasies in the first place has not been answered satisfactorily, although causes such as childhood sexual assaults, feelings of inadequacy and poor social relationships are suggested as possible factors. What does seem likely is that the reality of a normally-socialised man's life is rewarding enough for him to keep his reveries locked up in his head, whereas the sadistic killer's real life is so unsatisfactory to him that the addictive fantasies devour him, assuming a disproportionate importance and coming to take the place of reality. We find that in childhood and adolescence the sadist has retreated into his violent imagination instead of forming relationships with others, until one day the fantasies cannot be contained and he ritually acts out his dream. As Colin Wilson points out in his 1990 book *The Serial Killers*: 'For the sexual criminal, the most important step is the one that bridges the gap between fantasy and actuality.' And for the criminal investigator, the nature of a man's fantasies is a valuable forensic key to identifying the sadistic killer, as was outlined in a 2014 article about violent offenders' fantasy histories: 'Importance of Finding the Offender's Pornography Stash'.[19]

A sexual sadist's fantasies can sometimes be so rich that they alone can induce orgasm. During one of his terms of imprisonment, Peter Kürten had no need to masturbate or indulge in homosexual acts with his fellow-prisoners, but perfected a technique whereby he imagined sadistic acts or scenes of death and this would cause him to ejaculate. The 'imaginative revolution' – an advance in our imaginative capacity over the past couple of centuries – can, suggests Colin Wilson, account for the rise in fetishism (sexual stimulation derived from a non-erotic, inanimate object) and other sexual perversions. 'Hundreds of years ago,' he claims in his 1988 book *The Misfits: A Study of Sexual Outsiders*, 'imaginative powers concerning sexuality were more limited.' (Although the wealth of erotica and evidence of deviant behaviour to be found among all ancient cultures could challenge this postulation.) Quoting Tolstoy's view that there is so much leisure in the modern world that people spend a large part of their time dreaming about sex and distorting and exaggerating the sexual image, Wilson studies various forms of sexual abnormality and concludes that sexuality has evolved to a 'higher' level beyond that of mere reproduction, to a 'symbolic' plane, where people can be stimulated by ideas to nourish their imaginations.

The optimistic hope that these ideas will always augment or benefit the lives of the general populace is dashed as Wilson focuses on the opposite, especially the sexual cruelties – both imagined and real – which inflamed the Marquis de Sade, resulting in a thirty-two-year incarceration until his death in the early nineteenth century at the Paris asylum, where his last five years had been spent in solitary confinement. Pornography increasingly became available during the Victorian era and its sometimes bizarre nature proved instructive for the general public, Wilson suggests. While many were galvanised at the discovery of an imaginative world of promised satiation, a fault-line simultaneously materialised during that period according to Wilson – and this was the significant appearance of sex-crime. The debate about the correlation between sex-crime and pornography continues today, especially since the advent of the internet, which permits any imaginative or deviant desire to be nourished, either in secret or among others with a similar appetite.

If we were to identify a logical link between pornographic images and the thought-processes of rapists and sex killers, the most obvious would likely be the depersonalisation and degradation of the female, for it is inarguable that pornography portrays women as non-threatening objects to be manipulated sexually for male gratification, comparable to the way that rapists, sadists and murderers objectify them. Yet, despite studies like that in 1983 by American sociologists Straus and Baron, which showed that rates of forcible rape were higher in states where the soft porn 'girly pic' magazine *Playboy* sold better, during the intervening thirty-eight years, empirical research has found sparse evidence to support a relationship between adult males' exposure to non-violent pornography and sex crime. On the contrary, several researchers suggest that the liberalisation of a growing pornography industry in recent decades correlates with an overall decrease in rape and sexual violence (although dissenters from this view point to other contributory factors such as more assiduous law enforcement and punishment). Certainly, research figures from as far back as 1970 show that while sexual criminals invariably collect pornography, so indeed do many non-criminals – and although repeated exposure to porn is generally judged to have negative social and personal effects on users, ninety-nine per cent of them do not commit sex crimes.[20]

From the start, however, most researchers asked the wrong question. Back in 1984 psychologists Edward Donnerstein and Neil Malamuth asked the right one. It was not specifically about sex criminals but about the wider effect of pornography, especially aggressive pornography, upon male attitudes. They asked: could it increase observers' acceptance of sexual aggression towards women? And their answer was a confident 'yes': the quantity of this sort of violent pornographic material viewed by men influenced their perceptions of women and was positively correlated with the degree to which they endorsed sexual assault, leading to an increase in their aggressive sexual fantasies.

Malamuth and Donnerstein, working either together or with other academics, have recorded this result consistently in their subsequent research into the impact of media violence upon human nature. For example, in 2010 Malamuth, Hald and Yuen declared a link between the consumption of violent pornography and 'rape-supportive' attitudes in certain populations of men, while in 2014 Donnerstein wrote in the *Encyclopedia of Media Violence* that, after viewing violent pornography, men not only displayed desensitized 'calloused attitudes' about rape, but that a common pornographic theme – that women derive pleasure from sexual aggression – produced in them a justification of aggressive behaviour and a reduction of 'aggressive inhibitions'. This carries an echo of the 1976 pornography research by Gager and Schurr concerning the misrepresentation of sadism as a source of sexual pleasure for women who, after their initial resistance is overcome, thereafter 'wallow in physical abuse and degradation'. They noted: 'It is the pattern of horror which we have seen in our examination of sex cases translated again and again into actual assaults.'

In 2011 the first of an 'erotic romance' series of novels expressing precisely this theme became the fastest-selling paperback of all time. Although amateurishly-written by first-time author E. L. James, the novel *Fifty Shades of Grey*'s explicit scenes of sado masochism captured the attention of the world and resulted in 100 million sales. In 2015 a film adaptation came out on general release in cinemas and made a record-breaking $85 million in the USA during its first weeks; its 2017 and 2018 sequels performed similarly. E. L. James published four more 'Grey' novels, such was the popularity of the work.

The Marquis de Sade, then, turned out to be something of a prophet from his lonely cell. The man who gave his name to sexual torture and mutilation stories – which will sicken any reader who naively imagines they feature only a little consensual bondage and light spanking – died in 1814. Sexual sadism may not be new, but much has changed in 200 years. In the early nineteenth century, a devotee of sadism dreaded exposure and feared the law. Widespread illiteracy ensured a limited readership for books such as Sade's and aside from medical or legal professionals, relatively few educated citizens would have had much awareness of such depraved inclinations.

Even until a few decades ago, when violent pornography was starting to become more widely available in the Western world, obtaining it was not easy, the enthusiast having to slink shamefully into sleazy shops, have brown-paper packages arriving by mail order or, with the very extreme material, having to risk legal punishment by smuggling such material through customs. When I wrote the first edition of this book in 1993, it would have seemed preposterous to predict that within ten years such covert purchasing methods would be rendered redundant by a device installed in every home which can nurture the specific fantasies of all the deviants on the planet – in secret, involving no shame and no recriminations. Easy access to the internet has ensured that there is little sexual behaviour which remains a mystery – even to the very young – and that includes online pornography, which presents the fusion of aggression and sexuality as just another option for the sexually adventurous.

The assumption that the pornography industry is all about sex is erroneous; its primary purpose has always been to make money. More pornographic movies are produced each year than those which go on general release. On the World Wide Web, as we enter the third decade of the twenty-first century, porn is far and away the most prolific and lucrative business in operation, representing thirty per cent of profits across the entire internet industry. There are now more than 300,000,000 pages of pornography on the Net and these attract more visitors each month than Amazon, Twitter and Netflix put together. At any one moment, according to CBS News, almost 30,000 people are viewing online pornography and this includes children and teenagers, who are unhealthily influenced by it. Such viewing by teenage girls, conditions not only their dissatisfaction with their own physical appearance compared to that of the 'actresses' they see, but also influences their expectations of the sort of audacious sexual behaviour which is required of them in normal relationships. Social media sites such as Facebook have created a theatre for the 'selfie' photograph, where scantily clad girls can model themselves on porn stars, both in the overtly sexual pouts and intimate poses they display and the unambiguously sexualised language which is used when conversing with males. Frequently there is a lack of understanding that once in the public arena, these photographs and 'chats' will be eternally accessible to everyone, not just to their own contacts.

Even very young teenage girls in the Western world now seek or yearn for cosmetic surgery in a quest to perfect their bodies in alignment with those of the females who perform in pornographic videos which are freely available on the internet; one of the most significant results of this is girls' now-commonplace removal of their pubic hair – a relatively modern phenomenon in screened pornography, introduced for reasons of visual explicitness. Young males, whose real-life desires are similarly influenced by the pornography they watch, concur with this view, concluding that pubic hair is unsightly, unclean and even repulsive. (A commercial response is reflected in beauty clinics: where once there was bikini-line waxing, now there is the full 'Brazilian' and its variations.) The way that this recent craze infantilises the female body is particularly disturbing, especially since there is an elision of boundaries on the internet between so-called 'teen porn' – which accounts for one-third of total searches at 500,000 per day – and child pornography, for which there are 116,000 daily searches. The US's National Center for Missing and Exploited Children (NCMEC) estimated in 2003 that twenty per cent of all pornography traded over the internet was child pornography, and that since 1997 the number of child pornography images available had increased by 1,500 per cent.

In 2007, the British-based Internet Watch Foundation charity reported a fourfold rise in brutal and graphic child abuse images on the internet and in 2018, this figure was up by another third. Internet grooming of children surged to an all-time high during the Covid lockdowns of 2020 and 2021: the Foundation confirmed that in 2021 they identified 252,000 web-pages, each depicting thousands of images of sexual abuse including sadistic violence and the rape and torture of children – including infants, babies and toddlers, eighty per cent of the child victims being female. This was nearly double the 2020 figure. The fastest-growing increase in such material occurred among seven- to ten-year-olds. Thanks to the work of the Foundation, the majority of the web-pages they uncovered were removed from the internet.[21]

It is indisputable that the internet, which held so much glittering promise at its inception, has become a playground for sociopaths and paedophiles, its boundaries seemingly impossible to control. Trying to get this ever-expanding evil genie back into the bottle is an exercise in futility and the pre-electronic ways in which paedophiles used to obtain their illegal material – which were easier for the authorities to police – are all but obsolete. According to the US Department of Justice, the radical changes in reproduction and distribution of child pornography are to blame for the 'massive increase' in the availability, accessibility, and volume of it. This includes the use of digital cameras and credit cards and the ease of transferring images across national borders. The proliferation of child-abuse sites, together with the online grooming of children and teenagers by predators or 'web-stalking' paedophiles who use chat-rooms and social media sites as a means of entrapping a child or teenager, is proving a legislative and expensive challenge for governments to control.

Distribution and possession of child pornography is a criminal offence in almost all Western countries and there are international movements to try and globalise this criminalisation, but identifying and convicting online predators involves crime-fighters in lengthy undercover operations with no certainty of conviction or punishment – sometimes the operators' work can avert a planned crime but this can result in a 'catch-22' situation, where because of the investigators' success, the intended crime is not committed, and a perpetrator's true intent becomes difficult to prove. As Joseph V. DeMarco, an internet lawyer and former head of the cybercrime unit in the federal prosecutor's office in New York says: 'As much as we like to think of things happening "in cyberspace", the reality is that internet and email are simply new methods of communication and that when those communications involve planning crimes, the fact that the planning is done online is fundamentally no different than when it happens on the telephone, or for that matter, in person.'

It is worth noting that even non-sexual screen violence has a brutalising effect, especially on those whose emotions have already been flattened by their experience of life. Albert Bandura and Alberta Siegel's famous experiments way back in 1969 were the first to show conclusively how aggressive behaviour in children increased after they had been exposed to violent scenes in films. Yet every year scores of 'slasher' movies – with a teenage target market – continue to go out on general release, a tribute to those special-effects wizards who have ceased creating 'screen magic' in favour of 'screen mutilation'. The explicitness of the images in these films is subject to more control than the sadistic pornography which can be accessed on the internet, but in either case, screen violence feeds the imagination in entirely the wrong way.

Considering that sadistic pornography was a preoccupation of all the killers who appear in this book, might we blame it for actually directing their fantasies? Gein's dark crypt was stacked with it – and so was Dahmer's bedroom. Chikatilo claimed that sadistic pornography had incited his acts and an FBI survey of sex murderers showed that seventy per cent of them felt 'sexually incompetent' and relied heavily on visual stimuli such as pornography. But saying that such images may reinforce the acceptability of sexual aggression in someone's mind is not the same as blaming violent pornography for actually causing a man to become a sadistic cannibal killer. Ed Kemper pored over detective magazines for pictures of corpses, read pornographic magazines and watched 'snuff' movies (where real-life murder is purported to be depicted), but said, with some honesty: 'That didn't make me mean. It just fuelled the fire.'

But what starts this particular fire in the first place? We might be able to attribute most crime – including murder – to social conditions, psychodynamics, personality disorders, resentments and lusts, but an overwhelming majority of even the most amoral of criminals would balk at the idea of being sexually stimulated by disembowelment, blood-drinking and flesh-eating ... wouldn't they? But consider: how many of these would find the idea of committing rape arousing? How many would still find it stimulating if the rape was accompanied by injury which draws blood, because the sight of blood sparks some excitement in their instinctive response? The number of men who do respond to such images will be proportionately fewer as the images increase in violence and depravity, finally degenerating into cannibalism – but theoretically maybe it's simply a matter of degree. There is certainly no shortage of cases within psychiatric and psychoanalytical literature – or on the internet, of course – which confirm the sensual fascination which blood and pain exert upon some people.

If we acknowledge that vampirism and cannibalism played a part in human evolution, then we should perhaps accept that at the deeper levels of the psyche, common to all modern humans must be vestiges of these inclinations and desire for supernatural beliefs, in the same way that the human body contains physical vestiges of our evolutionary stages. Psychologist Carl Gustav Jung called this concept the 'collective unconscious', identifying various archetypal images that make contact with some primitive aspects of man – and one of these archaic vestiges is likely to be an appetite for blood. 'An archetype is like an old watercourse along which the water of life has flowed for centuries, digging a deep channel for itself. The longer it has flowed in this channel the more likely it is that sooner or later the water will return to its old bed,' said Jung.[22] The combined spiritual and sexual power attached to blood runs like a secret underground stream in the primitive depths of the human subconscious dating back to man's early religions and superstitions and harnessed to his desire to eat human meat and drink human blood. We conclude that cannibal killers function at this same primitive level.

In sexual relations, biting is not considered to be abnormal and neither is the love-bite – but at what point does a love-bite come to be considered deviant? Vampirism usually occurs in association with another psychiatric condition like schizophrenia or mental deficiency, but blood-drinking which does not necessarily result in death is suspected to be more common than most of us imagine. A research trawl on the internet offers enlightenment. In addition to the inevitable fan sites devoted to a cult inspired by so many vampire heroes and anti-heroes of written fiction and movies, there are sites to be found which claim to be run by and for 'real' vampires. Some are dating sites for 'real' vampires. Another offers advisory tit-bits such as 'The best way to get a willing donor for human blood is to find an Emo'. An Emo, the website states confidently, will willingly cut him or herself and will enjoy the attention of a 'real vampire'. But, the text cautions: 'Make sure they are of legal age'.

In the non-cyber world of crime and medicine, however, few patients or offenders are likely to confide such activities on their own initiative, said Professor Herschel Prins of the University of Leicester, England, who spent more than sixty years working and lecturing in criminal justice and forensic mental health until his death in May 2016. Professor Prins was one of Britain's foremost researchers into vampiristic activity as part of bizarre sexual behaviour, speaking of the 'dual but highly related worlds of mythical and clinical vampirism', and explaining sadistic, biting fantasies as an extension of the vampire's 'kiss', linking the subconscious urges which feed such fantasies and behaviour with the notion of being able to perpetuate life, which the vampire in its 'undead' state, has achieved, able as it is to balance life and death. In his 1990 book *Bizarre Behaviours: Boundaries of Psychiatric Disorder*, Professor Prins gives several examples of people with no apparent associated mental disorder whose desire to drink blood had brought them to the attention of the police or psychiatrists, one nineteen-year-old man saying he believed fresh human blood had a 'supernatural quality' which would grant him immortality. As sexologist Havelock Ellis said in 1903:

'The result of the love-bite in its extreme form is to shed blood... the mingled feelings of close contact, of passionate gripping, of symbolic devouring ... with some persons ... the love-bite is really associated with a conscious desire, even if more or less restrained, to draw blood, a real delight in this process, a love of blood. Probably this only occurs in persons who are not absolutely normal ...'[23]

A pair of researchers[24] in 1971 reported a ritual practised by a married couple: as a prelude to sexual intercourse, the young man would draw blood by cutting a small incision on the palm of his wife's right hand. She would then stimulate his penis, using the blood of her right palm as a lubricant.

Among other reported cases are those of a twenty-year-old man in prison for larceny who submitted to homosexual acts in return for being allowed to suck his partner's blood, because blood had excited him sexually since, as a small child, he had felt stimulated by the sight of road-kill dogs; men and women who reported violent sexual excitement when sucking blood from an incision in a partner's flesh and a man who enjoyed drinking his own blood so much that he perfected a technique of directing blood from an artery directly into his mouth. More unusual still was the disturbed woman whose fantasy was to capture a docile young girl, 'to kiss her breasts, then tear or bite them off and eat them ... I would at last find my way to the heart and then drink the heart's blood, then pluck out the heart and perhaps eat it.'[25]

Many researchers besides Herschel Prins are of the opinion that erotic vampiristic and cannibalistic impulses are by no means rarities.[26] Professor Prins posed the question: is vampirism merely a pathological extension of the 'love-bite' which is practised in normal sexual relations, possibly serving to satisfy very basic oral/sadistic needs which are present, to a greater or lesser extent, in all of us?

But then, what is 'normal'? What is the point at which vampiristic behaviour begins and ends on the 'normal' continuum? Could all sexual behaviour be placed on such a continuum, with loving, reciprocal, non-injurious sex placed at the top, and with the imaginary graph-line plunging downwards through behaviour such as so-called date-rape (a possible term for 'non-sadistic' rape) to rape with excessive violence, infliction of injury, mutilation. On such a continuum, which is also irrevocably tied up with the assertion of power, deviant behaviour like vampirism, sadism, and cannibalism would be down at the lowest point as urges which are only enacted by the few ... down, as into the depths of man's unconscious, down towards the primitive, the ungodly, the unspeakable: the depraved cannibal killers at the bottom of the pit.

Writers of fiction have exploited our subconscious primeval urges towards blood-letting and blood-drinking and, when the vampire took centre-stage, the sexual aspect was powerfully reinforced. The myth of the male vampire was a pervasive form of inspiration for the romantic poets and gothic writers of the late eighteenth and early nineteenth centuries, producing a romantic male archetype, a 'Fatal Man' who, according to Mario Praz in his book of the same name, can be identified in works ranging from Milton's Satan (in his book *Paradise Lost*) to Byron's heroes. By the time that Bram Stoker wrote Dracula in 1897 there were also other nineteenth-century concerns to exploit. Charles Darwin's evolutionary theories published between 1859 and 1871 served to heighten fears that 'higher' and 'lower' urges struggled for primacy within a single individual and that the more savage and degenerate side of human nature constantly bubbled beneath the surface façade of civilisation. Such ideas inspired other books from that period, such as Oscar Wilde's *The Picture of Dorian Gray* in 1891 and Robert Louis Stevenson's *The Strange Case of Dr Jekyll and Mr Hyde* in 1886.

The evolution of the vampire from historical legend into nineteenth-century fiction created a fiend quite unlike all other fearsome supernatural monsters because of the mesmeric seduction and blatant forbidden pleasure of sexuality involved in the blood-letting process, inspired, one can speculate, by the Romanian vampire Nosferatu, which legendarily raped women at the same time as sucking their blood. As with the real-life cannibal killers contained in this book, the three main components of sexuality, blood and death became fused in Stoker's vampire. For instance, when the half-asleep Jonathan Harker is surrounded by three beautiful vampire women at Dracula's castle, his feelings are ambiguous in this extract:

'There was something about them that made me uneasy, some longing and at the same time some deadly fear. I felt in my heart a wicked, burning desire that they would kiss me with those red lips ... I lay quiet ... in an agony of delightful anticipation ... The fair girl went on her knees and bent over me, fairly gloating. There was a deliberate voluptuousness which was both thrilling and repulsive.' (*Dracula*, pp. 37–8)

The blatant sexual symbolism in the above passage leaves nothing to the imagination of the sophisticated twenty-first century reader, any more than does the scene where, in a curious reversal of the usual relationship between vampire and victim, Dracula forces Mina Harker to drink blood from his chest – symbolically an act of enforced fellatio with blood being a substitute for semen:[27]

'With his left hand he held both Mrs. Harker's hands ... his right hand gripped her by the back of the neck, forcing her face down on his bosom. Her white nightdress was smeared with blood, and a thin stream trickled down the man's bare breast ... The attitude of the two had a terrible resemblance to a child forcing a kitten's nose into a saucer of milk to compel it to drink.' (*Dracula*, p.282)

Historically, this suggestion of sexual symbolism has much to commend it in explanatory terms. If we glance backwards through the sort of tribal belief-systems catalogued in an earlier chapter, including modern-day cultist activity, one learns that blood, semen, urine and other bodily substances play a part, each thought to be endowed with special mystical or medicinal powers which could be absorbed by others to their benefit; for example, seminal fluid from animals was thought to ensure virility (alas, similar absurd Eastern beliefs still persist about animal substances such as rhino-horn, resulting in a great many endangered species). According to folklore, vampires and succubi craved human semen as well as blood. And as has been shown, the most significant spiritual life-essence, assigned a special importance, was blood.[28]

Fictionally, vampirism is also used as a metaphor for interpreting interpersonal dynamics, in which one person absorbs the energy, exploits or destroys another – something else which finds its roots in primitive human practices such as eating one's enemies or the corpses of venerated tribal elders. As in myth, the victim of a vampire's bite also becomes a vampire – there is a merging of the feeder and the victim. Interestingly, this merging delusion has been offered by cannibalistic and other murderers as a 'reason' for their actions. Just as Britain's infamous necrophile serial killer Dennis Nilson declared that he killed, sexually violated and dismembered fifteen young men because he wanted company and his actions ensured they would always be with him, a similar symbolic explanation came from Jeffrey Dahmer. He too tried to control and keep his victims around because they wanted to leave.

Dr Judith Becker, hired by Dahmer's attorney Gerald Boyle, said at the murder trial that Dahmer admitted that cannibalism gave him a sexual thrill. 'He felt that the man was a part of him and he internalised him. He reported having an erection while eating,' she revealed. Ed Kemper said he cut flesh from his victims' legs and ate it because 'I wanted them to be a part of me – and now they are,' explaining at his trial that it was 'the only way they could be mine. I had their spirits. I still have them.' The German cannibal Armin Meiwes, who is the subject of the next chapter, claimed that his ability to speak English improved after he had eaten his fluent English-speaker victim – and it is not such a leap of logic to interpret Issei Sagawa's sexual and cannibalistic preference for large, healthy women as a desire to absorb the robustness of a victim who would counter his own weakness and sense of physical insignificance.

As the anthropologist M. Sahlins observed: 'Cannibalism is always "symbolic" even when it is real.'[29]

'Genghis Khan with a telegraph'

(Nineteenth-century Russian dissident Alexander Herzen's warning against equipping non-advanced societies with progressive technology)

The marvellous innovation of that global communications system known as the World Wide Web is evolutionary evidence of cumulative brilliance, the creative geniuses and prodigies of the modern world standing upon the shoulders of history's intellectual giants. Yet it has taken no time at all for this exalted networking instrument to have been exploited and debased by the greedy, corrupt and malevolent to disseminate their individual brands of awful propaganda. In 2019 actor and writer Sacha Baron Cohen denounced online social media's 'free speech' advertising policy, which permitted the transmission of lies such as Holocaust denial as 'the greatest propaganda machine in history'. If Facebook had been around in the 1930s, he said, 'it would have allowed Hitler to post thirty-second ads on his "solution" to the "Jewish problem".'[30] His view appeared to gain authenticity when, in 2021, data scientist Frances Haugen, a former Facebook employee, disclosed to *The Wall Street Journal* and US news TV shows including *60 Minutes* that the organisation was well aware of the harmful effects caused by the misuse of its platforms to amplify misinformation such as conspiracy theories, hate speech and divisive political material. But she alleged that the company hides this knowledge in order to protect its profits.

Thirty-seven-year-old Haugen – who also testified before the Senate committee with her claims, backed by tens of thousands of copied pages of Facebook internal research into algorithms – also drew attention to the damage caused to teenage girls' body image perceptions in the case of the Facebook subsidiary, Instagram. Claiming that the company incentivises 'angry, polarising and divisive content', Haugen said that she believed the founder of Facebook, Mark Zuckerberg, had not intended to create a 'hateful platform' but that data choices were made with the side-effect that such content gets more distribution and reach. She commented: 'The thing I saw at Facebook ... was there were conflicts of interest between what was good for the public and what was good for Facebook ... Over and over again [Facebook] chose to optimise for its own interests, like making more money.' Facebook, she said, 'is tearing our societies apart and causing ethnic violence around the world.' She offered as evidence the genocide in Myanmar (formerly Burma) in February 2021, when the military used Facebook to propagandise its coup. She also cited the 2020 US election and its historical aftermath, the January 2021 violent insurrection at the US Capitol building – a far-right crowd whipped into a frenzy by former president Donald Trump seemingly trying to mimic the Myanmar methodology to overturn his election loss – demonstrates the fragility of Western democracies. It reinforces Frances Haugen's remark: 'It's easier to inspire people to anger than it is to other emotions.'[31]

As my previous chapter indicated, the mediaeval savagery of genocidal terrorists who have broadcast videos of their bloody deeds using web technology far exceeding the 'telegraph' of Alexander Herzen's nightmare, is just the tip of the primal iceberg. On the 'deep net' Tor networks, constructed of complex nodal connections which conceal a person's IP (Internet Protocol) address, there is satisfaction available to be discovered by society's cyber-savvy outcasts, perverts or felons, whether their interests lie in obtaining weaponry or other illegal items and substances, hiring assassins or accessing extreme outlawed sexual material and sharing their particular obsessive cravings with similar enthusiasts in near-anonymity, thereby obtaining mutual or group validation of their sexual aberration. 'The Web' is fittingly named, for the forbidden 'deep net' sites are located amid an infinite complexity of interlinked strands in cyberspace, routing paths in an ungoverned network of networks. This presents cyber-investigators with time-consuming problems in establishing criminals' identity, proof of intent and also of boundary-definition for legal systems anchored in the real world – known by some users as 'Meatspace' or 'Real Life'.

For Armin Meiwes – who was a computer expert – it was simplicity itself to access the dark and hidden reaches of cyberspace which reflected his own psyche and, left alone after the death of his mother in 1999, he began to do just that. Psychiatrist Heinrich Wilmer, who examined Meiwes after his arrest, speculated that the motivation for his actions was not so much sexual but more to do with childhood devastation at paternal and family abandonment – his father had emptied the family bank accounts and departed when Meiwes was a child, followed later by Armin's two half-siblings. The psychiatrist believed that being placed in a position in which he bore all responsibility for his mother was something for which Meiwes had not been prepared. Could this have created a deviant urge in him? It was an urge which was to be sated – for a while – after his online exchanges and subsequent meeting with Bernd Brandes at his home, Wüstefeld Manor, in 2001.

To those who met him, Brandes was a likeable man who had the respect of his work colleagues at Siemens in Berlin. No one was aware of his sexual masochism. An ex-girlfriend later talked on a German TV station about their healthy sex life, while his gay lover told detectives that he and Brandes had been very happy together and were making travel plans. Brandes did not have a death wish, nor was he suicidal, he said, upset and bewildered; Brandes had certainly never revealed that he wanted to be slaughtered and eaten. It would later emerge that Brandes had made a will two months prior to his internet encounter with Meiwes. The subsequent online conversations between Brandes and Meiwes conjure up a grotesque parody of a courtship. Early on, they made small-talk about themselves and their excitement at meeting each other, although, said Brandes, 'I would have rather met you yesterday and felt your teeth.' Subsequent chats concerned slaughter, the difference in consistency of a raw and fried penis, the taste of blood (Meiwes described sampling his own blood and finding it 'quite tasty ... a real treat'), and what would happen to Brandes's body after death. They arranged to meet at Meiwes's home a few days later and, after selling all of his belongings including his car, on 9 March 2001 Brandes left work early 'for personal reasons' and set off on his final journey on this earth.

The two men kissed and behaved affectionately with each other for a little time, until Brandes asked Meiwes to fulfil his personal fantasy and bite off his penis. It was a mission which met with failure. So after accepting a large dose of painkillers and much alcohol from Meiwes, Brandes placed his penis on a table and, taking a knife, Meiwes amputated it. Amid a profusion of blood and the screams of Brandes, there was an attempt by both of the men to eat the organ, but finding it fibrous and hard to chew it was instead fried with wine and garlic. However, it became burnt and inedible and, Meiwes said later, he ended up feeding it to his dog. With Brandes in pain and weakened from blood-loss, Meiwes insisted he take a huge overdose of sleeping pills with a bottle of schnapps, then he left Brandes to bleed to death in the bath. It was nine hours before Brandes lost consciousness, hours which Meiwes whiled away by reading a *Star Trek* adventure book. Eventually, Meiwes kissed the unconscious Brandes before stabbing him in the neck to kill him. Then he hung the corpse on a meathook in the 'slaughter room' and, following some butchery instructions for cannibals which he had found on the internet, he cut it into manageable chunks to store in the freezer. These would provide him with food over the next ten months.

Finally, Armin Meiwes turned off the video camera.

The video movies which had been removed from Wüstefeld Manor ended any initial notions which the investigators had entertained that, together with Meiwes's confession, they had a straightforward, open-and-shut murder case. True, the films were evidence of Meiwes's actions, being a visual record of the ghastly events of March 2001 – the previous year – but they also included footage at the beginning where Brandes stated his voluntary agreement to everything which had been planned and thereafter his collusion in it. There was footage in which Meiwes suggested calling an emergency doctor when Brandes was bleeding to death – and Brandes's recorded refusal to allow this. So was this murder after all? And if not, then what criminal charge were they going to level at Meiwes? While prosecutors mulled over this dilemma, Meiwes's defence lawyer, Harald Ermel, reminded them that cannibalism was not a recognised criminal offence in Germany. And, he added, since Brandes had been a willing participant, the only crime with which Meiwes could be charged was that of assisted suicide, punishable by a maximum five-year prison sentence. Meanwhile, as the legal quandaries were lengthily grappled with, Meiwes was held in custody and psychiatrists queued up to interview and examine him.

Was he mad or bad? This was a vital issue to be addressed by the assessing clinicians. 'For to define true madness, what is't but to be nothing else but mad?' asks Polonius in Shakespeare's play *Hamlet* and it is certainly tempting to declare as mad the terrorists, tyrants and sexually sadistic murderers – or anyone, in fact, who commits acts so unthinkably heinous and challenging to our concept of humanity that our gut reaction is to declare that these people must be deranged. But there is also the question of whether a truly insane person is capable of systematic, carefully-planned and chillingly-executed murder. These types of killers share certain traits which make them dangerous, such as single-minded certainty of purpose and the conscience-free ruthlessness to carry out that purpose and reap its reward – the reward being, in the case of sexual sadists and cannibal killers, erotic gratification.

So, are they really sick or just sickening? It is common for criminals to claim that insanity drove their actions, especially in a country or state where there is still capital punishment which they hope to side-step. And certainly it is hard to imagine in what way can a man be judged sane who talks, as Ed Kemper did, of the sexual thrill obtained from decapitating somebody: 'You hear that little pop and pull their heads off and hold their heads up by the hair. Whipping their heads off, their body sitting there. That'd get me off.'

The compulsion to murder for a motive such as greed or jealousy or revenge can be acknowledged by the average person, if not condoned. But many people would declare that such a man as Meiwes, or Kemper, or Chikatilo must be crazy to do what they did. However, the legal criteria used to define insanity can differ significantly from the medical criteria and will frequently clash with common opinion. The burden of proving insanity lies with the defence. At Jeffrey Dahmer's trial, his attorney Gerald Boyle contended that his client's extreme perversions showed he was a mentally diseased human being, and explaining that he was: 'not an evil man but a sick man whose acts grew to a level of a mental illness, an illness that has been growing and growing to the point where he was not able to conform his conduct to the law... he was isolated in his own mind.' At that trial District Attorney Michael McCann countered by reminding the jury that they must consider Dahmer's state of mind when he killed, not his unnatural acts, because these do not necessarily point to insanity in the legal sense. 'You may feel sex with a dead body is an unnatural act,' McCann told the jury, but added: 'This is a lawsuit about responsibility for killing fifteen men. Not responsibility for dismemberment. Not responsibility for having sex with a dead body.' And he pointed out that Dahmer acted rationally and in his own self-interest – for instance, he always wore a condom. 'Mr Dahmer knew at all times that what he was doing was wrong ... The issue here is going to be responsibility,' McCann said.

The responsibility factor also arose after Andrei Chikatilo was found guilty and sentenced to death in 1992 and his defence lawyer Marad Khabibulin attempted to have the conviction overturned. The lawyer's 'insanity' claim was to deny that Chikatilo had actually committed the murders, claiming that the guilty verdict was mainly based on Chikatilo's confessions, which were unreliable. 'He is not sane, therefore his evidence is inadmissible, so the verdict should be overturned,' said the lawyer – and it was true that much of the evidence in the investigation did indeed come from Chikatilo's own highly detailed confessions and facts about the killings, which concurred with the forensic evidence. But despite Chikatilo's bizarre courtroom behaviour, which included ranting incoherently and drooling, Judge Akubzhanov said the killer's remarkable self-control during and after his crimes indicated otherwise: he had fastidiously prepared for his attacks by carrying spare clothes in case the ones he was wearing became covered in blood. 'Literally, several minutes after committing a bestial murder and mutilating his victims, he walked calmly out of the forest and began a conversation about mushrooms with people at the bus stop,' said the judge. 'At every stage of his crimes, he was in total command of his actions. His conscience didn't bother him at all. He has an iron psyche and nerves of steel.'

The sanity argument has been the source of legal dispute since mediaeval times. When dangerous behaviour could not be attributed to demonic possession, witchcraft or werewolfery, the courts of thirteenth-century England operated a 'wild beast test', for people judged to be either 'idiots' or 'lunatics'. An 'idiot' was born with below-average intellectual function and judged not to be responsible for criminal acts: idiocy was tested by asking a person to count twenty pennies, name his mother or father and give his age. For someone to be judged a 'lunatic' (madness manifesting later in life), it had to be proved that his mental abilities were no greater than those of a wild beast. A few centuries later it became accepted that 'lunatics' could be suffering from temporary insanity – not having understanding at the time of the crime – and then the test of understanding became 'whether or not the accused hath yet ordinarily as great understanding as ordinarily a child of fourteen years hath.'

In 1839 a distinction between the insane and the sane murderer was drawn up by American psychiatrist Dr Isaac Ray. The difference, he claimed, was in method and motive and in the subsequent behaviour of the killer. The insane murderer, he said, does not plan methodically, but falls prey to his homicidal impulses 'and then voluntarily surrenders himself to the constituted authorities.'

The present system of rules, which became adopted in many jurisdictions throughout the world, dates back to the 1843 trial of Daniel McNaghten in Britain. McNaghten fired a gun at police chief Sir Robert Peel, but was found not guilty by reason of insanity and spent twenty-one years in an institution. Since then, the 'McNaghten Rules' have applied, designed to exclude from criminal responsibility those who 'at the time of the committing of the act' are suffering 'a defect of reason' or 'disease of the mind, as to not know the nature and quality of the act ... or, if he did know it, that he did not know he was doing what was wrong.' Such a lack of blameworthiness, meaning the lack of an ability to distinguish between moral and immoral behaviour, right and wrong, is still applied to young children and the mentally ill who require hospitalisation rather than imprisonment. Thus the insanity plea in court is black and white: you are either sane or you are not; you are either controlled and organised, or irrational, impulsive and out of control.

There are dissenters in the ranks of forensic psychiatrists to this attempted resolution of conflict between the legal and medical criteria. Dr Donald Lunde, who wrote in-depth studies of Edmund Kemper, claims that mass murderers and serial killers are 'almost always insane', believing they fall broadly into two groups: the sexual sadists and the paranoid schizophrenics. Paranoid schizophrenia is a psychosis that is often characterised by an aggressive, suspicious attitude, by delusions of grandeur and/or persecution, and by hallucinations, such as auditory hallucinations in which the killer 'hears voices' ordering him to kill. This experience was claimed, for instance, by Britain's 'Yorkshire Ripper', Peter Sutcliffe, who killed thirteen women and attempted to murder seven others over a period of five years until his arrest in 1981. Sutcliffe said that God had told him to kill prostitutes (and, presumably, to mutilate them sexually, too). Similarly, New York's 'Son of Sam', David Berkowitz, who killed six people during 1976 and 1977, told psychiatrists that he had been ordered to kill by his neighbour Sam's dog, which was speaking to him with the voice of a demon.

As I write this, in 2022, a court in Florida is still grappling with its decision about the insanity or otherwise of Austin Harrouff. He was a college student aged nineteen with no criminal history when one hot evening in August 2016 he wandered into the driveway of a nearby home in his suburban area of Florida wearing his red MAGA baseball cap (to indicate his support for the then presidential nominee Donald Trump), and who launched an apparently unprovoked cannibalistic attack on a middle-aged couple who had been sitting outside, companionably drinking.

John Stevens and Michelle Mishcon were stabbed to death in their garage and Harrouff injured another neighbour who came to help them. After killing the couple, he bit into the stomach and the head of John Stevens and attempted to eat his face, grunting and howling as he did it – under the impression, it was revealed at his 2019 trial, that he was half-man and half-dog. It required several police officers, an electric stun gun and a snapping police dog to drag the killer from Mr Stevens's body. Blood tests revealed that Harrouff had taken no drugs, but according to his family he had been behaving strangely for weeks before the attack. He believed he had super-powers, he wrote songs about cannibalism, he was preoccupied with the 'Illuminati' and stated that he heard the voices of 'monsters and stuff' talking to him. His mother told the police that his bed had been moved into the garage because he thought there were demons in the house. As well as 'loving' Trump, he was a great fan of actor Arnold Schwarzenegger; his Fitbit, he had told his family, made him feel like Schwarzenegger's screen character, The Terminator.

Evidence-gathering has continued for almost six years while Harrouff has remained incarcerated in this American state where a murder conviction carries the death penalty. He expressed great remorse on a TV show interview over the internet with celebrity psychologist Dr Phil McGraw, saying he had little recollection of the motiveless killings, but felt that he was fleeing a demon-like creature, a 'dark figure' which scared him, 'then it's a blur.' His attorneys plan an 'insanity' plea, armed with a clinical report that declared Harrouff to be legally insane at the time of the crime, having experienced a 'decompensated mental state associated with an emerging mood and/or thought disorder resulting in an acute psychiatric episode.' As a result of this, the doctor concluded that Harrouff 'was unable to distinguish right from wrong'. Historically, a psychotic episode which is shown to have met these criteria could constitute insanity. However, in May 2020 the double-murder trial was held up after prosecutors asked for the opinion of a second mental health expert, despite the protests of the defence counsel. Harrouff, now twenty-four, is still awaiting trial in 2022, his psychotic episode apparently behind him.[32]

But many psychiatrists would also agree that most serial murderers are neither psychotic in that sort of accepted sense, nor, notes Richard Rappaport, a Northwestern University psychiatrist in the USA, do they go through the sort of emotional breakdown experienced after the event experienced by many 'spree' killers (meaning a person who kills a number of people at one particular time and location in a frenzied, random and apparently unpremeditated way). It is a vexing problem: sadistic and serial killers invariably fall into the category of having an antisocial personality disorder – but is this due to an intrinsic neural impairment which prevents them from assessing the needs of others and can it therefore be deemed insanity? Criminal psychologist Dr Silvano Arieti said, after examining Boston Strangler Albert DeSalvo, who killed thirteen women in a frenzied eighteen months up to January 1964, that he was not 'insane in the legal sense, nor psychotic in the medical sense. He is a sociopath, and only that. The law does not recognise a sociopath as having a mental illness which will excuse criminal responsibility. I thoroughly disagree with the law on this point.'

* * * *

'Sociopath' is an interchangeable word for 'psychopath' and 'antisocial personality' is a generic term frequently used for this personality disorder. Its diagnostic roots lie in the early nineteenth century, when French doctor Philippe Pinel studied an aristocrat who had whipped a horse, kicked a dog to death and tossed a peasant woman into a well. He declared the man to be suffering from 'manie sans délire' – insanity without apparent derangement. This was translated as 'moral insanity' in 1835 by English psychiatrist James Prichard, because it fell outside the usual ethical and legal codes. The term 'psychopath' was first coined by German psychiatrist J. L. A. Koch in 1888. A psychopath is not necessarily a criminal but – according to Hervey Cleckley, the most influential modern figure in psychopathy clinical research – he will meet some or all of the diagnostic criteria which were listed in Cleckley's 1941 book *The Mask of Sanity* and which he continued to develop in further editions until 1976, just before his death.[33] Cleckley's classic model for identifying the psychopath is still in use today: a constellation of symptoms including gross egocentricity, callousness which demands self-gratification regardless of the cost to others, no sense of responsibility, no capacity to experience or feel guilt or empathy with others, untruthfulness, absence of delusions, poorly-integrated sex-life, low frustration tolerance, easy arousability and sometimes explosiveness, considerable superficial charm, above-average intelligence and a failure to learn from experience or punishment. (Although it can be argued that serial killers do learn from experience when they wish: as can be seen from the murderers in this book, they note their mistakes and learn how to be more successful killers without getting caught.) There is a complete absence of remorse with psychopaths. They are so emotionally flattened that they are chillingly indifferent to any suffering they have caused. Note the words of David Bullock, aged twenty-one, who murdered six people at random in Manhattan and told the judge he did it because it 'makes me happy ... It was in the Christmas spirit ... something to amuse myself.'

One aspect of sociopathy is 'narcissistic personality disorder', in which the totally self-centred person has a grandiose view of his own uniqueness and abilities. Killers like many of those under discussion in this book display tremendous vanity, relishing the fame which their crimes ultimately win them. Sometimes they proclaim themselves 'experts' and offer their self-absorbed opinions and thoughts. Chikatilo, for instance, believed that because of his conflicting blood and semen type, he was unique and possessed two souls. John George Haigh was a monstrously narcissistic man, vain about his forgery skills and his disposal of the bodies of those he murdered. His vanity extended to his desire to be commemorated in wax at Madame Tussaud's Chamber of Horrors – and he even bequeathed the waxworks a suit of his clothes, to make sure the model of him looked elegant enough. Often it is this very vanity which ensnares murderers, for in their narcissism, they believe they are more clever than those who try to catch them. Sometimes they are so keen to reassure themselves of this superiority that they take risks by sending taunting letters to the police, or associating with officers who are conducting the murder hunt. Edmund Kemper spent time hanging around a Santa Cruz bar with off-duty policemen, asking them questions about murders which, unknown to them, he had committed – and he even applied to join the police force. Peter Kürten went to a bar near the scene of one of his crimes to listen to people talking with horror about the murder he had committed.

Arrest frequently offers these men an opportunity for recognition and notoriety for the first time in their lives. Police interviews enable them to talk in minute (and sexually stimulating) detail about their crimes, reliving the events in the glow of attention. Sometimes killers – like Issei Sagawa and Armin Meiwes – enjoy writing autobiographies containing detailed accounts of their sex crimes. Other killers confess to more crimes than they have committed in order to be 'the best' murderer. For example, Chikatilo told the police chief who had arrested him of another prisoner boasting about having killed five people. 'How would he have felt if I'd said I was in for fifty-five?' said Chikatilo, laughing heartily.

The illogical thought processes which killers sometimes display also sets them apart. Righteous indignation is often expressed about the reporting of comparatively trivial details of their appalling crimes. Albert Fish was hurt and angry when a New York newspaper called him 'a sixty-five-year-old ogre'. He was also shocked when he learned that he was being charged with kidnapping Grace Budd. But

Mr and Mrs Budd had given him their permission to take Grace away with him, he protested to his psychiatrist, so how could he have kidnapped her? David 'Son of Sam' Berkowitz displayed the same lack of logic when one of his victims displayed fear. 'I wasn't going to rob her, or touch her or rape her. I just wanted to kill her,' he said. Andrei Chikatilo was insulted at any suggestion that he stole from his victims and Ed Gein was similarly outraged at the police accusation that he stole the cash register at the hardware shop where he had killed the elderly woman whom he would later dismember and eat. Just as Issei Sagawa spoke of his terrible crime as though it was a piece of mischief, Jeffrey Dahmer never seemed to grasp the full horror of his acts. Milwaukee police detective Dennis Murphy, who conducted sixty hours of interviews with Dahmer, said Dahmer reminded him of a guy who had been caught doing 'something wrong and was a little embarrassed about it.'

Psychopaths are probably the largest group of recidivists, and attempts to cure them are always unsuccessful, said Cleckley. After more than thirty years' work with this group using a variety of therapeutic approaches, he reached the depressing conclusion (depressing, because psychiatrists do not like to confess the failure of their methods): 'There is no evidence to demonstrate or to indicate that psychiatry has yet found a therapy that cures or profoundly changes the psychopath.' So we come back to the legal core of the matter: does this make them insane, according to the McNaghten Rules? It is, after all, not that psychopaths are in such mental disarray that they are unable to distinguish between right and wrong; just that they don't care. Their mental impairment robs them of the ability to care. Does that mental impairment then make them insane? Or are they, as Jack Levin says in his book *Mass Murder*, 'evil, not crazy'?

And what hope is there for citizens on juries to reach balanced conclusions when there is disagreement about terminology among the professionals? While it is a risk that the jury may pass judgement on the criminal based on the repulsiveness of his act rather than the mental state he was in when he committed it, another hazard is when killers do not exhibit the accepted signs of insanity: look at Dahmer, look at Sagawa – yes, look even at Chikatilo, who only began behaving like a madman in court when he perceived that in this way he might escape execution.

And certainly one must look at Armin Meiwes, who, when held in custody pre-trial was variously diagnosed by psychiatrists and psychologists as firstly having no mental disorder whatsoever, then as having a schizoid personality disorder, and finally – contrarily – as not having a schizoid personality, but instead suffered from a recognized 'sexual sadism' disorder. Psychiatrist Heinrich Wilmer commented on Meiwes's lack of displayed emotion, saying that a session with him 'was like sitting opposite a scientist ... conducting an experiment.' Another psychiatrist, Professor Georg Stolpmann, described Meiwes as being smug, self-assured and incapable of showing 'warm and tender feelings towards others'. Where the psychiatric evaluations were in agreement – possibly because Meiwes admitted still entertaining fantasies about killing when he saw pictures of attractive young people – was that his behaviour would not be controlled by therapy, that he was psychologically sound enough to go to trial and that he did not need to be kept in a mental institution.

In January 2004 Meiwes was convicted of manslaughter. At his trial, several men who harboured fantasies of eating human flesh testified that there was a large network of like-minded individuals who connected through cyberspace in a bid to satisfy their fantasies.

Judge Volker Muetze described Meiwes as indulging in behaviour 'which is condemned in our society, namely the killing and butchering of a human being' but he indicated that it was not murder in the legal sense, rather it was 'killing a person without being a murderer.' It was, the judge said in conclusion, 'an act between two extremely disturbed people who both wanted something from each other.' Meiwes was sentenced to eight-and-a-half years in prison, while out on the streets and in the media the debate rumbled on about whether he had been treated too leniently or whether he should have been convicted at all. Among prosecuting lawyers, however, there was a strong feeling that a conviction for murder would have been more appropriate. In April 2005 they appealed against the sentence and at a re-trial a year later, Meiwes answered a murder charge in a Frankfurt court. The appeal judge gave much consideration to the motives and the desired satiation of both men's individual needs. In particular, he dismissed the defence statement that since Brandes's goal was to be eaten, that necessitated being killed so therefore it could not be classed as murder. Meiwes had insisted that it was murder on request: euthanasia, in fact. Presenting the slaughter of a human as if it were almost an occupational hazard, he said the act of killing had been a very unpleasant experience for him. He would have preferred Brandes to have killed himself, he suggested. In fact, this was actually a mercy killing, Meiwes's lawyer Joachim Bremer told the court.

The judge had no sympathy with the 'mercy killing' argument, despite the offered opinion of a sexologist – Klaus Beier – who said that Meiwes displayed no signs of psychiatric illness but that he was 'above all fascinated by the act of cutting up corpses ... Killing was a necessary evil to achieve that end.' But having also heard the prosecutor speak of Brandes being killed and cut up 'like a piece of livestock', the judge remarked on the disdain and lack of pity which Meiwes had shown for Brandes in making a video-film of his own inhuman post-mortem actions.

The judge considered Meiwes's particular sexual desires and speculated upon whether the strategy of drawing in a volunteer for sadomasochistic and cannibalistic 'play' was a way of obtaining the video 'proof' he needed in order to show that he did not enjoy killing and thereby it could be portrayed as a mercy killing. Brandes's only sexual motivation was the castration of his penis, said the judge. There had been no agreement to being slaughtered and he had not foreseen the consequences of his decision; upon discovering that castration did not provide the extreme sexual gratification he had expected, he was left with no choice other than death. The heavy doses of alcohol and drugs, his desperation due to the failed experiment and a wish not to break his promise meant that death was the only way Brandes could escape the horrible situation he was in, declared the judge. He found Meiwes guilty and ordered that he should serve a life sentence – which is fifteen years. This meant that according to German law Meiwes could have been freed early – in 2021, but in 2018 the Frankfurt State Court rejected his appeal, judging that expert advice was that there was 'currently no favourable outlook' for his future behaviour.

In the maximum security jail where he was held, Armin Meiwes worked in the prison library, became a vegetarian, admitted that eating people was wrong, warned other people against making the same mistakes he had and, with an interest in the environment, became the leader of a prison branch of the Green Party. According to a 2006 *Times Online* story by David Crossland, (entitled 'Cannibal Goes on Charm Offensive'), Meiwes maintained a good relationship with other inmates, who declared that he seemed harmless and smiled a lot: 'All the people who've met him, the people he worked with, the psychiatrists who have examined him, don't have the impression that he's a dangerous person, that he's some kind of crazy serial killer,' Crossland wrote. In a 2008 book about Meiwes – *Interview with a Cannibal: The Secret Life of the Monster of Rotenburg* – Gunter Stampf said much the same thing; Meiwes's lawyer had even said he would trust Meiwes to look after his own children. In February 2020, heavy metal singer Ozzy Osbourne included a song called 'Eat Me' on his album *Ordinary Men*. The song was, he said, inspired by Armin Meiwes.

Forensic psychiatrist Willem Martens points out in his case report on Meiwes that in such cases smoothness, charm and self-assurance are very much characteristics of psychopaths. Martens has previously written books and studies of other murderers, including Jeffrey Dahmer, and can identify parallels to be drawn with Meiwes: 'The most dangerous among them [are] able to give a deep impression of harmlessness linked to a lack of internal conflicts, lack of nervousness, open-mindedness and self-knowledge.' Even experienced therapists and psychiatrists are inclined to believe psychopaths, he reminds. This has been shown to be disastrously true on several occasions, especially in America, where even though proportionally fewer murderers are judged to be insane than in, say, the United Kingdom, there appears to be an understanding among criminals that an 'insane' killer will spend only a short time incarcerated in a psychiatric hospital before being freed. In US states where there is still capital punishment, there is logic to a killer's wish to be found insane – but balancing the scales of justice also involves considering the public's desire for revenge, which also comes into play particularly in sadistic cases. Interestingly, when Albert Fish was found sane and guilty and sent to the electric chair in the 1930s, it was later revealed that the jury did not really believe him to be sane, but there were few people in New York who wished to see Fish escape with his life, as an insanity verdict would have ensured.

Yet there are some who would say that the death penalty is preferable to a lifetime of incarceration. As Douglas Clark, the sadistic murderer of six women, said – and he was fearfully well-qualified to say it – 'There are a hell of a lot worse things that can happen than to die in the gas chamber.' In fact it is not necessarily true that people sent to prison are deprived of their liberty for longer periods than if they are judged insane and sent to a secure psychiatric unit for treatment: statistics demonstrate that generally the reverse applies. The median time served by people convicted of first-degree murder in the USA is ten-and-a-half years and 'life imprisonment' in both Britain and the United States is frequently an oxymoron. But statistics contain exceptions. Public fear is justified when they learn of frightening instances on both sides of the Atlantic where psychiatrists and psychologists ignore the advice of experts on psychopathy like Cleckley. In those cases, perpetrators of the most abominable crimes are allowed out of high-security hospitals on unaccompanied shopping trips or are released on parole after mental health tribunals take the word of optimistic psychiatrists that the patient is 'safe' – that is, cured of his deviant impulses. Not infrequently we hear of people committing the most grotesque murders almost as soon as they have been released from hospital.

In this book alone we have several glaring examples of psychiatric complacency. Police records show that at one hospital – from which he escaped – vampire killer Richard Chase was described as a 'violent mental patient'. Nevertheless, he was allowed to re-enter society – and obtain a gun. In Germany, Peter Kürten was repeatedly set free or sentenced to only a few years for attacks on women, despite having a history of such attacks – and the story is similar regarding Fritz Haarman. At Albert Fish's trial, his defence attorney, James Dempsey, indicated the shrunken, grey-haired old man peeping fearfully through the open fingers of his hands spread across his face, and declared that Fish 'was insane in 1928 and is insane today.' New York's Bellevue Hospital, which had discharged Fish as safe in 1930 had a lot to answer for, he said. Issei Sagawa was released as cured from the Japanese hospital to which he had been transferred; he is a free man today.

Dr Donald Lunde has suggested that assessing someone on the grounds of 'treatability' and 'dangerousness' would be more worthwhile than trying to label them as sane or insane, for if someone was found to be dangerous but suffering from a treatable mental disease, he could then be treated in a hospital. Sadly, though, this 'treatment' sometimes has clever killers laughing up their sleeves at the psychiatric experts who attend them. Fooling the professionals has proved a remarkably easy task for a glib psychopath, whether it is before or after they have been tried and sentenced. The smart, educated criminal can fake schizophrenia, epilepsy, amnesia and even Multiple Personality Disorder (now termed Dissociative Identity Disorder) in pursuit of an insanity verdict and, he hopes, incarceration in a hospital with his imagined prospect of earlier release.

The aforementioned sadistic killer David 'Son of Sam' Berkowitz convinced two court-appointed psychiatrists that he was delusional in his belief that his neighbour's dog, possessed by a three-thousand-year-old demon, had barked instructions at him to kill because demonic forces wished to drink the victim's blood. Another psychiatrist, David Abrahamsen, remained unconvinced and it was he who persuaded the court that Berkowitz was sane, saying he had failed to display any other indicators of insanity, especially demonstrating 'clear-headed cunning' in avoiding detection for a whole year. Berkowitz was found sane and given a twenty-five-year sentence. Three years later, in 1979, he admitted he had invented the talking devil-dog story which had given him infamy in order to try and fool the authorities into believing he was insane. Far from being seized by an uncontrollable compulsion to kill, Berkowitz – like Andrei Chikatilo, Joachim Kroll, Ed Kemper and others in this book – would roam around for hours searching for suitable victims and stalking them. Every night Berkowitz was out hunting, but only attacked when he thought it was safe to do so.

Such careful premeditation defies the legal definition of insanity. But just as cunning killers are able to fake insanity and fool psychologists, they are equally well able to feign normality and rehabilitation in order to win their liberty. Jeffrey Dahmer, on bail awaiting a court hearing on an enticement and assault charge, so convinced the psychologist who had monitored him for months that he was recovering from his social problems that his jail sentence was kept to a minimum. But during the time that the psychologist had been seeing Dahmer, the cannibal had killed several people, the last one only a matter of weeks before he was due to be sentenced. As he appeared in court to hear experts declare him a changed and repentant man, at home in his Milwaukee flat was his latest souvenir: Anthony Sears's boiled head.

Similarly, some years after Ed Kemper had been released as cured from Atascadero mental hospital where he had been 'treated' after he had murdered his grandparents, his mother – whom he was later to slaughter grotesquely – poignantly fought to have his juvenile record set aside, or 'sealed', so he could begin life afresh without a blot on his character. Soon afterwards, in September 1972, he was seen by two psychiatrists who remarked on the excellent progress he had made and recommended the sealing of his records. One of them said he was pleased that Ed had given up riding a motor-cycle 'since this seemed more a threat to his life and health than any threat he is presently to anyone else.' At the time of the interviews, Kemper had already killed, mutilated and fed upon the corpses of several women. Indeed, his latest murder had been four days prior to his visit to the psychiatrists. He had dismembered the victim's body and flushed the body fluids down the drain before burying the hands in one county and the torso in another. He did not get rid of the head, but kept it in the boot of his car, where it rested during his interview with a psychiatrist who was to declare him 'a very well-adjusted young man who had initiative, intelligence and who was free of any psychiatric illness.'

An intelligent killer like Kemper who has had dealings with psychologists or has undertaken research on clinical psychology is more than capable of putting his acquired knowledge to use, either to entertain himself, to give him reassurance of his own superiority or for other devious purposes. Just as Kemper enjoyed toying with interviewers and reporters (ghoulishly amusing himself on one occasion by telling one shocked woman that when he saw a pretty girl: 'One side of me says, "Wow, what an attractive chick, I'd like to talk to her." The other side of me says, "I wonder how her head would look on a stick?"'). He also tried to confuse psychologists by offering varying and conflicting explanations for his acts on different occasions. He would begin interviews by giving psychologists the Minnesota Multiphasic Personality Inventory, a personality assessment device which he had learned inside-out during his teenage years in the mental hospital.

It is concerning that some psychiatric professionals have been dangerously misled into interpreting a sociopathic killer's exhibited compliance as a real change of inner personality especially since they, of all people, should be aware of the psychopath's legendary charm, intelligence, cunning and ability to lie or flatter convincingly. As Hervey Cleckley says, the psychopath 'is much more likely than others who have committed serious crimes to convince his psychotherapist that treatment has been effective, that it has brought true insight and profound changes that make him no longer a danger to society' and he is also clever enough to 'make the therapist feel also that the cure was specifically effected through cherished items of the therapist's creed of psychiatric theory.' But, adds Cleckley: 'The daily papers report many cases of armed robbery, rape and murder resulting from such confidently optimistic estimates of therapeutic success.'

Psychopathic serial killers have the ability to blend in with society, arousing no suspicion. The so-called 'impulse to kill' can be interpreted as a desire which gets out of hand and becomes a habit or an addiction. Abnormal, of course, but it is a habit over which they exert control when they choose, and psychiatrists agree that it takes high intelligence or a large amount of low cunning to get away with murder repeatedly. FBI consultant Professor Park Elliott Dietz puts it succinctly: 'In order to be serially successful with murder – that is, simply, not to get caught, a person has to have both the intelligence and the means to evade detection. He has to be reasonably well-integrated socially. He is not likely to be an alcoholic or a drug user. And he usually owns a car.' He adds: 'One of the reasons serial killers have been so hard to catch is our old assumption that they must be frothing at the mouth... If that were true, they would be easy to spot. What is really disquieting is that people who act normal can commit these unspeakable crimes.'

But what if the person 'acting normal' is actually professionally responsible for the safeguarding and protection of the rest of us? And what if the 'unspeakable crime' of cannibalistic murder appears to have been planned meticulously but – so far – has not been committed? If there's enough evidence of intent, can someone be judged guilty of something they might do? This, as the next chapter illustrates, was the diabolical riddle which a New York jury were faced with unravelling in 2013.

Dark Matter

> *'De Sade lived in an atmosphere of unreality, a world of dreams inside his own head. He was one of the privileged few who could afford that indulgence. Two centuries later, an affluent society has created conditions that could spawn potential de Sades by the thousand'*
>
> Colin Wilson and Donald Seaman, *The Serial Killers*

As she was sitting and feeding the baby on a bright summer's day in 2012, Kathleen Mangan-Valle just could not stop her mind from wandering. Unsettled and unhappy, she knew she had a problem with her marriage, but could not fathom out what had gone awry between herself and Gil. The future had seemed promising three years ago when they found each other via the dating website *OKCupid.com*. Both in their mid-twenties, both with good jobs – she as a teacher in the Bronx and he as a patrol officer with the New York Police Department – they made a good-looking and happy couple and, she recalled, he had seemed so nice: he had a sweet old-fashioned charm about him – opening doors for her and so on.

Was it the pregnancy last year that changed things between them? After all, at one point he had said 'I can't do this' when she had talked to him about their impending parenthood. She smiled at their beautiful little girl and chattered playfully along with her while she racked her brains. No, how could that be? Anyone who saw them together could see that Gil adored his baby daughter. The wedding that followed the birth, then? Did he feel trapped? Was that the point when things starting turning sour? No, she reflected, he had definitely begun to show a less appealing side to his nature long before they made it official: in fact, she could remember him grizzling and complaining when she went to her ante-natal medical appointments and then, when she actually went into labour, he deliberately delayed taking her into hospital because he insisted on taking a shower while she anxiously dealt with the contractions. Not a capital crime, sure, but still, pretty spiteful at a time when she really needed his support. And these days, it just seemed as if he didn't want to spend time with her. As soon as he could after he came home from work, he got on the computer – some nights he stayed up until five o'clock in the morning. Was it police work he was doing? What on earth could be occupying him online until the early hours, night after night? Her mind whirling with possibilities, she decided to check out her husband's website history as soon as the baby took her nap.

The picture of a dead woman which she found almost immediately could well have been a piece of evidence from a crime scene, but in fact it was not. The photograph appeared on a bondage site. 'I know S&M is popular – with *Fifty Shades of Grey* – but this seemed different,' Kathleen was later to tell a reporter from the *New York Daily News*, 'because the girl on the front page was dead.' Kathleen was not naive – she was well aware of the darker aspects of human behaviour which officers like her husband encountered regularly, especially in an urban sprawl like New York – so asking Gil straight out about the bondage site was, she considered, the most open approach. But instead of the discussion bringing about an improvement in their relationship, over the next few months it deteriorated further. They were still maintaining a social life together – for example, that summer they travelled with the baby to Maryland to have brunch with some old college friends of Gil's – but at home their sexual intimacy was a failure and her husband became even more distant and strange, sometimes asking her peculiar questions about her daily routine: where she liked to jog, what the lighting there was like and how many people were around: 'weird stuff', as Kathleen was later to describe it.

Anxious, she downloaded spyware onto their computer to check his online actions. What she uncovered left her numb with shock. There were gruesome pictures showing what she described in a later news interview as 'feet not attached to bodies' and other photographs of dead, tortured and mutilated women, including one of somebody 'hog-tied, naked, with blood all over her'. Most disturbing of all were the photos she found of herself and of several of their female friends, attached to messages sent from a secret email account. In the 'thousands' of emails which her husband had exchanged with other men, he plotted to torture and kill women in a variety of ways, including his wife. 'I was supposed to be tied by my feet, my throat slit and they were going to watch the blood rush from my body,' Kathleen said. When one of the email correspondents wrote: 'If she cries, don't show her mercy', her husband's reply had been: 'Don't worry. We'll just gag her.'

His plan for one of their female friends apparently included stuffing her in a suitcase and delivering her to a co-conspirator to be raped and murdered; two others were to be raped in front of each other 'to heighten their fears' and yet another was going to be roasted alive on a spit over an open fire and eaten. 'The suffering was for his enjoyment and he wanted to make it last as long as possible,' Kathleen said, recalling the nightmarish horror of her discovery. Shattered and terrified, she hurriedly packed a bag for herself and her baby daughter, grabbed her laptop and flew immediately to Reno, Nevada, where her parents lived. On arrival, she contacted the FBI and handed over the computer, the keys to the apartment where they lived in the quiet residential area of Queens and gave the FBI permission to take an older computer and hack its contents for incriminating material.

What the FBI discovered were crime-scene pictures of dead and mutilated women and images of women being tortured and sexually abused, together with 'human meat recipes' and a trail of emails, instant messages, fetish chatroom posts and computer files outlining plans to kidnap, rape, slaughter and cannibalise more than one hundred women whose names, addresses, heights, weights and photographs – sometimes taken from their Facebook profile pages – were meticulously recorded. Valle's own Facebook page presented an image of a caring family man complete with happy photographs of his wife, baby girl and pet puppy. Valle had more than 600 Facebook friends, including dozens of young women. Meanwhile his alter-ego – 'Girl-Meat Hunter' – was subscribed to one website with 38,000 members called *DarkFetish.net* where regulars discuss the sadistic killing and cannibalisation of women. Online, Valle shared his desires and schemes with three other men in particular, including a fetishist from England who used the alias names 'Moody Blues' or 'MeatMarketMan'. Just before Valle's arrest in autumn 2012, he had informed 'Moody Blues' of his ambitions for November: 'I'm planning on getting some girl meat ... for Thanksgiving.'

One document uncovered by the FBI was entitled *Abducting and Cooking Kimberley: A Blueprint* and focused on Kimberley Sauer, one of the college friends with whom the Valles had enjoyed the reunion brunch in Maryland only a few months earlier. 'When I see her Sunday my mouth will be watering,' Valle had written to 'Moody Blues' three days before the summer event, saying how he 'longed for the day I cram a chloroform-soaked rag in her face.' Along with a picture and personal details about Kimberley and her lifestyle, the file also contained a list of materials needed – a car, chloroform and rope (Valle claimed he was able to make chloroform at home). 'I can knock her out, wait until dark and kidnap her right out of her house,' Valle wrote in one exchange that July. 'I was thinking of tying her body onto some kind of apparatus ... cook her over low heat, keep her alive as long as possible.' With disturbing irony, during the later trial of Valle it emerged that his wife Kathleen, during the traumatic period when she had seen some of the material her husband had gathered about Kimberley Sauer's lifestyle, had emailed a warning to their friend. However, Kimberley had considered the email so bizarre that she concluded it had come from a hacker and instead of responding to Kathleen, she contacted Gilberto Valle to pass on the strange information she had received.

Valle's online interactions with other apparent predators included discussing his intended role in a plot to kidnap a certain woman for another man or men to rape, torture and murder. He told the 'buyer' that he was an aspiring professional kidnapper and asked for a fee of $5,000, adding that he wanted no involvement in the rape or murder, but would 'really get off on knocking her out, tying up her hands and bare feet and gagging her ... then she will be stuffed into a large piece of luggage and wheeled out to my van.' Cellphone data revealed that Valle made calls on the block where the woman lived, but she told the FBI that she did not know Valle well and he had never been in her home. In another online message Valle had told his fellow-fetishist that him being acquainted with the women he had targeted would aid his scheme: 'The abduction will have to be flawless ... I know all of them ... I can just show up at her home unannounced, it will not alert her, and I can knock her out.'

New York Police Department Commissioner Ray Kelly called the case 'bizarre' and released a careful statement saying: 'We suspended the officer immediately upon his arrest and a review is now underway to determine whether there was anything in his background that should have alerted the department to his alleged proclivities.' The FBI found no evidence that any of the scores of women who featured in Valle's sick online schemes had actually been harmed, but there was the question of how he had obtained his highly detailed information about the women, their lives and their contact details. It was alleged that Valle had abused his privileged position as a police officer by illegally accessing a law enforcement database to discover much of his information about the women he was 'explicitly targeting' and that he had followed two of them, once while on-duty. He had attempted to contact potential victims, including a New York City schoolteacher, to find out more about their jobs and their homes. He also made a cellphone call from near the home of one woman, it was alleged. When Valle's trial opened in February 2013 at Federal District Court in Manhattan, the charge he faced was plotting on the internet to abduct, rape, kill and cannibalise female victims. A further charge of online kidnapping and conspiracy, jointly with motor-mechanic Michael Van Hise, aged twenty-two, concerned Valle's emails to Van Hise about kidnapping a Manhattan teacher and delivering her to Van Hise's home to be raped and murdered, a crime which also carries a life sentence.

As the prosecution prepared their case, an issue arose about the fair selection of strong-stomached jurors for a case which had already received much media attention, the *New York Post* having dubbed Valle 'The Cannibal Cop' and, since nobody had actually died or suffered injury, felt it enjoyed the freedom to use such creative headlines as 'Cook 'em Danno'. Understandably, these 'negative' stories were of concern to the defence, as were various images stored by Valle and filed by the prosecution – one of a naked woman being spit-roasted over a fire, another of an oiled, bound, naked woman face-down in a roasting-pan with an apple in her mouth (Valle's long-held favourite fantasy-image, his defence attorney Julia Gatto was later to tell the court, helpfully). Such pictures might prejudice jurors, said Ms Gatto, requesting that they be not made public in case they perpetuated 'a smear campaign' against Valle, making the selection of objective jurors 'nearly impossible'.

While the defence was unsuccessful in its bid to suppress these images, certain other pieces of the prosecution's evidence were destined to be ruled inadmissable by Judge Paul G. Gardephe to avoid causing prejudice in jurors. For instance, the 'evidentiary value' of gruesome images, such as a video showing the slaughtering of a goat and an online chat between Valle and another man about devouring a child, 'was far outweighed by its unfair prejudicial effect' he decided. Also removed from the prosecution evidence were some cell-phone records which had placed Valle near victims' homes.

At Valle's trial, his attorney argued there was no proof of crime, that the charges were 'pure fiction' and that Valle never posed a threat but had merely been engaging in harmless internet fantasy. 'He participates in what is a very vibrant subculture on the internet of fantasy role-playing,' Julia Gatto declared. 'He's thought some bizarre thoughts and shared them with others who share the same fetishes.' At worst, she claimed, Valle was a man 'who has sexual fantasies about people he knows and he talks about it on the internet, but ... nothing has happened ... it's just talk.' She told the court that Valle had been 'Googling a host of awful things, because that's what he fantasises about; that's Gil's porn.' It quickly became apparent that this was the crux of the case: does an individual's online fantasy behaviour direct or describe his real-life inclinations and behaviour?

The defence introduced evidence from the fetish website's co-founder Sergey Merenkov, who described *DarkFetish.net* as 'a clone of Facebook ... oriented to people with fetishes that are not considered standard,' and called upon expert witnesses, including psychologists, who said that a person's bizarre compulsion to create horrific and sickeningly violent scenarios did not necessarily mean he posed a danger to the public. A prominent forensic psychiatrist, Dr Park Dietz had, said the defence, evaluated Officer Valle and concluded he lacked certain risk factors for violence. The prosecution team, meanwhile, claimed that the detailed dossier Valle had compiled on the women, together with his raid on the police database for more information, amply demonstrated that his fantasies had turned into a very real threat and, alleged Assistant US Attorney Hadassa Waxman, at the time of his arrest Valle was on the verge of 'kidnapping a woman, cooking her and actually eating her.' Assistant US Attorney Randall Jackson declared: 'Make no mistake, Gilbert Valle was very serious about these plans.'

The internet apart, anyone who has been reading about the methodology of the murderers described in previous pages of this book will be conscious of the patterns to which organised sadistic killers conform, meticulous planning being one crucial indicator and an obsessive use of pornography appropriate to the ultimate crime being another. Usually, however, both of these indicators only become known to the investigating authorities after the corpses have been gathered and the prime suspect's secret stash of sadistic pornography has been discovered. At this point there is much hand-wringing disappointment: if only there had been some advance clues about the sick state of the killer's mind, cry the homicide detectives. If only. So while the argument in court, in the media, among the citizens of New York and further afield became one of whether a free society built upon the principle of justice should be able to convict people for their thoughts – no matter how depraved those thoughts might be – the prosecution, in possession of some very significant indicators about the obsessive state of Gilberto Valle's mind, said he was a sexual sadist and that the 'detailed and specific' steps he had taken – such as surveillance of his chosen victims – meant that his 'grotesque' plans were real, despite his never having committed the actual crime of killing or cannibalising a single victim. Said Preet Bharara, prosecution attorney: 'The internet is a forum for the free exchange of ideas ... but it does not confer immunity for plotting crimes and taking steps to carry out those crimes.' In his summing-up to the jury, prosecutor Randall Jackson said that in relation to reality, Valle's fantasies were 'not OK.' He asked the jurors if they would feel comfortable dining with a chef who had fantasies about poisoning food, or travelling on a plane where a fellow-passenger fantasised about hijacking.

Valle was found guilty on all the charges. Sentencing was deferred. After the trial some members of the jury said that for some time there was not unanimity among them and it was only after two of the jurors role-played Valle's online chats with Moody Blues that the doubters decided upon a 'guilty' verdict. The 'turning point', as described by a juror interviewed on a website for lawyers,[34] was the realisation that when Valle got home from the college reunion lunch in Maryland, the first thing he did was to go online to tell his chat-room cohorts that he had successfully cased his first place of attack. That he had staked out a victim's home and office and had formulated plans on how to do the deed was the overt act necessary to make the jury decide upon the guilty verdict – for if it was just fantasy, they believed, Valle would not have rushed immediately to report the results of his trip. Coupled with Valle's use of real names and real pictures of his 'wish list' victims, this changed a 'thought crime' into a real crime, they decided.

Valle was facing a life-term and appealed. One of his legal team's arguments was that Randall Jackson's remarks about chefs or plane passengers who entertained poisoning or hi-jacking fantasies were aimed at encouraging a conviction based on speculative fear of what Valle might do instead of offering proof beyond a reasonable doubt. Filing their motion for a new trial, Valle's lawyers said that Jackson's closing remarks played on the 'very human fear' of the jurors that 'if they didn't convict Valle now, someone with such a deviant imagination could potentially harm someone in the future.'

Then in July 2014 the jury's 'guilty' verdict was overturned by the District Court Judge Paul Gardephe, who had presided over Valle's original trial and who now produced a 118-page report opining that it was 'more likely than not' that all of Valle's internet communications about kidnapping were fantasy role-play. He said the government had failed to prove beyond a reasonable doubt that Gilberto Valle 'entered into a genuine agreement to kidnap a woman, or that he specifically intended to commit a kidnapping.' Judge Gardephe's view was that 'once the lies and the fantastical elements are stripped away, what is left are deeply disturbing misogynistic chats and emails written by an individual obsessed with imagining women he knows suffering horrific sex-related pain, terror and degradation.' While acknowledging that Valle's 'depraved, misogynistic sexual fantasies about his wife, former college classmates and acquaintances undoubtedly reflected a mind diseased,' the judge said that no matter how disturbing Valle's fantasies, chats and emails, might be: 'these interests are not sufficient – standing alone – to make out the elements of conspiracy to commit kidnapping.' The internet activities were not, of course, 'standing alone' on the charge-sheet: he had also been found guilty of using a law enforcement database to get information about women – and this conviction was upheld, although since the sentence for the crime was one year and Valle had already been in custody for almost twenty-one months, this was judged to be 'time served' and he was released into the care of his mother, electronically-tagged and subject to a $100,000 home detention bond. He was barred from using the internet, from leaving New York, from contacting the women he fantasised about and was ordered to have mental health treatment.

The jurors were aghast and one of them called the ruling 'abominable', saying that based upon the evidence of Valle's actions during and after the Maryland visit, they had followed the rules of law and believed they got the verdict right. However, defence attorney Julia Gatto declared that the judge's decision validated the defence argument and that Valle was guilty of 'nothing more than very unconventional thoughts ... we don't put people in jail for their thoughts.' The government immediately announced that there would be a further appeal to decide whether the judge had overstepped his bounds and to attempt to get the jury's original decision reinstated: 'We do respectfully believe the activity went far beyond imagining,' prosecutor Randall Jackson told Judge Gardephe. 'It went to actual planning and conspiracy.' But Valle himself told the judge: 'You made the right decision ... I am incapable of violence. I would never do the things I talked about on the internet ... What I needed was help, not prosecution

... I clearly have some issues that I need to address and I am addressing them, but at no time did anything extend beyond cyberspace.'

Julia Gatto expressed her concern about Valle's return to a normal life. 'Prison has been hard. He has to pick up the pieces of his life. He has lost a lot during this case: his liberty for twenty-one months, his wife, his child, many of his friends, his job. He lost his reputation and anonymity.'

The more cynical among us might consider that expecting sympathy for such misfortune is rather like someone killing his parents then bewailing his orphanhood. Immediately upon release, Valle declared his intention to do charity work for his local Catholic church and to seek visitation rights with his daughter, by then aged three. His experiences had given him 'a new passion in life' which was to become a criminal defence lawyer, he said, and he also decided to seek a new girlfriend by advertising on *Match. com*, writing on his online dating profile that he hoped to find a 'non-judgmental' woman, going on to say: 'I am spending my energy rebounding from the errors I made in my past and rebuilding my life.' He does not, he says, want to be known forever as 'the Cannibal Cop'.

But the media sobriquet cannot be evaded so easily. In April 2015 a documentary called *Thought Crimes: The Case of the Cannibal Cop* was premiered and was widely broadcast on American TV and later worldwide. Then in December that year Valle was back in the news as the US Circuit Court of Appeals in Manhattan rejected the appeal by the government to get Valle's original conviction by the jury reinstated and to put him back behind bars. By two-to-one, the ruling in Manhattan was that Judge Paul Gardephe had been correct to reverse the 2013 jury's guilty verdict on the kidnapping conspiracy charge. In addition, they also reversed Valle's conviction on the charge that he used a law enforcement database to look up personal information about women he knew. One of the three judges on the appeal panel, Circuit Judge Barrington D. Parker, said: 'We are loath to give the government the power to punish us for our thoughts and not our actions ... That includes the power to criminalise an individual's expression of sexual fantasies, no matter how perverse or disturbing. Fantasising about committing a crime, even a crime of violence against a real person whom you know, is not a crime.'

Meanwhile, there were other loose ends to be tied up following Valle's release. During the two years following Valle's trial, three more American men who had chatted with him on *DarkFetishNet.com* – Michael Van Hise, Richard Meltz and Christopher Asch – were charged and convicted of Conspiracy to Commit Kidnapping, having allegedly schemed in emails and online chats to carry out gruesome fantasies of kidnapping, raping, torturing and killing women, among them Van Hise's wife, his sister-in-law, his four young nieces and his nine-year-old stepdaughter. The FBI said the trio had abandoned this scheme after Valle was arrested separately on the cannibalism charge, after which Meltz and Asch plotted to kidnap a female FBI agent and at Meltz's direction, Asch allegedly purchased a Taser weapon at a Pennsylvania gun show for the planned abduction. The same defence as Valle – that they only participated in internet fantasy role-play and never planned to harm anyone – was not accepted by Judge Paul Gardephe when he sentenced Meltz – a former Massachusetts hospital police chief – to ten years in prison. Meltz's lawyer Peter Brill said afterwards that he had hoped the judge's reversal on Valle would be a positive sign for Meltz because, out of the three co-defendants, his case was the 'most similar' to Valle's. However, although Judge Gardephe had ruled that Valle's actions were merely fantasy, he believed that the same could not be said of sixty-six-year-old Meltz who 'represents a danger to the community.' Similarly the appeal instigated by Van Hise and Asch reached completion in August 2017. Judge Gardephe upheld the pair's convictions.

On the other side of the Atlantic, UK cyber-investigators identified Valle's online correspondent Moody Blues as Dale Bolinger, a fifty-seven-year-old hospital nurse from Canterbury who, as Valle's jury trial was taking place in 2013, was arrested on suspicion of conspiracy offences, grooming and the possession of child-abuse images. Police discovered on Bolinger's computer indecent pseudo-images of children aged between four and sixteen which had been digitally manipulated to display his cannibalism interests. When questioned about the pictures, he told detectives: 'I do not find children sexually attractive but I do find them interesting as a food source.' Police officers dug in Bolinger's garden seeking clues after reading his email correspondence with Gilberto Valle, in which Bolinger had recounted how he had eaten a woman and a five-year-old boy, saying: 'I also love roasting whole pelvises, mind you only did with the little one so far.' Bolinger had also offered to fly to New York to help Valle kill and butcher a woman, offering to bring anaesthetic gas and a meat cleaver. 'I'd love to eat another child,' said Moody Blues to 'Girl-meat Hunter' Valle.

However, these sordid remarks made by Bolinger to Valle were not the cause of his ultimate undoing. He had also exchanged emails with a young Mexican teenager called 'Eva' in which he described the sex acts he planned to perform with her prior to killing and preparing her 'for the table'. At his UK trial in July 2014, it was revealed that he made an arrangement to meet 'Eva' at a railway station in Kent and some days earlier had purchased an axe from a Homebase DIY store in Broadstairs, writing to the girl the evening before the intended meeting, saying: 'Got the axe, you ready to get that train?' Bolinger waited at the station, but 'Eva' did not turn up. Bolinger was found guilty at Canterbury Crown Court of grooming and attempting to lure a fourteen-year-old girl because he allegedly wanted to kill and eat her. Before the trial, he admitted other charges, including administering a poison or noxious substance after he put a cloth soaked in dry cleaning fluid over his friend Urlene King's mouth in July 2010. He also pleaded guilty to one count of making indecent pseudo-photographs of children and seven counts of publishing an obscene article. In September 2014 he was jailed for nine years and was also made the subject of a sexual offences prevention order to stop him using the internet without permission.

After Bolinger's conviction, Detective Inspector Rob Chitham, of Kent Police, said that the investigation was long and complicated because much of the evidence was in the USA. 'In addition, the people who use fetish chat-rooms go to great lengths to hide their identity and specialist knowledge and equipment is needed to determine who they are and where they live.' Thousands of pages of chat logs between Valle and Bolinger had been sent to England. 'It's some of the worst stuff I've ever seen and I've been in child protection for seven years,' DI Chitham said. 'Over time you think you have witnessed the depths of depravity, but he plumbed it again.'

During the trial Bolinger's lawyers, like Valle's, claimed he was a fantasist – 'more Walter Mitty than Hannibal Lecter' – but DI Chitham said: 'Where the fantasy defence ceases is when the individual steps outside the virtual world and takes action within the real world ... Bolinger stepped outside the virtual world when he made specific plans to meet the girl and purchased an axe to decapitate her.' Bolinger, however, claimed that had 'Eva' turned up at the railway station, he would have taken her home and contacted social services. This was met with raised eyebrows from the police. 'I have heard more convincing defences,' was DI Chitham's wry comment. 'Cannibal fantasies have been around since the earliest times, but the difference in the modern era is that before it was difficult to share them.'

Gilberto Valle, meanwhile, stays in the public eye, claiming in interviews that not only was he an innocent victim who had been 'thrown into prison for his thoughts' but that he intended to sue for wrongful imprisonment. During February 2017 he gave several interviews to promote his autobiography *Raw Deal: The Untold Story of NYPD's 'Cannibal Cop'* in which he said he still immerses himself in flesh-eating fantasies on his favourite sadistic websites and feels no sense of shame about his 'fetishes'. The book tells of how he progressed from bondage porn during his teenage years to the *Dark Fetish Network* which 'covered the whole spectrum ... cannibalism ... torture, castration, pissing, shitting, slavery, leather, executions, mummification, it just went on and on ... it was obvious there was something there for everyone with an unusual sexual fetish ... the intro to DFN said it all: "Welcome to the social network where you won't feel like an outcast because of your dark fetish ... because this place is created by people like you, FOR people like you!"'

Valle wrote the book to 'set the record straight' about his life for the benefit of his young daughter, he told the *New York Post*.[35] 'One day my daughter will be old enough to look into all this stuff on her own and I want her to read something that came from me,' he said. A couple of months later, in May 2017, he appeared on *Crime Watch Daily* to tell of his popularity with the women he meets through dating sites and announced that he had been 'a very good husband'. He issued an on-screen plea to his wife Kathleen, whom he hasn't seen since that day when she took their baby girl and fled the New York apartment after reading about her 'good' husband's fantasies to kill and eat her. 'I'm just so incredibly sorry that this all happened,' Valle declared. 'You know, I wish we had our old life back.'

Valle now works in the construction industry. In 2019 he told an audience at a CrimeCon convention in New Orleans that he still received death-threats: 'I understand that people don't like what I did, but the question is, is not liking me reason enough to have me in prison for the rest of my life?'

Celebrity Culture

'Murderers have become online broadcasters – and their audience is us'

Steve Lillebuen, *Globe and Mail*, Canada, 2 June 2012

Anna Yourkin and Donald Newman were just troubled teenagers in 1982 when their first child, Eric Clinton Kirk Newman, was born. The couple from Scarborough, Ontario, gave him the middle names of their two favourite actors: Kirk Douglas and Clint Eastwood. Two more children followed, but it was not a happy home. Donald Newman was diagnosed with schizophrenia and divorced Anna, leaving the family home when Eric was twelve. According to Anna, her ex-husband was a Nazi and an abuser; according to the boy himself, his mother was the abuser; an obsessive-compulsive germophobe, strong on discipline, who refused to send her son into formal education which she perceived as dangerously germ-laden – so Eric did not go to school until he was eleven years old, where, he claimed, he was bullied.

Eric had obsessions of his own: old movie pin-ups like Marilyn Monroe and Ava Gardner, newer film icons like Sharon Stone, star of *Basic Instinct*. As a child he played with Barbie dolls and wanted to be a girl – and his maternal grandmother, who helped to raise him, would dress him in her clothes. But, he alleged, she also called him 'a faggot' – and so did his younger brother. Friendless, withdrawn and emotionally unstable, Eric was later to tell psychiatrists of suffering paranoia, a fear of abandonment, the need for love and an enduring feeling of emptiness. His first medical diagnosis of paranoid schizophrenia was made when he was seventeen – after which he dropped out of school and eventually left his home behind. He was treated for schizophrenia intermittently over the following years: there was talk of psychosis.

But as one century passed into the next, Eric realised that what he really ached for was fame: he wanted to be a celebrity, an actor, a model – and he thought he had the good looks for it, even blaming his narcissistic obsession with his appearance as the reason why he had alienated other people during his school years. He had cosmetic surgery – a nose job – and in 2008 was thrilled when the possibility of celebrity materialised: he was offered an audition for *Plastic Makes Perfect*, a TV reality show that follows individuals through cosmetic surgery. 'People would say to me all the time, even when I was a teenager … every time you pass a mirror, all you do is glance in it,' he told a producer. He claimed he worked full-time, 'whether it's doing films, magazines or internet shows in Montreal, Toronto or Los Angeles.' This was untrue. His application for the show was rejected. Hopes of stardom dwindled.

With the internet, though, the enchanted world of social media chat-rooms and dating sites continued to beguile him, offering another fantasy route to a disturbed young man trying to invent his own personal mythology. During almost a decade on Facebook he used a variety of false names to create literally scores of alluring profiles, the imaginary characters frosted with intrigue and grandiose self-puffery. He invented an untrue rumour about himself which went viral, suggesting he had once dated a Canadian female murderer who was in jail – then he put himself in the spotlight by arranging interviews to publicly deny the rumour, saying it was someone else's attempt to destroy his life.

Offline, meanwhile, reality was different. He rattled through a series of sleazier life-roles: he worked as a stripper, an escort, a participant in porn movies, a rent boy. He was found guilty of several credit card fraud crimes, given a suspended sentence and put on probation. In 2007 he declared bankruptcy, owing $17,000 in debts. He advertised on gay dating sites, including *Craigslist*, describing himself in much the same way as he did in his TV show audition. He adopted two tiny kittens to keep in his apartment and named them Jasmin and Kenny. In April 2012 he was to tell a psychiatrist at a Montreal hospital – who referred him for therapy and anti-depressants – that he had been sexually assaulted by a male cousin when he was fourteen, that he heard voices in his head and that he was often convinced he was being followed. Later he would claim his actions were being controlled by someone called 'Manny Lopez', a former lover from New York.

But by then Eric wasn't even Eric anymore: he had changed his name by deed poll in 2006. The majority of his innumerable fake online identities contained his new name, a name which would ultimately give him the notoriety he yearned for. It contained a surname he had casually pilfered from one of the largest vineyards in Ontario: Luka Rocco Magnotta. Only weeks after that psychiatric consultation in April 2012, he posted in the *Men Seeking Men* section of the *Craigslist* classified advertisement website for a 'Prince Charming ... a single white male, 28-38 years of age ... in shape ... one who is loyal, preferably educated, financially and emotionally stable, for a long term committed relationship.' Lin Jun, a gentle, thirty-three-year-old Chinese student is thought to have responded to this or another online dating ad, for he went to Magnotta's Montreal apartment, where Magnotta tied him up and then filmed himself stabbing Lin Jun to death before dismembering and grotesquely sexually abusing his victim. Then, producing a steak knife and fork, Magnotta cannibalised the young man's corpse and fed some of the flesh to a puppy he had just acquired, before packaging-up the victim's severed hands and feet, ready for mailing to public organisations in several Canadian cities. On May 25, 2012, Magnotta uploaded the eleven-minute video to a website called *BestGore.com* and entitled it *1 Lunatic 1 Ice Pick*.

★ ★ ★ ★

The internet has greatly expanded the hunting ground for predators, paedophiles, child traffickers and other perverts, some who need look no further than the sort of online dating sites used by Magnotta. Tens of millions of people use dating sites – forty million in the United States alone, according to one internet survey[36] which gathers statistical data from several crime and cybercrime monitoring organisations. A recent study by Stanford University and the University of New Mexico shows that almost forty per cent of relationships are believed to start online. These are alarming figures when it is also suggested that ten per cent of sex offenders use online dating to meet people. Reported crimes related to online dating have also risen dramatically over the last five years. A study by Sky News found that crimes connected with two of the biggest organisations, Tinder and Grindr, have an especially dark side, as for many users the emphasis has moved away from relationships to an expectation of no-strings sex with strangers – something that has a particular prevalence among gay men.

In the world of adult consensual dating there is a higher incidence of fake online profiles, of 'catfishing' (where a pursuer pretends to be someone else online), of stalking and of sexual, abusive or violent crimes occurring more frequently. Internet predators are estimated to commit over 16,000 abductions, one hundred murders and thousands of rapes annually. In the UK, between 2011 and 2016, there was almost a 400 per cent increase in such internet-linked crimes, with the National Crime Agency detecting that the number of reported rapes rose six-fold during that five-year period. Since the police believe that only sixteen per cent of rapes and sexual assaults are actually reported, this figure is regarded as 'the tip of the iceberg,' said the head of the NCA's investigation team, Sean Sutton, cautioning internet daters to meet in public. 'Over seventy per cent of the stranger rape cases we see are from people going home with their date or taking their date back to their own accommodation on the first date,' warned Mr Sutton.[37]

Among the countless internet-linked murders worldwide, the victims – both male and female – have been stabbed, strangled, beaten to death, tortured, dismembered and even buried alive by sadistic and sometimes cannibalistic killers. In 2008 Canadian Mark Twitchell posed as a woman on a dating site called *Plenty of Fish* to lure a man to his home, where he bludgeoned and stabbed him, then cut his body into pieces. On Twitchell's laptop police found a file called 'Serial Killer Confessions' purporting to be a fictional story of his fantasy of becoming a serial killer. 'I've always had a dark side I've had to sugarcoat for the world ... On my journey of discovering my disorder, I've discovered my killer instinct,' he wrote, before detailing how the story's protagonist used online dating sites to select victims. In December 2019, when twenty-five-year-old Kevin Bacon went missing from his Michigan home on Christmas Eve, police went to check on Mark Latunski, a fifty-year-old who had set up a meeting with Bacon via the dating website Grindr. They found a scene of horror at Latunski's house. The young man was suspended naked from a rafter by his ankles. Allegedly Latunski had stabbed him in the back, slit his throat, then cut off his testicles and eaten them. He has been imprisoned for two years awaiting trial, which is set for 2022. Latunski has reportedly confessed to the murder.

In November 2017 a twenty-four-year-old Nebraska woman, Sydney Loofe, never returned from a date with Bailey Boswell, a woman whom she had met on Tinder. A month later her dismembered body was found in garbage bags dumped by a roadside: she had been killed by Boswell and her fifty-three-year-old boyfriend Aubrey Trail, a 'sex cult' leader who called himself a vampire, and claimed that he could read minds and fly, and who taught his 'witch' followers that they would gain powers if they tortured and killed. All of these women had been recruited by Boswell on Tinder. One of them told the Nebraska court in July 2019 – when Trail was found guilty – that Trail had wanted them to make snuff movies (films where a real-life murder is purported to be portrayed) for him to sell. Other testimony held that Trail bragged about the murder and said he had drunk Loofe's blood. In June 2021 Trail was sentenced to be executed by lethal injection, the judge saying that his was a crime of 'exceptional depravity'. Nebraska is a state which still maintains the death penalty, although it is rarely applied. Trail's sentence will be automatically appealed under state law. Boswell was also convicted on first-degree murder charges and in November 2021 she was sentenced to a lifetime in prison.

For criminal investigators pursuing such grotesque perpetrators, those who select their victims via mainstream dating websites instead of concealed *Dark Net* sites do at least provide a first foothold when it comes to tracking down the guilty after the crime has been committed. But what made the Luka Magnotta case so very different, what made his story extraordinary, was his identification and capture. His use of the mainstream internet for personal narcissistic propaganda meant that his murderous intentions were unwittingly revealed well in advance and he became trapped in a net which spread further than he could have envisaged, one constructed not by professional crime-fighters but by worldwide web-surfers: amateurs who became cyber-sleuths. Long before Magnotta murdered Lin Jun, he was actually identified as potentially dangerous, his name and even his Canadian address was determined – and an alert was sent to the police in that city: 'This man would become a killer,' they were told. The tragedy was that the police failed to pursue that line of investigation and the day came when the amateur internet detectives were to switch on their computer screens and realise with sickened horror that they had been right all along, that their warning had not been heeded and that Magnotta had now done exactly what they had most feared.

* * * *

Deanna Thompson and John Green lived hundreds of miles apart in the USA and did not know each other. But one night in December 2010 they, along with many other people from all over the planet, had clicked on a video which had been uploaded to YouTube under the title *1 Boy 2 Kittens*. It was a title suggestive of a cute cat video, one of thousands which circulate on social media – and at first it appeared benign. With a background soundtrack of John Lennon's song 'Happy Christmas, War is Over', into the frame came a young male in a hoodie-jacket affectionately petting and stroking two tiny wide-eyed kittens. Moments later, though, he could be seen pushing the little wriggling creatures into a large polythene clothes storage bag – the sort with an airtight seal which enables all the air to be extracted from the bag using a vacuum cleaner. Slowly and deliberately he sealed the bag while the animals mewed and tried to escape, then he attached a vacuum hose and turned it on, slowly suffocating the struggling kittens until they no longer moved. Then the camera was turned off. Deanna Thompson, who was winding down after another long day's work as a data analyst at a Las Vegas casino was stunned, distressed and horrified – and she wasn't alone, for the YouTube comments box beneath the video was exploding with the fury of hundreds of animal-lovers. 'Does anyone know who this motherfucker is?' asked one. 'He should rot in hell,' declared another. 'You're going to go to jail,' roared another. But reading the comments and threats of these angry people, the only thing Deanna could remember thinking was: 'But who are you going to call? This guy could have lived in Siberia for all we knew.'

In Los Angeles, John Green said to himself: 'What type of individual would do that?' The video had two thousand worldwide views and soon a link appeared on one, to a newly-created Facebook page called *Find The Kitten Vacuumer ... for Great Justice*. It already had ninety-three members. John and Deanna joined up. So did someone else – assumed to be the kitten-killer himself – who posted an anonymous link to a movie called *Catch Me If You Can*. 'I took that as a challenge,' said John. 'This person wanted to play a game of cat and mouse and I was up for that.' Their resolve strengthened by the Facebook group friendship, John and Deanna began to work together to identify the torturer of the kittens.

Carefully they studied the cramped room in the video and drew up a diagram of it. Then they enlarged individual shots of the bed, the door, the light, the table, the bedspread with a distinctive wolf's head design, the electric wall sockets and asked all the Facebook group members to identify a specific country by these items. They discovered that the bedspread had been bought on Ebay and was the only one of its kind – but were unable to discover the buyer's country. They called out to the group members to identify the language of a voice which could be heard in the background of the video – and someone from Russia did, but this lead died when another Russian member identified the speech as taken from a recording of a Russian situation comedy show. There was great frustration. 'We thought: "this person is trying to mislead us",' said John. Deanna said wearily: 'We spent weeks on this Russian bullshit. I spent sixteen hours looking at doorknobs from Lithuania.'

Then suddenly, another video was posted to the Facebook page. This showed the killer, his face blurred-out, playing with the stiff bodies of the dead kittens and it contained a link to a fake profile account in the name of 'John Smith'. While some of the group members were concerned for their safety, knowing their group had been infiltrated by the killer, John and Deanna turned to the new video for more clues. They noted a cigarette packet, a yellow vacuum cleaner, a clearer view of the plug sockets. Cigarette packets are shaped differently depending upon the country; more importantly, they have a written health warning – in the language of that country. These packets – and the exact model of the vacuum cleaner – were only sold in North America.

Then Deanna and John found themselves working with a new set of animal-loving supporters called Rescue Ink: a group of tough leather-clad bikers from New York. 'We have an in-your-face approach to rescuing animals from bad situations,' the leader – codenamed 'Joe Panz' – explained cryptically in a Netflix documentary about the sleuthing mission of John, Deanna and the other Facebook group members.[38] 'Joe' was anxious to track down the perpetrator of this animal torture. His sister, a psychologist with knowledge of criminal profiling, had told him – quite correctly, as is outlined in Chapter Ten of this book – that the kitten-killer was highly likely to graduate eventually to murdering humans. 'She said this wasn't the first time he had done this and it wouldn't be the last time – it would get progressively worse,' said Joe. 'This is an early warning of somebody who is going to become a serial killer ... who needs to be stopped immediately.'

Rescue Ink joined the Facebook group and brought its 100,000 followers with it. They also offered a $5,000 reward to anyone who found the man who slaughters kittens. The world responded. 'We had tens of thousands of people sending us photographs from all over the globe,' said Deanna. 'It was chaos.' A third video was posted on the internet, showing a kitten in a cage with a man pouring petrol over it and burning it alive. He looked remarkably like the hooded killer in the previous videos. Joe sent a message to the person who had posted it: 'Are you the 1 Boy 2 Kittens killer?' and he received a chilling reply: 'Yes, I kill kittens. LOL', accompanied by a video of fireworks being set off. The disgust that this video engendered sent the group on a quest to expose the killer by using reverse-imagery of still pictures from the videos, but apart from turning up one possible match on a pornography website, the group found itself going down more rabbit holes, including one which led to an innocent young man in Africa being 'trolled' online. He was a depressive person and was later to commit suicide.

After this tragedy the Facebook group lost impetus and months passed. Its membership halved from the 16,000 people whose fury had peaked in early 2011. Then in December 2011, a year after the first video had appeared, another one was posted for the group to see. It bore the title *Bathtime lol* and showed a desperately frightened cat immobilised with parcel-tape tying it to the end of a pole. The pole was then lowered under bathwater until the cat drowned, while in the background a jaunty piece of pop music played.

Then later the same day a further YouTube video was uploaded, one which bore the username *Lesley Ann Downey*. It is a name infamous in the UK – that of a ten-year-old who was tortured, raped and killed on Boxing Day 1964 by the 'Moors Murderers' Ian Brady and Myra Hindley. Five children were murdered by them in the 1960s and the bodies were buried under Saddleworth Moor near Manchester in north-west England. And during this follow-up cat-killing video, the musical track was 'The Little Drummer Boy' – a Christmas song which had also played on a tape recorded by Hindley and Brady as they carried out the sadistic murder of little Lesley Ann Downey while she begged for her life. So distressing was that tape that it reduced policemen, news reporters and lawyers to tears when it was played in court at the trial of Brady and Hindley in 1966. They were found guilty just six months after the death penalty for murder had been abolished in the United Kingdom, meaning that the most severe penalty for them both was life imprisonment.

And here, on this internet video in 2011, that music was playing again. The cat-killer was wearing a Santa hat and sunglasses and more of his face was visible. The kitten being stroked affectionately in this film appeared to be very afraid of something under the sofa and as the camera rolled, the threat became visible: it was a python. The terrified kitten was fed to the snake, which slowly consumed it, and the innocent Christmas song 'The Little Drummer Boy' played horrifically in the background. The Facebook group were galvanised into action yet again, using image and facial recognition searches to scroll through a multitude of online photographs of young men wearing sunglasses similar to the ones in the latest video. Then, out of the blue, Deanna received a message from an unknown sender calling themselves 'Beverly Knight', announcing that the name of the person for whom the group was looking was 'Luka Magnotta'. There is little doubt that 'Beverly Knight' was Magnotta himself and a Google search instantly turned up 'hundreds and hundreds' of astonishing results, said Deanna. 'It was a slide-show of him posing.' A clip of an audition tape from a TV show called *Cover Guy*, a Canadian reality series about male models, showed Magnotta announcing to the camera: 'A lot of people tell me I'm really devastatingly good-looking.' From the array of Magnotta photographs, it seemed, John said, as if he was leading a jet-setting lifestyle: 'There were pictures of him in Bermuda, Sweden, Russia, in front of the Eiffel Tower, in Rome and Miami.' The internet search also threw up a plethora of fan sites in his name. Said Deanna: 'A lot of the comments on these sites said really flattering things about him, like "You are so hot and sexy." There was story after contorted story about Luka online, about him becoming a model, a suggestion that he was a long-lost cousin of River Phoenix, or Marilyn Monroe's son, or that he was dating Madonna.' A wedding picture appeared on one 'fan site', with Magnotta declaring that he had just married the girl in Russia.

But John worked out that Luka wasn't quite the jet-setter he appeared to be: he discovered that a large proportion of the photographs were originally of other people: Magnotta had edited them by placing his head on the bodies of random men posing in stylish clothes in glamorous places. After hours of searching online John was able to find many of the original photographs – including the wedding picture. Then John studied the countless Magnotta 'fan sites' – police were later to establish that there were at least seventy Facebook pages and twenty websites about Magnotta – and he grasped that these, together with all the comments and responses from 'fans' which they contained, were identical across all the sites and that they appeared to have been written by the same person with a thirst for internet fame, including the fake rumours and hoaxes which suggested he was being cyber-stalked.

'I gradually realised that they were all created by Luka himself,' John said. However, for a patient researcher with John's computer skills, the genuine Magnotta pictures, including one 'selfie' taken on the balcony of a high-rise apartment block of flats, were to prove useful. Using metadata he was able to discover the exact GPS co-ordinates which dated the photographs as having been taken in Toronto, Canada, in October 2010 – just a month before Magnotta had uploaded his first *1 Boy 2 Kittens* video onto the internet site. Behind and below Magnotta's balcony picture was a street-view with a petrol station and other buildings and by cross-referencing the landmarks with all the data he had gathered, John was able to deduce Magnotta's building and his exact apartment in it. Excitedly, he and Deanna informed the Toronto police of Magnotta's name, address and his online cat-killing activities, together with their fears about what Magnotta might do when he no longer got his kicks from animal torture. But it was now December 2011, more than a year after the photograph had been taken. The police checked the address: Magnotta had lived there, they told John and Deanna, but he was there no longer; they thought he had moved to Russia.

Whether Magnotta had ever been in Russia at all was not certain, but after the last two videos had been posted online during December 2011, he turned up in England. *The Sun*, a popular tabloid newspaper, had run a story about the cat-killing film with the python under the splash headline *Catch the Sicko*. Days later, journalist Alex West received an anonymous message telling him that the name of the person he sought was Luka Magnotta, who happened to be in London, staying at a certain hotel; he wished to meet West for an interview. Wearing a hidden microphone, West went to the hotel. Magnotta denied any involvement in the kitten videos and said he had moved to London to avoid harassment, claiming to have been framed. Alex West described the encounter: 'I looked into his eyes and did not like what I saw,' he wrote. 'It wasn't just his appearance that was weird – his behaviour was very odd as well. In a strange, high-pitched voice, he spent twenty minutes denying that he was involved in killing the kitten.' Then Magnotta abruptly ended the interview.

Two days later, the newspaper received an email purporting to come from 'John Kilbride'. (John Kilbride was, in fact, the name of another of the child victims of the Moors Murderers.) Magnotta was later to confess to the Montreal police that he was the author of this email. 'I will continue to make more movies,' Magnotta announced. 'Next time you hear from me it will be in a movie I am producing that will have some humans in it, not just pussies. You see, killing is different than smoking. With smoking you can actually quit. Once you kill and taste blood, it's impossible to stop. The urge is just too strong not to continue ... Getting away with all this, now that's genius.'

Magnotta returned to Canada and at the end of January 2012 he moved into an apartment in Montreal. He paid up the rent until 1 June – which was to be a week after the 25 May murder of Jun Lin. During the first few months of 2012 Magnotta ceased posting films of himself torturing animals, although his online presence continued to expand. A blog site named *Necrophilia Serial Killer*

Luka Magnotta contained photographs of himself with his views about having sex with corpses: 'It's not cool to the world being a necrophiliac,' he wrote, in something of an understatement. 'It's bloody lonely. But I don't really care, I have never cared what people thought of me. Most people are judgmental idiots.' Magnotta posted on two white supremacist sites about his hatred of other races, particularly the Chinese. An online article believed to have been posted by Magnotta was called 'How to disappear completely and never be found' and shared a six-step process for escaping and changing one's identity – which included severing all ties to personal relationships, liquidating one's assets and creating fake documents – and warning that it was not 'an undertaking to be entered into lightly' because at least four months' planning was needed to 'successfully carry out the heroic actions necessary to leave your old life behind.'

Attention-seeking Magnotta was certainly signalling his intentions transparently, but no one other than the Facebook group who recognised his dangerousness appeared to be taking it seriously. On a website forum called *Orato*, which invites people to speak about their experiences, could be found a 2007 post from 'Luka Magnotta' who claimed to be 'a citizen journalist' telling how he overcame mental illness after a traumatic childhood and teenage experimentation with drugs and alcohol which ended in his hospitalisation for 'a depressive disorder'. He said that after leaving home to live on the streets, his life eventually turned around when he went into an assisted living facility and got the right medication. In his trademark boastful tone, he added: 'I am now successful beyond my wildest dreams. I travel the world, ride around in limos, have only the most expensive clothing. I've come a long way from eating out of old pizza boxes on the streets.'

But in April 2012, Magnotta walked into the Jewish General Hospital in Montreal, asking for help with his mental problems, talking about his previous diagnoses of schizophrenia with a psychiatrist who suggested a further appointment and medication. However, what Luka Magnotta did instead was to increase his presence on gay dating websites. Ten days in advance of his upload onto *Bestgore.com* of the eleven-minute video of his grotesque murder of Jun Lin, Magnotta promoted it online. The promo video contained a photograph of a man who looked like him holding an ice pick, together with a hooded figure leaning forward in front of a wall-poster of the 1942 film *Casablanca*. The title *1 Lunatic 1 Ice Pick* was based upon a graphic snuff movie from 2008 called *3 Guys 1 Hammer*. During the communications with Jun Lin before they met, Magnotta told him he wanted to make a movie and the gentle Chinese student went to Magnotta's apartment on that understanding.

The cultural media and movie 'clues' which Magnotta had long used to try and enhance his mystery as a catch-me-if-you-can killer were prominent in the snuff video of Jun Lin's death which Magnotta was to upload to *Bestgore.com* on May 25. The *Casablanca* poster from the promotional trailer was prominently placed over the bed where, after drugging Jun Lin and caressing his face in a comparable manner to his petting of the kittens in previous videos, Luka Magnotta slaughtered him as he lay supine in a crucified position, hands bound. The 1987 New Order song, 'True Faith' plays as the camera captures Magnotta frenziedly stabbing his captive more than a hundred times in the abdomen, chest and face with a screwdriver which he had sharpened and painted to resemble an ice pick, such as the one used by Sharon Stone's character, Catherine Tramell, in the opening scene of the film *Basic Instinct*. The New Order song was also a reference to another movie: it was used prominently in *American Psycho* (2000) about a sadistic serial killer, played chillingly by Christian Bale. Magnotta can be seen hacking off Jun Lin's head, placing it in a box and then, for the camera, he dreamily swings the box around in an abstracted manner. After cutting off the arms and legs, he masturbates with one of the limbs and then commits other necrophiliac sexual acts with the victim's corpse, including sodomising him with a wine-bottle. Then Magnotta produces a steak knife and fork and removes pieces of flesh from the body to eat. Moments later, a small black-and-white puppy appears in the shot and Magnotta feeds it some flesh.

Watching this carnage, Deanna and John shared the horrified revulsion of thousands of other online viewers, but in their case there was an added dimension: they had been following Magnotta's deviant activities for a year-and-a-half and had even reported their concerns to the Toronto police on one occasion. 'Why didn't they listen to us?' asked Deanna. 'Everything we said was going to happen, he did.' They immediately wrote to the same Toronto detective with whom they had previously communicated, to alert him regarding Magnotta's video and while waiting for his response, John moved back into online sleuth mode. He looked in detail at some of the recent photographs posted on the internet by Magnotta and quickly realised that the background to Magnotta's selfies was no longer Toronto; some more work confirmed to John that this was Montreal. They emailed the Montreal police department to offer to tell them what they already knew about the video and the killer featured in it. But although the *Bestgore.com* film had been seen by 70,000 people, apparently none of them worked for the Montreal police department. Numerous other viewers – including an American lawyer – tried to report the online murder to the police and the FBI, but no corpse had been discovered and the police paid little attention. 'How do we establish credibility with the Montreal police now?' was John's query during the documentary series which tracked the private internet manhunt spearheaded by himself and Deanna, *Don't F*** With Cats*. 'We're just internet nerds.' (Later, Montreal police would actually ask to join their Facebook offshoot site in order to access the extensive catalogue of information and clues they had gathered on Magnotta and their speculation about his motives and delusions.)

As time passed, Jun Lin's university friends were becoming anxious about him: he had not attended classes since 24 May, and he had disappeared from his apartment, leaving behind his much-loved – and by now very hungry – cat. This was not something a caring animal-lover like Jun Lin would do, they agreed, and their concern deepened. Then something happened: a bloodstained package was delivered to the headquarters of the Conservative Party of Canada, containing a severed foot, accompanied by a note which said that six body parts had been distributed altogether and declaring that more murders were planned. During the ensuing days several political and educational establishments in Canada received packages mailed from Montreal containing severed body parts. The news made headlines all over the world, but it was not until 29 May – days after Luka Magnotta had already fled Canada – when a janitor found a suitcase containing a decomposing torso in a pile of garbage at the back of a Montreal apartment block that the police got their first lead – assuming one discounts the very precise lead emailed to them several days earlier by Deanna Thompson and John Green, which had been ignored. Among the garbage at the apartment block there were bags containing more human remains, bloody clothes, the weapons used to kill, a blood-spattered cinema poster advertising *Casablanca* and the dead body of a small black-and-white puppy. They also found papers, letters and a driver's licence on which there was Magnotta's name and address. But, as Magnotta had probably intended, the murdered corpse was at first thought to be that of Magnotta himself.

'I didn't have a clue who this person was,' said Detective Inspector Claudette Hamlin, who was in charge of the case. 'I concluded that this was Luka Rocco Magnotta who had been killed.' Later the CCTV footage in the public areas of the apartment building told another story: the arrival of Magnotta at the building with Jun Lin on 24 May, Jun Lin in a bright yellow teeshirt following Magnotta through the door; Magnotta in the early hours of 25 May making twenty trips to the building's garbage station to calmly deposit large black bags there – wearing the yellow top which had been Jun Lin's; Magnotta's subsequent departure from the front of the building carrying a travel bag and pausing to pout and check himself in the lobby mirror on his way out.

But still the police – who had not seen the online snuff movie – lacked certainty about what had happened inside the apartment and to whom. It took more CCTV footage obtained from the Montreal post office used by Magnotta to send out his macabre parcels to produce a clear image of the person at the counter, which matched that of the surveillance film within the apartment block. Magnotta himself was long gone, of course, but there was a cryptic message from him scrawled in red ink on the inside of his closet: 'Don't look in the mirror. I don't care' (sic). It was confirmed that the body parts were those of Jun Lin, but it was not until July 1 that his head was recovered from a lake in a Montreal park. By then, Magnotta had been in custody in Canada for two weeks – but only after an international manhunt involving Interpol had tracked him down to Europe.

Magnotta, presumably following his own online advice on 'how to disappear and create a new identity' had flown from Montreal to Paris on May 26, 2012, just after his murder of Jun Lin. He used a false name at the first hotel he checked into: Kirk Trammel. This was one of his own original birth-names coupled with the surname of the female killer in *Basic Instinct*. In later check-ins, he used the Magnotta name. The Parisian police force, alarmed that a sadistic murderer dubbed by French newspapers as 'The Butcher of Montreal' was somewhere in their city, were spurred into action and pursued him from one hotel to another by tracking his mobile phone – until eventually they learned that Magnotta had travelled by bus to Berlin. Once there, Magnotta headed to an internet café and settled down with one of the computers to enable him to find out what the world was saying about him. It was saying plenty. Enough, in fact, for the café owner to recognise him and put in a call to the German police. They arrested Magnotta as he gazed at a screen showing his favourite things: pictures and stories about himself. The date was 4 June 2012.

Magnotta was extradited and flown back to Canadian custody on a military plane, one reason for this choice being the fear that passengers on a routine flight might identify him and be disturbed at the memory of his horrific acts. At his jury trial – which eventually took place in December 2014 – he pleaded not guilty to 'murder, suffering indignities to a human body and using the postal service to distribute obscene materials'. His defence attorney claimed that he had been in a 'psychotic state' at the time. Six psychiatric expert witnesses diagnosed him variously as having a borderline personality disorder, a narcissistic or an antisocial personality disorder, paranoid schizophrenia and paraphilia – which describes extreme sexual fetishistic deviance.

This insanity defence was countered by the prosecution, who pointed out that the premeditated 'purposeful, mindful, ultra-organised' nature of the crime made him responsible for his actions. An example of this could be inferred in Magnotta's curious claim that he had been controlled and persecuted for years by someone called 'Manny Lopez' from New York, who had forced him into committing all his crimes. More than a year before the murder of Jun Lin, Magnotta had visited a New York lawyer to say that he was very afraid of 'Manny' and he listed the abuse he had received at the man's hands. His improbable story was that among many awful acts, he had been forced to 'eat animal parts' and 'have sex with dogs' and that he had been kidnapped, raped and drugged by 'Manny'. (After Magnotta's conviction, the lawyer marvelled that by trying to make this case to him, Magnotta had been setting up an alibi long in advance of his crime.)

'Manny' appeared in one of the psychiatrists' court reports, Magnotta claiming that 'Manny' had forced him to kill the kittens and film it, but that he was very 'scared' and 'couldn't stop shaking' as he was doing so. Magnotta said that on the night of the murder of Jun Lin, 'Manny' had turned up in Montreal to direct in detail the filmed killing because he believed the young man to be 'an agent'. Afterwards, said Magnotta, it was 'Manny' who took the film away and uploaded it onto the internet. A police and legal search was instigated to find 'Emmanuel Lopez' using Magnotta's information, but they could find no proof of his existence. Meanwhile, Magnotta expanded on the 'Manny' story to his mother, saying that 'Manny' had been parked outside the apartment during the murder and had repeatedly phoned Magnotta to instruct him on what he must do to his victim during the slaughter. The police checked Magnotta's phone records and found no calls had been received during the evening of the murder. Additionally, the surveillance videos obtained from the building showed a calm and unruffled Magnotta after the murder, strolling alone through the corridors and making some twenty journeys to dispose of the garbage bags containing body parts.

Magnotta was found guilty of all charges and sentenced to a mandatory life sentence, eligible for parole in 2039. The detective inspector in charge of the case, Claudette Hamlin, said she believed that Magnotta had achieved what he wanted, which was celebrity. 'He was playing a movie and he was the star of the movie,' she said. John Green – who, with Deanna Johnson had played a significant role in their Facebook tracking of Magnotta agreed: 'He just wanted to be a famous serial killer.' John and Deanna, trying to make sense of this motive, together with the 'Manny' story, looked back at their masses of stored information for some clues – and they were there in the movies. The film poster of *Casablanca* posted above the bed where Magnotta killed Jun Lin was a hint about where Magnotta would flee to, Deanna believed. 'There's always Paris,' says Bogart in the final frame, and to Paris Magnotta went. But the main source of the cannibal killer's sick inspiration came from *Basic Instinct*: the screwdriver modified to look like an ice pick; the surname of Sharon Stone's character Catherine Tramell when he was creating a fake identity in Paris; even Tramell's cryptic remark which he adapted for his message to *The Sun* newspaper in 2011: 'Killing isn't like smoking. You can quit.' Deanna noticed that there was someone called 'Manny' in the film too: Manny Vasquez was Catherine Tramell's former fiancé, who had died during a boxing match.

Deanna and John's sense of satisfaction at this sort of successful sleuthing was instead of certainty, pervaded by doubts. In the Netflix movie they express concern that in following Magnotta's murderous trail of clues they allowed themselves – and the other outraged people on social media who were in pursuit – to be manipulated by him.

'Maybe we were pawns,' said John. Deanna fretted: 'Did we feed the monster?'

And of course, Magnotta did achieve the fame he craved. Efforts were made to crush this in Canada: the leader of the Liberal Party at the time declared that Canadians should mourn Jun Lin rather than recognise Magnotta's notoriety 'in any way, shape or form' and the government expressed its condolences to Jun Lin's family and to the Chinese ambassador. An award was created in Jun Lin's honour at the Montreal university he attended. Additionally, *Bestgore. com* owner Mark Marek faced an obscenity charge for corrupting public morals by allowing the snuff movie to be shown online and was given a six-month jail sentence. The case drew comparisons with that of Mark Twitchell, another convicted North American murderer who had been arrested the previous year (see above). Twitchell also used social media to promote his crimes by writing *Serial Killer Confessions*, which was about luring a man using fake online dating profiles as bait. He also dismembered the body. Soon after the discovery of Jun Lin's murder, Canadian author Steve Lillebuen, whose book *The Devil's Cinema* was about Twitchell, made an accurate assessment of narcissistic killers – and specifically Magnotta – who seek notoriety by using direct internet access to a global audience:

'The internet has eroded the judiciary's role as gatekeeper, leaving the door open to a morbidly curious community that seeks out the very kind of filth once considered taboo – some of it produced by the killers themselves ... now it's gone mainstream, making celebrity-seeking killers into broadcasters who use Google and social media to self-promote.'

Steve Lillebuen, *Globe and Mail*, Canada 2 June 2012

Present Imperfect, Future Tense

> *'The question had come into my mind abruptly: were these creatures fools? ...You see I had always anticipated that the people of the year Eight Hundred and Two Thousand odd would be incredibly in front of us in knowledge, art, everything ... I have thought since how particularly ill-equipped I was for such an experience. When I had started with the Time Machine, I had started with the absurd assumption that the men of the Future would certainly be infinitely ahead of ourselves in all their appliances'*

> H. G. Wells, *The Time Machine*, 1895

Futuristic science fiction, by writers such as H. G. Wells, George Orwell and Isaac Asimov, frequently begins with Utopian hopefulness and ends in disappointment or catastrophe. Their best guesses at how a scientifically-advanced future may improve the lives of humans also have to take account of the unchanging nature of those same humans, some of whom – as we have seen – have primitive appetites. Since Wells wrote *The Time Machine*, more than a century of knowledge gathered by psychologists, psychiatrists, sociologists and criminologists has still failed to find a secure method of identifying such people until they have perpetrated terrible crimes, sometimes again and again. But keeping society safe from a potentially dangerous person appears to be well-nigh impossible if that person has not yet committed a crime.

One science fiction story suggested a fictional solution to this dilemma. Written in 1956, *The Minority Report* by Philip K. Dick (adapted as a 2002 movie starring Tom Cruise) is set in a future where a government 'Department of Precrime' has virtually eliminated the crime of murder. This is achieved by using 'precogs' – a group of captive mutant precognitive humans who can see into the future and predict murders and those who will commit them. This enables the department to identify, sentence and punish those who are destined to kill before they have actually done so, the philosophical irony being that once the murder has been prevented, it is no longer in someone's future – ergo, the imprisoned person is actually innocent. The other ethical question raised by the story concerns the issue of human error: what if the 'precogs' get it wrong – or provide conflicting data? Most good science fiction occupies its own speculative 'precognitive' space where the author extrapolates existing dilemmas or ideas from their own society and historical time by imagining how the future for humans might look, given that scientific and technological advances are forever striding ahead. Not infrequently, we look back at what these remarkable writers have created and marvel at their perspicacity. Aldous Huxley's *Brave New World*, written in 1931, is a perfect example.

Advances in social and psychiatric research continue to provide knowledge which enables us to name the paraphilia for sexual cannibalism and vampirism as 'Vorarephilia', which we may define as necrophilia combined with infantile oralism and sadism. We can say that this deviation from normality occurs where myth, fantasy and reality converge, and we can predict, with a high degree of informed accuracy, that a sadist will never lose interest in his sexual predilection, any more than a psychopath can be rehabilitated or 'cured'. But that is just assembling indicators in order to put a condition in a pigeonhole; it is not dealing with the cause. The essential question 'What makes these monsters?' has no succinct answer, but research material has been able to speculate with some authority: genetic predispositions and childhood influences; modern-day expectations conflicting with social deprivation, maternal failings and wretched loveless childhoods; the gratuitous violence in the media – especially sexual violence – and of course, the increase in sadistic pornography. All of these may combine to form a perverse continuity with the shadow of man's innate primitive aggression and blood-beliefs, providing easy arousal in certain individuals whose dark side – 'the invisible saurian tail that man still drags behind him' as Jung described it – casts a darker shadow than it does in the majority of people.

And having speculated about common causes, there are more specific indicative clues to be gathered based upon adult interests and certain childhood behaviours such as animal cruelty, fire-setting and bed-wetting which, as a triad, are thought to be predictive as regards sexually sadistic murderers. It should be a source of optimism that our information age enables increased sharing of such knowledge between police departments, criminologists, psychiatrists and psychologists, yet logic still tells us that, for example, while all lust-killers may torture animals when young, childhood cruelty to animals is more widespread than sadistic murder, therefore not every child sadist will grow up to be a sadistic killer. Using childhood behaviour to predict adult criminality is thus strewn with pitfalls and requires caution, for what is to be done if a 'murder-prone' child has not committed a 'serious' crime? It might be recalled that Fritz Haarman's father had tried to have his son committed when he sensed the child's potential dangerousness, but doctors refused the request, declaring him to be safe.

Is it possible that offering treatment or in-depth counselling to such a young male after the first manifestation of his sadistic impulses might deflect him from worse crime? And if, ultimately, it does not, then is that not more reason for the authorities to maintain a long-term, non-intrusive watching brief? This suggestion – to which I drew attention in the 1993 edition of this book in an effort to leaven the sense of gloomy 'what-is-to-be-done' hopelessness at a time of rising murder rates – was first proposed in 1966 by two psychiatrists, Daniel S. Hellman and Nathan Blackman. They thought that 'the detection and early management' of such children 'might well forestall a career of violent crime' in the adult,[39] while Hervey Cleckley, the 'father' of psychopathic theory, was also an advocate of early identification and positive action, pointing out that if a child shows signs of schizophrenic illness or any other psychiatric disorder (apart from psychopathy) he can usually be dealt with, which may prevent his committing possible future crime. Something similar should be available for psychopaths who display disturbing behaviour, he says, for 'perhaps all or nearly all of these patients will ... eventually commit antisocial acts.' But it is difficult to see how this could be achieved without infringing an individual's rights and liberties and also risking the stigmatising of the child, perhaps thereby inclining him even more towards dangerous behaviour.

Fifty-five years ago – when Hellman and Blackman began offering their ideas – computer technology and information-sharing methods had not reached a level where 'pre-crime' monitoring strategies could have been covertly applied. In the present century, however, police departments have begun setting up their own futuristic 'Pre-Crime' units. In the UK, many people with human rights concerns began complaining in the 1990s about our 'surveillance society', in particular with regard to closed circuit television cameras (CCTVs) of which there are now approximately six million throughout Britain, with around 700,000 of them in London alone. Despite the 'Big Brother' accusations, in 2006 London Metropolitan Police's Homicide Prevention Unit began compiling a database of psychological profiles of the one hundred men in the country most likely to commit murder in the future based upon information gathered from their personal relationships, mental health or criminal history together with statements made by those who have encountered the individuals. One of the hopes of the Homicide Prevention Unit is that with the involvement of other government agencies the targeted individuals will be encouraged into deflective programmes in a bid to divert impending disaster.

In 2009 Philadelphia's Adult Probation and Parole Department advanced even further into the cyber world of crime-divination in order to try and predict future recidivists among US parolees. In the absence of any precognitive mutants like those in *The Minority Report*, a new computer system was developed which, beyond mere data-analysis, was programmed with independent 'machine learning'. This computer processes its own information using decision-making and faux-human judgement in order to find patterns or factors that predict criminal behaviour. Using a sample of 30,000, the computer identified predictive homicidal patterns in several hundred people – and it proved to be correct in forty-five per cent of the cases.

Observation and supervision is one thing; crime analysis is another. Some crimes may not appear to be obviously sexually-motivated, but contradictory evidence demonstrates the need for broad knowledge and alertness in our police forces when someone is apprehended.[40] As Brittain said of those who are arrested for lesser sexual crimes: 'It does not follow that all who commit such acts are potentially sexual murderers and many may only be social nuisances; it does follow, however, that such offenders should be examined most carefully because a proportion, however small, are potentially very dangerous.' Carrying out thorough background research on offenders – from sources other than the criminal himself – might reveal information which could influence the way the authorities deal with him. For instance, the American sadistic killer Duane Samples had his application for parole supported by psychologists until FBI man Robert Ressler discovered that Samples had fed them lies and had a long history of disembowelment fantasies. Sometimes, the most comprehensive background information about a killer is revealed after his arrest and it is discovered by journalists or writers immersed in research of the case; how much more useful it would be for investigating officers to have a fuller picture of the psychology and life of the murder suspect they are tracking.

For those like the cannibal killers in this book whose deviant fantasies have led to sadistic murder, in a humanitarian country or state which has outlawed the death penalty it actually becomes irrelevant whether they are tagged 'mad' or 'bad' or whether sociopathy can be labelled 'insanity' or not. What is important – and where the system has frequently failed society in its anxiety not to victimise the criminal – is that a highly dangerous killer should be able to be recognised as beyond redemption and incarcerated for the rest of his natural life – which, in practical terms, makes an 'insanity' defence redundant. And at the risk of stating the obvious, terrible sexual fantasies do not abate just because a man is imprisoned for carrying out the murderous joys of his twisted imagination. His claims that he no longer fantasises should be disbelieved by those with the power to release him. Psychopathy expert Hervey Cleckley's reminder still applies: 'There is no evidence to demonstrate or to indicate that psychiatry has yet found a therapy that cures or profoundly changes the psychopath.'

As if establishing how best to prevent violent homicide is not challenge enough to modern psychologists and law-enforcers, the goalposts have shifted to infinity now there is the internet. In 2014, Tom Winsor, the Chief Inspector of Constabulary for England and Wales, warned that the force was 'policing the crimes of today with the methods of yesterday' and his annual *State of Policing* report urged that 'every officer' must understand computer-based offences, because 'the force that many of them joined bears little resemblance to the force that is required now and in the future.' In cyberspace thousands of highly dangerous potential killers may loiter among the multitude of those whose unnatural and sadistic proclivities can only be disclosed by skilled cyber-investigators and ethical hackers with the time and the budget to do so. Yet in the end, plentiful evidence of an individual's obsession with the sort of sexual barbarity for which the Marquis de Sade was jailed – evidence which once would have been unanimously regarded by psychologists and law-makers as indicative of a high-risk dysfunctional human – can these days be described by Gilberto Valle's lawyer as merely participation in 'a vibrant subculture ... of fantasy role-playing' which, though repulsive, is not illegal.

We like to imagine the aspirations of humanity include civilised principles like reason, compassion, benevolence, fairness and justice, but the truth is that our technological achievements count for little when it comes to primal instincts: our planet is still one of proliferating violence with zones of internecine and close-up warfare, rape, pillage and shocking cruelty. It is a world where one in three women experience sexual violence[41] and where the weakest and most vulnerable are oppressed, exploited and destroyed by those whose survival strategy resembles that of Jack London's wolf-dog, White Fang, in the eponymous book he wrote: 'There were the eaters and the eaten. The law was: eat or be eaten' (p.65). Were the Marquis de Sade alive today, it goes without saying that at the very least he would be an enthusiastic blogger on the sort of websites used by Valle, Magnotta or Meiwes.

And who can even begin to hazard a guess at how many of these sexual deviants there are, surfing cyberspace's 'deep web' along with the black-market drugs and arms dealers, the terrorists, child-pornographers and activists, the hit-men for hire? Reinforcing and validating each others' diseased fantasies, how many de Sades or Meiwes, posing as normal humans, are circulating among us? *Darkfetish. net* maintains that it has 38,000 subscribers – and this is a mainstream site, not one of the 'invisible' websites where online content is not indexed or catalogued and where users are said to be untraceable. The 'Cannibal Café' claimed it had tens of thousands of subscribers until it was closed down by the authorities after the trial of Armin Meiwes in Frankfurt disclosed his use of this website. At the time, police estimated that in Germany alone there were ten thousand people who shared Meiwes's enthusiasm for cannibalism.

'Perro Loco' (translation: 'Mad Dog'), the man who had started up *The Cannibal Café* website in 1994, presently runs one of several websites – again, these are accessible sites – where visitors invent fantasy tales about the rape and mutilation of females. The pneumatic women in the stories are usually ludicrously delighted to be the victims of sadistic or cannibalistic sacrifice, which feeds into the old nauseating falsehood that women enjoy being brutalised. Perro's site is partly devoted to 'Dolcett', a sexual fantasy cartoon artist (or, it seems, artists) whose favorite depictions are described elsewhere on the internet as 'asphyxiation (especially hanging) and gynophagia (the eating of women) especially after impalement, execution by gunfire, electrocution, decapitation, and several more exotic tortures (such as the use of honey and ants).' Perro's site allegedly has 53,000 members. It gets a million hits a month, he claimed in a 2011 online interview about the Meiwes case. Perro Loco said that he had no moral objection to what Meiwes did, because it was 'entirely consensual' and he approved of Meiwes's 'social responsibility' in seeking out a willing victim to kill and eat.

Some might claim that if there are hundreds of thousands of cannibalistic sadists at large, then it is better that they express and satisfy their sexual desire to mutilate and feast upon the bodies of their fellow-humans via extreme online fantasy rather than by killing real people. They might, indeed, suggest that the Western World's lower murder rates this century have more to do with the modern pervert's ability to access sadistic porn than with improved policing and detection strategies. For practical purposes, it is an interesting view, as is another argument: that having the bulk of the world's potentially dangerous deviants herded together in cyberspace clusters could prove a useful monitoring and apprehension aid. For that to be successful, however, government agencies must be prepared to invest heavily in the expert manpower and cutting-edge computer technology needed to enable the accurate mapping of those clusters, for at present most are hidden in the ninety-six per cent of the internet which is beyond the reach of search engines like Google or Bing.

Can we surmise that the internet encourages potential cannibals by giving them somewhere safe to plot and plan, its more pernicious websites providing a fertile soil in which aberrant individuals can blossom? Possibly, but to blame the internet and its remarkable progress is akin to blaming oxygen for allowing itself to be breathed by the wicked; it is throwing out the infant prodigy with the bathwater. In the century or so since psychoanalysis explained the nature of the unconscious with its complex network of desires and drives, we must acknowledge that those with repressed cannibalistic and sadistic longings have always infested human society. Our best hope for the future is to identify early, divert successfully or contain permanently those whose primal yearnings mark them out as evolutionary throwbacks, akin to Jack London's outwardly-domesticated fictional dog in the book of the same name, *White Fang*:

'The Wild still lingered in him and the wolf in him merely slept.'

Endnotes

1   Paul Barber, in his book, *Vampires, Burial and Death*, suggests that cut-marks on these bones might have been caused not by cannibalism but by a tribal burial practice called excarnation, in which the flesh was routinely separated from the bones of corpses both to facilitate disposal and to ensure the destruction of the body, which hastened the soul on its journey into an afterlife.

2   Interestingly, 'moon-madness' might well exist. Scientists believe that the waxing and waning of the moon can substantially affect behaviour, noting that there is an increase in all crime – including murder – on nights of the full moon. During the period of the lunar cycle when the moon is closest to the earth, homicides are more ruthless and bizarre. A New York study found a dramatic rise in the number of admissions to psychiatric hospitals on days of the full moon. This theory is called the 'Transylvania Hypothesis'.

3   Ray Biondi and Walt Hecox, *The Dracula Killer*, 1992.

4   https://www.nhtsa.gov/sites/nhtsa.gov/files/2021-09/Early-Estimate-Motor-Vehicle-Traffic-Fatalities-Q1-2021.pdf

5   https://edition.cnn.com/2021/09/19/politics/gun-violence-spike-2021-explainer/index.html

6   https://www.houstonpublicmedia.org/articles/news/
politics/2021/08/30/407291/here-are-the-new-texas-
gun-laws-going-into-effect-on-sept-1/

7   'Rape: An Analysis,' *The Evening Star* (Washington DC) 12 November 1971.

8   See: Hollenberg and Sperry, Sears and others, Gluecks, Bandura and Walters, Eron and others, Duncan and others, Sattin and others.

9   That sado-necrophilia and necrophilia is not a new phenomenon can be seen in the sixteenth-century writings of the jurist Damhoudere who recommended the death penalty for lower-class people and exile if the culprit was an 'honorable' – or upper-class – person, on the grounds that such a person does not 'respect the goal and the measure of natural love, but uses the dead body sexually, behaving as if he copulated with a piece of wood or stone.'

10 Serial killers are distinct from mass murderers in that serial killers kill one or two people at a time, repeating this until they are caught, whereas mass murderers wipe out crowds of people at one time, for instance, by shooting – and may frequently turn the gun upon themselves after such an act of slaughter.

11 In Richard von Krafft-Ebing's *Psychopathia Sexualis*, published in 1886, the psychiatrist classes the 'lust-murderer' as 'cruelty, murderous lust extending to anthropophagy', Krafft-Ebing tells of Leger, a 19-year-old who 'wanders about eight days in a forest, there catches a girl twelve years old, violates her … tears out her heart, eats of it, drinks the blood, and buries the remains.'

12 Ressler, Burgess, Hartman, Douglas and McCormack, 'Murderers who Rape and Mutilate', *Journal of Interpersonal Violence*, Vol. 1, No. 3, September 1986.

13 McGuire, R.J., Carlisle, J.M. and Young, B.G. 'Sexual deviations as conditioned behaviour: a hypothesis.' *Behaviour Research and Therapy*. 3, 1965.

14 Lewis F. Richardson, *Statistics of Deadly Quarrels*. *London*: Stevens and Sons, 1960, p.153.

15 Raju, G. C., *The Balkan Conflict and International Reaction: American and Serbian Options*. Thomas, 1992.

16 Among the world-changing fall-out from this sense of horror was the knee-jerk reaction to be seen when, in America's 2016 presidential election, a far-right non-politician was elected: property developer and TV reality show host Donald Trump. Trump's populist 'America First' strategy was created to foster unrest and divisiveness, tapping into xenophobic fears and whipping up the latent racism in grassroots Republican voters. Among the authoritarian pledges he made was the deportation of large numbers of the US immigrant population, a proposal to build a wall along the southern United States border to keep out Mexican would-be immigrants and a 'Muslim travel ban' on visitors from selected Islamic countries.

17 Castle, T. and Hensley, C., 'Serial killers with military experience: applying learning theory to serial murder'. *International Journal of Offender Therapy and Comparative Criminology* 2002, 453–65.

18 Crepault, C. and Couture, M., 'Men's erotic fantasies'. *Archives of Sexual Behaviour 9*, 1980, 565–81.

19 Johnson, S. A., 'Importance of Finding the Offender's Pornography Stash' in *Journal of Forensic Res 5*, 2014, 229.

20 In 1970, when aggressive pornography was rarer than it is now, the Commission on Obscenity and Pornography concluded that pornographic materials did not have a 'harmful' effect; in 1973, Howard, Liptzin and Riefler

concluded that pornography was 'an innocuous stimulus which leads quickly to satiation' and decided that public concern was misplaced; also in 1973 Mann, Sidmann and Starr concluded that viewing erotic films did not produce 'harmful social consequences.'

21 See online: https://www.theguardian.com/society/2022/jan/13/2021-was-worst-year-on-record-for-online-child-sex-abuse-says-iwf. Also: https://www.iwf.org.uk/news/record-number-of-images-showing-children-being-sexually-abused-removed-by-uk-internet-charity

22 Jung, C. G., 'Wotan' in *Collected Works Vol. 10: Civilisation in Transition*, 1964/70.

23 Havelock Ellis, quoted in Richard Noll, *Vampires, Werewolves and Demons*, Brunner/Mazel, New York. 1992.

24 Lazarus and Davison in *Abnormal Psychology*, Davison and Neale, 1971.

25 Quoted in Richard Noll, *Vampires, Werewolves and Demons*, Brunner/ Mazel, New York. 1992.

26 For example, R.L. Vanden Bergh and J.F. Kelly in 'Vampirism', *Archives of General Psychiatry, 11*.

27 According to C. F. Bentley, in his article 'The Monster in The Bedroom: Sexual Symbolism in Bram Stoker's Dracula'. *Literature and Psychology, 22*, 1972.

28 In some cultures one of the measures designed to prevent a corpse becoming a vampire was to drink some of the corpse's blood and eat its flesh, sometimes boiling the heart in oil. This was practised until as late as the nineteenth century.

29 Sahlins, M. 'Raw women, cooked men and other "great things" of the Fiji Islands.' In P. Brown and D. Tuzin (eds) *The Ethnography of Cannibalism*. Washington: The Society for Psychological Anthropology, 1983.

30 Sacha Baron Cohen, The Guardian, 22 November 2019. See: https://www.theguardian.com/technology/2019/nov/

22/sacha-baron-cohen-facebook-propaganda. See also: https://www.theguardian.com/film/2019/nov/22/sacha-baron-cohen-facebook-would-have-sold-final-solution-ads-to-hitler

31 https://www.cbsnews.com/news/facebook-whistle blower-frances-haugen-misinformation-public-60-minutes-2021-10-03/
See also: https://www.dw.com/en/facebook-whistleblo wer-reveals-herself-as-frances-haugen/a-59396302

32 https://eu.tcpalm.com/story/news/crime/martin-county/2021/09/30/austin-harrouffs-sanity-when-he-killed-tequesta-couple-unsettled/5907147001/

33 Based on Hervey Cleckley's classic model, Dr Robert Hare produced a 'Psychopathy Checklist' in 1980 to assess the condition, comprising twenty diagnostic items. In 2006, Hare and industrial psychologist Paul Babiak, co-wrote *Snakes in Suits: When Psychopaths Go to Work* which suggested that psychopaths who are not murderous frequently use their psychopathic and narcissistic traits to find success in business, particularly in the corporate world.

34 See: http://www.courtroomstrategy.com/2014/09/canni bal-cop-juror-speaks-out-about-overturned-conviction

35 See: http://nypost.com/tag/gilberto-valle/

36 See: https://www.highspeedinternet.com/resources/saf est-dangerous-states-online-dating-2019

37 See: https://news.sky.com/story/dark-side-of-online-da ting-crimes-rise-by-300-in-five-years-11073230

38 *Don't F*** With Cats: Hunting an Internet Killer*, 2020. Netflix mini-series, writer and director: Mark Lewis.

39 Hellman and Blackman, 'Enuresis, Firesetting, and Cruelty to Animals,' *American Journal of Psychiatry* 122 (1966) pp1431–1435.

40 For example, some burglaries are sexually motivated. William Heirens, who murdered and mutilated two

females, one of whom was a small child, had shown early and unusual signs of severe disturbance: he had begun stealing women's underwear from clothes lines at age nine and progressed to burglary three years later. He would experience erection and sometimes orgasm as he broke into a house through the window.

41 Campbell, B., *End of Equality (Manifestos for the 21st Century)*, Seagull Books, 2014.

Bibliography

BOOKS

Babiek, Paul and Hare, Robert D., *Snakes in Suits: When Psychopaths Go to Work* (HarperBusiness, 2007)

Barber, Paul, *Vampires, Burial, and Death: Folklore and Reality* (Yale University Press, 1988)

Berg, Karl, *The Sadist* (Electron Ebooks, 2015)

Biondi, Ray and Hecox, Walt, *The Dracula Killer* (Pocket Books, 1992)

Boar, Roger and Blundell, Nigel, *The World's Most Infamous Murders* (Bookthrift Co, 1983)

Cleckley, Hervey Milton, *The Mask of Sanity* (Houraki Publishing, 2016)

Conradi, Peter, *The Red Ripper* (True Crime Books, 1994)

Davison, Gerald C. and Neale, John M., *Abnormal Psychology: An Experimental Clinical Approach* (Wiley, 1982)

Dunning, John, *Strange Deaths* (Mulberry, 1981)

Gollmar, Robert, *Edward Gein: America's Most Bizarre Murderer* (Hallberg, Delavan, WI, 1981)

Heimer, Mel, *The Cannibal: The Case of Albert Fish* (Xanadu Publications, 1971)

Holmes, Ronald, *The Legend of Sawney Bean* (Frederick Muller Ltd, 1975)

Klein, Melanie, *The Psycho-Analysis of Children* (Vintage, 1997)

Krafft-Ebing, Richard, *Psychopathia Sexualis* (Otbebookpublishing, 2021)

Levin, Jack and Fox, James Alan, *Mass Murder: America's Growing Menace* (Da Capo Press Inc, 1985)

Leyton, Elliot, *Hunting Humans: The Rise of the Modern Multiple Murderer* (Running Press Adult, 2003)

Lloyd, Georgina, *One Was Not Enough: True Stories of Multiple Murderers* (Robert Hale, 1986)

Lourie, Richard, *Hunting the Devil: The Search for the Russian Ripper* (Grafton Books, 1993)

Lunde, Donald T., *Murder and Madness* (W.W. Norton, New York, 1979)

Malamuth, Neil and Donnerstein, Edward, *Pornography and Sexual Aggression* (Academic Press Inc, 1984)

Marriner, Brian, *Cannibalism: The Last Taboo* (Senate, 1997)

Martens, Willem, *The Firebirds Among the Psychopaths*. (W. Khan Institute Publishing 2014)

Nash, Jay Robert, *Encyclopedia of World Crime* (Crimebooks, 1990)

Nash, Jay Robert, *Compendium of World Crime* (Harrap, 1983)

Nash, Jay Robert, *Bloodletters and Badmen* (M. Evans, New York, 1972)

Noll, Richard (Ed.), *Vampires, Werewolves and Demons: Twentieth Century Reports in the Psychiatric Literature* (Brunner/Mazel, Inc., 1992)

Playfair, Giles, *Crime in our Century* (Sidgwick and Jackson, 1977)

Praz, Mario, *The Romantic Agony* (Oxford Paperbacks, 1970)

Prins, Herschel, *Bizarre Behaviours: Boundaries of Psychiatric Disorder* (Routledge, 2013)

Ressler, Robert K. and Shachtman, Tom, *Whoever Fights Monsters* (St Martin's Press, 1992)

Robbins, Rossell Hope, *Encyclopedia of Witchcraft and Demonology* (Girard & Stewart, 2015)

Samenow, Stanton E., *Inside the Criminal Mind* (Bantam Books Inc, 2014)

Schlesinger, L.B. and Revitch, E. (Eds.), *Sexual Dynamics of Antisocial Behaviour* (Charles C. Thomas, Pub Ltd, 1997)

Schwartz, Anne E., *The Man Who Could Not Kill Enough* (Birch Lane Press, 1992)

Stampf, Gunter and Brown, Pat, *Interview with a Cannibal: The Secret Life of the Monster of Rotenburg* (Phoenix Books, 2008)

Storr, Anthony, *Human Destructiveness: The Roots of Genocide and Human Cruelty* (Routledge, 2013)

Wilson, Colin, and Seaman, Donald, *The Serial Killers: A Study in the Psychology of Violence* (Virgin Books, 2007)

Wilson, Colin, and Seaman, Donald, *Encyclopaedia of Modern Murder* (Book Club Associates, 1983)

Wilson, Colin, *The Misfits: A Study of Sexual Outsiders* (Grafton Books, 1988)

Woodward, Ian, *The Werewolf Delusion* (Paddington Press, 1979)

Campbell, Beatrix, *End of Equality* (Seagull Books, 2014)

ARTICLES

Aamodt, M. G., 'Serial killer Statistics'. Radford University (2013). Retrieved 19 May 2014 from http://maamodt. asp.radford.edu/serial killer information center/project

Bentley, C.F., 'The Monster in the Bedroom: Sexual Symbolism in Bram Stoker's Dracula', *Literature and Psychology*, 22 (1972)

Black, M.C., Basile, K.C., Breiding, M.J., Smith, S.G., Walters, M.L., Merrick, M.T., Chen, J., and Stevens,

M.R., The National Intimate Partner and Sexual Violence Survey (2010)

Boukhabza, D. and Yesavage, J., 'Cannibalism and Vampirism in Paranoid Schizophrenia', *Journal of Clinical Psychiatry*, 42 (1981)

Brittain, R.P., The Sadistic Murderer', *Medicine, Science and the Law*, 10 (1970)

Burton-Bradley B.G., 'Cannibalism for Cargo', *Journal of Nervous and Mental Disease*, 163 (1976)

Buskirk, R.E., Frohlich, C. and Ross, K.G. 'The Natural Selection of Sexual Cannibalism', *The American Naturalist* 123, 612–625 (1984)

Castle, T. and Hensley, C., 'Serial killers with Military Experience: Applying Learning Theory to Serial Murder'. *International Journal of Offender Therapy and Comparative Criminology*, 453–65. (2002)

Crepault, C. and Couture, M., 'Men's erotic fantasies' in *Archives of Sexual Behaviour*, 9, 565–81 (1980)

Donnerstein, E., 'Effects of Violent Content in Pornography' in M. Eastin (Ed), *Encyclopedia of Media Violence*, 288–290. Thousand Oaks, CA: Sage (2014)

Donnerstein, E. 'The Media and Aggression: From TV to the Internet' in Forgas, Kruglanski, and Williams (Eds), *The Psychology of Social Conflict and Aggression*, New York: Psychology Press (2011)

Felthous, Alan R., 'Childhood Cruelty to Cats, Dogs and Other Animals', *Bulletin of the American Academy of Psychology and the Law*, 9 (1981)

Garelik, Glenn and Maranto, Gina, 'Multiple Murderers' *Discover* (July 1984)

Hellman, Daniel S. and Blackman, Nathan, 'Enuresis, Firesetting and Cruelty to Animals: a Triad, Predictive of Adult Crime', *American Journal of Psychiatry*, 122 (June 1996)

Hemphill, R.E., and Zabow, T., 'Clinical Vampirism: A presentation of three cases and a re-evaluation of Haigh, the "Acid-Bath Murderer"', *South African Medical Journal*, 63 (1983)

Johnson, S.A., 'Importance of Finding the Offender's Pornography Stash', *Journal of Forensic Research*, 5, 229 (2014)

Kingston, D., Malamuth, N., Fedoroff, P., and Marshall, W., 'The Importance of Individual Differences in Pornography Use: Theoretical Perspectives and Implications for Treating Sexual Offenders', *The Journal of Sex Research*, 46 (24 March 2009)

Levitt, Steven D., 'Understanding Why Crime Fell in the 1990s', *Journal of Economic Perspectives*, Vol 18 (Winter 2004)

Lykins A.D., and Cantor J.M., 'Vorarephilia: a case study in masochism and erotic consumption', *Archives of Sexual Behaviour*, 43, 181–186 (January 2014)

MacCulloch, M.J. et al., 'Sadistic Fantasy, Sadistic Behaviour and Offending', *British Journal of Psychiatry*, 143 (1983)

McCarthy, Terry, 'Japan's Dr Lecter: no straitjacket required', *The Independent* (February 9, 1992)

McGill, Peter, 'Portrait of a Cannibal' (Issei Sagawa), *Observer Magazine* (May 24, 1992)

McGill, Peter, 'And tonight, folks, meet the man who ate his girlfriend ...', *The Observer* (March 8, 1992)

McGuire, R.J., Carlisle, J.M., and Young, B.G., 'Sexual deviations as conditioned behaviour: a hypothesis', *Behaviour Research and Therapy*, 3 (1965)

Pfafflin, F., 'Good enough to eat', *Archives of Sexual Behavior*, 37, 286–293 (2008)

Pitman, Joanna, 'How I tasted tea and whisky with a cannibal' (Issei Sagawa), *The Times* (January 25, 1992)

Prins, Herschel, 'Vampirism — a Clinical Condition', *British Journal of Psychiatry*, 146 (1985)

Prins, Herschel, 'Vampirism — Legendary or Clinical Phenomenon?', *Medicine, Science and the Law*, 24 (1984)

Ressler, Robert K. et al., 'Murderers Who Rape and Mutilate', *Journal of Interpersonal Violence* (September 1986)

Starr, Mark et al., The Random Killers', *Newsweek* (November 26, 1984)

WEBSITES: CANNIBALISM IN PAPUA, NEW GUINEA AND ALBINO KILLING IN AFRICA

http://www.thecitizen.co.tz/News/19-face-death-penalty-over-albino-killings-in-Tanzania/1840340-3117938-54nrj9/index.html

http://www.bbc.co.uk/news/world-africa-31849531

http://www.ibtimes.com.au/its-fatal-be-albino-tanzania-due-cannibalism-1423185

http://www.ibtimes.com.au/gangs-malawi-kill-4-albinos-april-skin-used-witchcraft-ai-calls-government-punish-perpetrators

http://www.nzherald.co.nz/world/news/article.cfm?c_id=2&objectid=10817610

http://www.telegraph.co.uk/news/worldnews/australiaandthepacific/papuanewguinea/9378038/Cannibal-killers-delay-Papua-New-Guinea-poll.html)